The Rest and the West

The Rest and the West

Capital and Power in a Multipolar World

Sandro Mezzadra and Brett Neilson

VERSO

London • New York

First published by Verso 2024
© Sandro Mezzadra and Brett Neilson 2024

1 3 5 7 9 10 8 6 4 2

Verso
UK: 6 Meard Street, London W1F 0EG
US: 388 Atlantic Avenue, Brooklyn, NY 11217
versobooks.com

Verso is the imprint of New Left Books

ISBN-13: 978-1-80429-605-9
ISBN-13: 978-1-80429-606-6 (UK EBK)
ISBN-13: 978-1-80429-607-3 (US EBK)

British Library Cataloguing in Publication Data
A catalogue record for this book is available from the British Library

Library of Congress Cataloging-in-Publication Data

Names: Mezzadra, Sandro, author. | Neilson, Brett, author.
Title: The rest and the West : capital and power in a multipolar world /
  Sandro Mezzadra and Brett Neilson.
Description: London ; Brooklyn, NY : Verso, 2024. | Includes
  bibliographical references and index.
Identifiers: LCCN 2024022968 (print) | LCCN 2024022969 (ebook) | ISBN
  9781804296059 (trade paperback) | ISBN 9781804296073 (ebook)
Subjects: LCSH: Multipolarity (International relations) |
  Globalization—Political aspects. | Power (Social sciences)—Political
  aspects. | Geopolitics.
Classification: LCC JZ1312.2 .M48 2024 (print) | LCC JZ1312.2 (ebook) |
  DDC 320.1/2—dc23/eng/20240627
LC record available at https://lccn.loc.gov/2024022968
LC ebook record available at https://lccn.loc.gov/2024022969

Typeset in Minion by Biblichor Ltd, Scotland
Printed and bound by CPI Group (UK) Ltd, Croydon CR0 4YY

Contents

Preface

The manuscript of this book was delivered to Verso in May 2023. What follows has only been altered slightly since that time. Conjunctural analysis entails the risk that things move on. *The Rest and the West* was written in the interchange between pandemic and war. We started in the long months of lockdown and allowed the writing to take a turn after Russia's invasion of Ukraine. Perhaps our awareness of time's passage is reflected by the title we chose for the first section of chapter 3, which develops the concept of regimes of war. We labelled that part of the book '24 February 2022', remembering the day on which Vladimir Putin launched Russia's so-called special military operation in Ukraine. Would the book be different if we had rushed to include another section called '7 October 2023', marking the day on which Hamas broke the prison walls of Gaza, violently attacked Israeli military personnel and civilians, and attracted the traumatized vengeance of Israel, leading to a war that has claimed over 33,000 Palestinian lives at the time of writing? Doubtlessly, so. But history is about more than dates, and conjunctural analysis involves more than providing a snapshot of a moment, however portentous that moment might prove. By titling this book *The Rest and the West*, and locating our analysis of geopolitical and geoeconomic conflicts in longer-run dynamics of capital and power, we hope to have provided resources for making sense of the diverse forces, causes, determinations, and temporalities that collide in the contemporary world.

We are not interested in rehearsing debates about conjunctural analysis. We are aware of the differing approaches of Antonio Gramsci and

Louis Althusser. Gramsci emphasized the immediate, periodic, and sometimes accidental play of political forces in specific social and economic circumstances. Althusser sought to disentangle the multiple lines of determination and dialectical interaction between primary structural contradictions and those that are historically particular or conjunctural. As the story goes, Stuart Hall charted a path between these perspectives, asking, 'What are the circumstances in which we now find ourselves, how did they arise, what forces are sustaining them, and what forces are available to us to change them?'[1] For us, this is a good enough description of conjunctural analysis, although we note that in the period when Hall was forging this approach he was responding to a sense of impending crisis in Britain, which was lurching towards Thatcherism. *The Rest and the West* grapples with a wider and more complex predicament, one sometimes referred to as polycrisis, in which multiple and critically intensifying conditions collapse in on each other – climate change, migration, health, geopolitical conflict, mounting economic inequalities, etc. Today, invocations of the conjuncture often signal attention to non-proximate relations, stressing the importance of influences from elsewhere and connectivity across geographical scales. There is growing emphasis on how social relations and processes intersect the biophysical condition of the planet, and a sense of how heterogeneous and conflicting determinations lead to conjunctural uncertainties that unsettle established hegemonies, opening possibilities for emancipatory political action or facilitating a turn for the worse.

Despite the events that have intervened since the completion of this book, we cannot be sure whether the increasing multipolarization of the world catalyses or hinders the emergence of enduring opposition to capital. Invocations of world disorder are as worn and unhelpful as claims for and directives to world order, whether based in legal or economic norms. Both, we postulate, are responses to a situation where nation-states struggle to control the circulation and reproduction of capital. By contending that war is central to capitalist globalization, we do not mean to suggest that capital accumulation cannot proceed without violent territorial conflict, as much as such confrontation is part

---

1   Stuart Hall, 'Epilogue: Through the Prism of Intellectual Life', in Brian Meeks (ed.), *Culture, Politics, Race and Diaspora: The Thought of Stuart Hall*, London: Lawrence & Wishart, 2007, 279.

of the wars in Ukraine and Gaza, and the more widespread rearmament triggered by these wars provides opportunities for enrichment. Both confrontations have complex historical roots, the study of which could occupy volumes. In the case of Ukraine, we can observe conflicts between different fractions of capital: the industrial capital invested in the Donbas versus the transnational informational capital centred in Kiev. For us, war, and the regimes of war evident in the wider militarization of politics and economy beyond sites of physical combat, are refracted through the global processes inherent to contemporary capitalism – logistics, finance, the spread of digital platforms, and the functioning of large infrastructural systems. As such, conflict in and through global spaces of capital circulation becomes at least as important as violent territorial struggles, as is clear from incidents such as the blasting of the Nord Stream pipelines in 2022 or the Houthi attacks on Red Sea shipping associated with the economic interests of Israel's Western allies. Likewise, the poles of today's multipolar world cannot be correlated with the territorial landmasses occupied by major state powers such as China, Russia, and the US. The shunting of war through irregular and shifting global spaces establishes new lines of conflict and amity, evident not only in the energy and other commodity flows that have been established to circumvent the sanctions against Russia but in the remarkable social solidarity for the Palestinian struggle that has emerged in almost every Western nation, notwithstanding the official and contrasting positions of governments.

As we explain in the introduction, *The Rest and the West* attempts to grasp powerful shifts in the distribution of power and wealth that are at the same time reconfiguring and disrupting the world system. While we follow the lead of Giovanni Arrighi and other world system scholars in taking the crisis of the global US hegemony as the common thread running through the current conjuncture, we are more cautious to identify emerging candidates to play the role of a new hegemon. This is not only because shifting formations of territorialism and capitalism seem to challenge the very logic of hegemony, but also because the decentring of the West we are currently experiencing may give way to new scenarios that we attempt to grasp though our elaborations on multipolarity. We stress that this category is not for us a fully fledged model, but rather a matrix that may generate completely different and even opposite developments. For now, the centrifugal and conflictual multipolarity that at least since the financial crisis of 2007–8 is the hallmark of our age is giving way to wars and to a proliferation of war regimes that seems to announce further wars.

As mentioned earlier, the Ukraine and the Gaza wars are in many respects completely different conflicts. Their histories and stakes are clearly distinct. Nonetheless, in the current conjuncture they are strictly *concatenated*. As we explain in Chapter 3, the Ukraine war is far from being limited to a regional setting. It rather touches upon the centre of the world system, intensifies already-existing dynamics of destabilization, and opens a space in which heterogeneous processes of militarization (what we call the proliferation of war regimes) concur to make war a concrete possibility in different parts of the world. Both the operation of Hamas on 7 October 2023 and the ongoing massacre in Gaza by the Israeli military are part of this new conjuncture of war and militarization. Although in different ways, the West is facing increasing difficulties in effectively managing the situation in Ukraine as well as in Gaza. While Putin's forces are slowly advancing in the South of Ukraine and in the Donbas, the US appears to be split in an electoral year with the prospect of Trump's return to the White House. While different views have emerged in European countries, these divergences do not hinder a general trend to rearmament, the establishment of a war economy, and preparations for war with Russia. Regarding Gaza, US politics appear weak with respect to the Israeli government, and the violence and brutality of Israeli bombardments are increasingly challenging the legitimacy of the West as such in the world. The wide international support for South Africa's genocide case against Israel at the International Court of Justice can be taken as a symptom of this legitimacy crisis.

While many other facets of the two wars merit closer scrutiny – such as the blend of old and new military techniques, the use of drones and trenches, artificial intelligence and urban guerrilla warfare, financial and economic measures, humanitarian efforts, and the spread of terror among civilian populations – we wish to focus on the implications of war for logistics and infrastructures. This nexus is by no means new, but we are convinced of its heightened importance today, both due to the relevance of these domains to contemporary capitalism and because it illuminates another key concatenation – namely, the link between the COVID-19 pandemic and war. As we argue in Chapter 1, the pandemic severely strained global logistics and supply chains, and the Ukraine war added new dimensions to what is widely seen as a crisis of globalization's infrastructural skeleton. The intertwining of geopolitics and geoeconomics is apparent here, and would become even clearer through an investigation of the new routes and channels that have enabled Russia to circumvent Western sanctions, at least partially.

The question of logistics and infrastructures is also crucial in the Gaza war, first of all – with catastrophic implications for the Gazans – with respect to the issue of humanitarian aid from land, from the sky, and from the sea, with related US plans to build new port infrastructure, whose hidden objectives are not difficult to imagine. But there is more to say on this issue, in particular with respect to the Houthi attacks in the Red Sea that we mentioned earlier and which build a kind of reverberation of another war (the Yemen war) within the scenario opened by Israel's response to the attack of 7 October. There is a need to remember that one of the major implications of the current situation of war is the stalemate and possible end of the so-called Abraham Accords, in particular with respect to Saudi Arabia. The Palestinian question, whose neutralization (or liquidation) was at the same time the premise and aim of those accords, is again politically unescapable. While the crisis in the Red Sea, with shipping companies renouncing to cross the Suez Canal and opting for much longer and more expensive routes, directly affects Europe more than the US, its wider implications come to bear on US strategic plans of global connectivity. Take the India–Middle East–Europe Economic Corridor (IMEC), launched in September 2023 at the G20 New Delhi Summit as a challenge to China's Belt and Road Initiative. The plan of a corridor from India to Europe through the Emirates, Saudi Arabia, Jordan, Israel, and Greece seems highly unrealistic less than a year after its official announcement.

These are scattered notes on the Gaza war, on its relations with the conjuncture opened by Russia's invasion of Ukraine, and on the multiple ways in which it relates to the wider shifts and tensions at the global level that we investigate in *The Rest and the West*. Our understanding of conjunctural analysis leads us to remain open to unpredictable developments and even enhanced prospects for radical political activity. Nonetheless, it is fair to say that while we write this preface, war is dominating political discourse and policy-making in many parts of the world. This dominance of war is particularly apparent in Europe, where, after the Second World War, war had become taboo in the Western part of the continent (which did not exclude multiple forms of intervention in wars being fought outside it or on its fringes, including in the former Yugoslavia in the 1990s). A direct participation of EU troops in the Ukraine war is explicitly discussed today, and as we mention above the same is true for the supposed need of a transition to a war economy. While the risk of a potentially catastrophic military escalation cannot be excluded in Europe, the notion of a war economy refers to a proliferation of war regimes that is far from being limited to this world region. Consider Japan's shift away from its defence-only principle, plans to almost double its military spending by 2027, and possible inclusion in the second pillar of the AUKUS technology-sharing agreements between Australia, the UK, and the US. The composition of public spending is drastically altered by rearmament in many parts of the world, notably to the detriment of welfare, an area of public investment which seemed to be experiencing an untimely revival at the height of the pandemic. In particular, the development of digital technologies and artificial intelligence is deflected by the ubiquity of military logics and related investment decisions. In the chapters that follow, we expand on the notion of war regime, critically analysing its multiple dimensions, which apply to far more than economy. We also maintain that today the opposition to wars and war regimes is crucial to forging an internationalist politics whose conditions we seek to outline. The stakes and task of imagining and enabling such a politics appears more urgent than ever, some months after we delivered the manuscript.

Our choice of the title *The Rest and the West* does not imply that the dynamics of contagion, war, capitalist transformation, and multipolarity can be explained by elaborating on or reversing a binary framework. Such a binary is, at best, problematic and, at worst, complicit in centuries of imperial ventures. The title is meant as a concise reminder of how today's tumultuous shifts in the world system have undermined the West's hegemony. The result is a situation where multiple other contenders compete for position in disunified ways, unable to establish clear alternative patterns of geopolitical or geoeconomic dominance. Nonetheless, the change is significant, calling into question the very categories of the Rest and the West. The signature of this transformed scenario is conflict surrounding the channelling of capital and power through highly interconnected logistical, financial, and infrastructural spaces that are incongruently overlaid with state or territorial boundaries. This, at least, is how we perceive the current conjuncture. In writing of the warring tendencies that culminate in the present, we do not mean to obscure longer-run trajectories or historical developments that play into this predicament. These change and move in relation to each other and the more immediate circumstances to which they connect. Our attention to the mutating roles of circulation and reproduction in capital operations should make this clear. Ultimately, our interest is neither in shifting conceptions of world order nor in the layered structure of historical time. Rather, we concern ourselves with how the geopolitical ordering of historical processes crosses the historical arrangement of geopolitical orders. In that sense, we hope that our engagement with the conjuncture has something lasting to say.

3 April 2024

Introduction

The rest?

In February 2023, one year after Russia's invasion of Ukraine, the European Council on Foreign Relations released a policy brief on the attitudes of 'global public opinion' towards the ongoing war. Authored by Timothy Garton Ash, Ivan Krastev, and Mark Leonard, the report bears a telling title: *United West, Divided from the Rest.* The authors highlight the fact that the Ukraine war has both reinstated the unity of the 'West' under US leadership and widened 'the gap between the West and the "rest" when it comes to their desired outcomes for the war and differing understandings of why the US and Europe support Ukraine'. We are at a 'turning point in world history', they write, with Russia's aggression in Ukraine marking 'both the consolidation of the West and the emergence of the long-heralded post-Western international order'.[1] To express it differently, what is emerging amid systemic chaos and war is a world 'order' in which the 'West' is just one part, however mighty and wealthy, and not the universal actor orchestrating some kind of liberal rules-based international order.

This book analyses some of the main questions raised by such a condition. *The Rest and the West,* while reversing a famous phrase

---

1 Timothy Garton Ash, Ivan Krastev, and Mark Leonard, *United West, Divided from the Rest: Global Public Opinion One Year into Russia's War on Ukraine,* European Council on Foreign Relations, Policy Brief, February 2023, 2.

coined by Stuart Hall, is meant to pay tribute to his prescient writings on globalization in the 1990s. As it happens, the title of Hall's essay has become a kind of shorthand that is often quoted without awareness of the argument that supports its formulation. Although the formula *the West and the Rest* is taken as a description of the binary structure of the world order since the inception of European colonial expansion, Hall's aim is to investigate 'the role which "the Rest" played in the formation of the idea of "the West" and a "Western" sense of identity'. Seen from this perspective, the crucial factor is a complicated and shifting set of entanglements between the 'West' – a notion whose emergence is located by Hall in 'the age of exploration and conquest' – and the 'Rest'.[2] This does not mean that the binary structure of Hall's formula had no material implications in the long centuries in which Europe and the West believed themselves to be at the centre of the world. The opposite is the case, but, according to Hall, the violence of conquest, colonization, and imperialism was played out against a fabric of entanglements that, in a certain way, included the 'Rest' in the 'West' through discursive and ideological operations and a kind of epistemic violence.

Between the 'West' and the 'Rest' was a kind of 'metaborder' that played crucial roles in the history of European colonial expansion and domination, as Carl Schmitt demonstrates in his celebration of the Eurocentric structure of global modernity.[3] Hall's insight allows us to grasp that, since its inception, the operations of this 'metaborder' had to organize processes of material and epistemic exploitation that, in important ways, made the 'Rest' internal to the 'West'. Significantly, Hall understands the postcolonial condition through the lens of decoloniza-tion processes that led to 'the subverting of the old colonizing/colonized binary'.[4] The challenge to the geopolitical architecture of colonialism raised by anticolonial movements 'marks the passage from one histori-cal power-configuration or conjuncture to another'. Although he is keen

---

2   Stuart Hall, 'The West and the Rest: Discourse and Power', in Stuart Hall, David Held, Don Hubert, and Kenneth Thompson (eds), *Modernity: An Introduction to Modern Societies*, Oxford: Blackwell Publishers, 1996, 188 and 197.

3   Carl Schmitt, *The Nomos of the Earth in the International Law of the Jus Publicum Europaeum*, New York: Telos Press, 2006.

4   Stuart Hall, 'When Was the "Post-Colonial"? Thinking at the Limit', in Iain Chambers and Lidia Curti (eds), *The Post-colonial Question: Common Skies Divided Horizons*, London: Routledge, 1996, 246.

to underscore the persistence of the problems of dependency, under-development, and marginalization in the new, postcolonial conjuncture, Hall calls attention to some unexpected implications of the 'subverting of the old colonizing/colonized binary'. In the wake of the Cold War, when the celebration of the US as a sole superpower and the projection of a 'New American Century' were common sense in public debates, Hall offers a substantially different analysis of globalization. Focusing on histories and routes of migration, he points to a powerful reshuffling of the relations among metropolitan centres and the 'margins', fleshing out a 'subaltern proliferation of difference' that exists alongside and in tension with 'globalization's homogenizing tendencies'. More impor-tantly still, he writes that 'what threatens to become the West's global closure – the apotheosis of its global universalizing mission – is *at the same time* the moment of the West's slow, uncertain, protracted de-centering'.[5]

It would be tempting to stage a dialogue in this respect between Hall and world-system scholars like Immanuel Wallerstein and Giovanni Arrighi, who began to talk about a crisis of US global hegemony in the 1990s (see below, Chapter 3). For now, we want to dwell a little longer on the concepts of the 'Rest' and the 'West' that figure in the title of this book. Hall's insistence on entanglements remains an effective antidote against essentialist understandings of these concepts, even in an age in which the rhetoric of 'decoupling' and 'friendshoring' is widespread, particularly in the West, and seems to foreshadow the establishment of new boundaries, often presented with civilizational overtones that demarcate 'democracy' from 'autocracy'. A critical attitude towards such rhetoric runs through the chapters of this book. At the same time, we recognize that the concept of the West is not simply going to go away, and even use the term ourselves.

Critical thinkers including David Graeber have argued 'there never was a West' and genealogists of the term have noted how its use has shifted to become 'shorthand for what now more usually goes by the name of the global North'.[6] However, claims such as the one opening this

5   Stuart Hall, 'Conclusion: The Multi-cultural Question', in Barnor Hesse (ed.), *Un/settled Multiculturalisms: Diasporas, Entanglements, Transruptions*, London: Zed Books, 2000, 213, 215 and 217.

6   David Graeber, 'There Never Was a West: Or, Democracy Emerges from the Spaces In Between', in *Possibilities: Essays on Hierarchy, Rebellion, and Desire*, Oakland,

introduction – that the Ukraine war has strengthened the West's unity
– underscore the concept's resilience even as its geopolitical referents
change, in this case, away from the contrast with colonial or Islamic
cultures prevalent after 9/11, and towards an opposition to Russia. In
fact, this is an old use of the term, which has resonances not only with
the Cold War period and the immediate aftermath of the Bolshevik
revolution but also with debates within pre-Soviet Russia, when 'Slavo-
philes' who advocated a return to pre-Petrine social and political norms
opposed 'Westerners' who espoused reform according to European
models.[7] In reality, the 'West' and the 'Rest' are rhetorical devices whose
repeated use screens out the plurality of cultural, social, and political
formations they subsume. Yet, even as we realize this, and associate the
distinction with past division, imperial ventures, and culture wars, its
mobilization is far from exhausted and, given the violent stakes surrounding what Hall calls the de-centring of the West, perhaps even
more dangerous in the present than the past.

Writing of the 'end of Pax Americana' from an East Asian perspective,
Naoki Sakai is another thinker who confronts the overarching issue of
the 'dislocation of the West'. Discussing the mutations and crises of the
'modern international world' (or 'internationality', a system of relations
among nation-states), he frames the 'West' and the 'Rest' as 'positionalities'
whose stability depends on a quest for civilizational or 'anthropological
difference'.[8] While Sakai offers a critical view on how the 'West'/'Rest'
divide has been employed historically and in the present, his observation about the 'proliferating sense of worthlessness' of these categories
today is even more striking. At issue is not only their growing irrele-
vance in the 'cartographic representation of the world' but also the
implausibility of the idea 'that the West is more developed than the
Rest in the chronological order of the world'.[9] Our challenge lies in
heeding these insights while negotiating the continual reemergence of

CA: AK Press, 2007, 329–74; Christopher GoGwilt, 'Reinventing the West: The Invention of the West 25 Years Later', in Christopher GoGwilt, Holt Meyer, and Sergey Sistiaga
(eds), *Westernness: Critical Reflections of the Spatio-temporal Construction of the West*,
Oldenbourg: De Gruyter, 2022, 224.

7   Christopher GoGwilt, 'A Brief Genealogy of the West', in GoGwilt, Meyer and
Sistiaga, *Westernness*, 239.

8   Naoki Sakai, *The End of Pax Americana: The Loss of Empire and Hikikomori
Nationalism*, Durham, NC: Duke University Press, 2022, 15.

9   Ibid., 3 and 16.

the 'West'/'Rest' division in political rhetoric, the media, and even critical discourse.

It should be clear that by reversing Stuart Hall's formula, our aim is not to describe the rise of an elusive 'Rest' in contrast to a presumed 'decline' of the 'West'. What is the 'Rest'? First, we note that it is *a* rest, what remains in the world once we have subtracted the 'West', which acts as a kind of master signifier in the initial formula. Shared experiences of slavery, colonialism, and 'humiliation' by 'Western' powers have prompted an important history of resistance and struggles in many parts of the world as well as the forging of 'metageographical' notions such as the 'Third World' and the 'global South'.[10] Today, there is a broad wariness of concepts that are constructed in a negative way ('what does *not* belong to the West'). Moreover, the powerful transformations reshaping contemporary capitalism seem to defy any established 'metageographic' partition of the world. For us, *The Rest and the West* signals precisely those transformations – a major shift in the distribution of power and wealth, and an open transition that needs to be investigated and theoretically grasped. Furthermore, asking what a rest is has important implications for understanding the current shape of the West. While the West may seem to be consolidating its unity, its increasing division from the 'Rest' may challenge and transform its nature in unpredictable ways. We draw inspiration here from James Clifford, who, in his review of Edward Said's *Orientalism*, astutely writes that the effect of this book's argument 'is not so much to undermine the notion of a substantial Orient as it is to make problematic "the Occident"'.[11]

The idea of reversing the formula *the West and the Rest* has been around for some time. In an influential book published in 2008, the Indian American journalist and political commentator Fareed Zakaria writes of an emerging 'post-American world', giving to the first chapter the telling title 'The Rise of the Rest'. What Zakaria intends to describe is the third of a series of 'tectonic power shifts' that have reshaped world politics over the past five hundred years. The rise of the West in early modern times, he explains, gave way to the rise of the US at the end of

---

10   See Anne Garland Mahler, *From the Tricontinental to the Global South: Race, Radicalism, and Transnational Solidarity*, Durham, NC: Duke University Press, 2018.

11   James Clifford, *The Predicament of Culture: Twentieth Century Ethnography, Literature, and Art*, Cambridge, MA: Harvard University Press, 1988, 271–2.

the nineteenth century, which is now superseded by 'the rise of everyone else'. The new world we are entering, he writes, will not necessarily be 'anti-American', but it will be 'defined and directed from many places and by many people'.[12] Written in 2006 and 2007, the power shift described in *The Post-American World* was accelerated by the financial crisis of 2007–8, which – as Zakaria contends in the preface to the 2011 edition – gave it 'new force and greater scope'.[13] And, while he explicitly claims that his book is not about the 'decline of America', he is also clear regarding the implications of the 'Rise of the Rest' for the West's position in the world system. This is a question that figures prominently in our book. While we take seriously the hypothesis of a crisis of US global hegemony, we echo Hall and Sakai in referring to a 'decentring' or a 'dislocation' of the West, steering clear from rhetoric about the 'decline' or 'disintegration of Western civilization'.[14] This is a rhetoric that emerged during the years of the Great War, with such works as Madison Grant's *The Passing of a Great Race* and Oswald Spengler's *The Decline of the West*, whose connection with the protean history of modern racism cannot be overlooked. Hence our wariness about invoking the notion of civilization when analyzing political and economic matters.

When we speak of a crisis of US global hegemony, we follow Giovanni Arrighi's lead by referring to a substantial weakening of its capacity to 'lead' and to orchestrate the distribution of power and capital accumulation at the world scale. As explained later in this introduction, we doubt that a straightforward 'hegemonic transition' – say, from the US to China – is imminent. However, we emphasize the fact that, for the first time in modern capitalism's centuries-long history, Western hegemony faces radical challenges and is highly improbable in the coming decades. This situation is not something we celebrate as a happy end: the world *after* the West may prove worse than the world the West built through colonialism and imperialism. We are living through an *open transition*, haunted by war and proliferating war regimes but also shaped by multifarious struggles for social justice. It bears remembering that the decentring and dislocation of the West has long been a dream and a

---

12   Fareed Zakaria, *The Post-American World*, 2nd edition, New York: Norton & Co, 2011, 7.

13   Ibid., 2.

14   Sakai, *End of Pax Americana*, 5.

political imperative for anticolonial, antiracist, and anti-imperialist movements. In the 1920s and 1930s, figures such as the Peruvian Marxist José Carlos Mariátegui and C. L. R. James found interest in Spengler's *Decline of the West*, connecting it to Trotsky and Lenin as inspiration for a world revolution.[15] However, we do not conclude this section by invoking Mariátegui or James, but rather with the words of W. E. B Du Bois from his 1906 essay 'The Negro Question in the United States', written at Max Weber's behest for a prestigious German social science journal. Du Bois ends by shifting perspective to the world beyond the US, warning: 'Above all consider one thing, the day of the colored races dawns. It is insanity to delay this development; it is wisdom to promote what it promises us in light and hope for the future.'[16] Stripped of the era's rhetoric, Du Bois's statement still echoes powerfully.

Polarities

The Rest and the West engages with the notions of multipolarity and multipolarism. These are, for us, descriptive tools, not ideals or political projects to be pursued. We concur with Adam Tooze that, at least since the financial crisis of 2007–8, we *already* inhabit a world characterized by 'centrifugal multipolarity'.[17] The COVID-19 pandemic and the Ukraine war have further entrenched this predicament while accentuating its 'centrifugal' dimension. At issue today is the future organization of multipolarity at a global scale, despite powerful forces seeking to simplify it according to territorial lines and blocs foreshadowing a so-called New Cold War between the US and China. While multipolarity may fuel new imperialist drives, inter-imperialist rivalries, and wars, it might also enable a more equitable distribution of wealth and power. This is what we mean by an open transition, and, in the following chapters we try to map the stakes and forces that shape this change. The notion of multipolarity guides our efforts, notwithstanding its use in

15   See Matthieu Renault, *C.L.R. James. La vie révolutionnaire d'un 'Platon noir'*, Paris: La Découverte, 2015, 67–9.

16   W.E.B. Du Bois, 'The Negro Question in the United States', *CR: The New Centennial Review* 6, no. 3 (2006), 241, 290, 287.

17   Adam Tooze, *Shutdown: How Covid Shook the World's Economy*, New York: Viking, 2021, 294.

rhetoric by Vladimir Putin and other reactionary leaders, which we view as a symptom of wider shifts requiring investigation.

Needless to say, the notion of multipolarity can be retrospectively projected onto the past. For instance, it can be adapted to the analysis of the systems of ancient city-states in Greece between the seventh and fourth centuries BCE or to the conflicts between Chinese warring states in the period between the fifth and third centuries BCE. In European history, multipolarity is often connected to the idea of a balance of power, as for instance in the case of the 'hundred years peace', as described by Karl Polanyi in his 1944 work *The Great Transformation* – which was disrupted by the rise of imperialism that led to the Great War. Today, parallels with 1914 abound, reinforced by images of trench warfare in Ukraine that recall the 'storm of steel' celebrated by Ernst Jünger in his 1920 book of the same title.[18] We acknowledge that the Second World War has often been invoked since the beginning of the Ukraine war, with the Russian propaganda mobilizing the rhetoric of the 'Great Patriotic War' against Nazism to justify the aggression on Ukraine, and Putin being occasionally portrayed as a 'new Hitler' in the West. In terms of a comparison between the present situation with the political and military scenarios of the Great War, however, there is much more than these gratuitous references to the Second World War imply. We agree with Raúl Sanchez Cedillo that historical processes such as the decline of British global hegemony, the qualitative leap in the technological development of war machines, and even the rise of a new nationalist discourse foreshadowing fascism, resonate in the present.[19] Some of the actors in the current drama even recall the 'sleepwalkers' at the centre of Christopher Clark's celebrated book on the outbreak of war in 1914.[20]

Having said this, we need to remain aware of the profound differences distinguishing present challenges from those of the early twentieth century. More generally, we note the limits of historical analogies. These limits are even more apparent when references to history nurture a kind of nostalgia for past configurations of power, often imagined and depicted with reference to multipolarity. To stay with the historical

---

18 Ernst Jünger, *Storm of Steel*, London: Penguin, 2016.
19 See Raúl Sanchez Cedillo, *Esta guerra no termina en Ucrania*, Pamplona: Katakrak, 2022, 149–50.
20 See Christopher Clark, *The Sleepwalkers: How Europe Went to War in 1914*, London: Allen Lane, 2012.

example of the Great War and the end of the Belle Époque, our critique of imperialism does not imply any sentimentality for the multipolar Europe of the nineteenth century or for a peace predicated upon war in Algeria and elsewhere, as well as on the massacre of countless rebels and revolutionaries, including the Paris Communards of 1871. To repeat, our interest in multipolarity does not lead us to idealize purported past instances of multipolar order. This is also why we are wary of attempts to draw inspiration for a 'decolonial' politics today from the 'inter-connected Old World, noncapitalist and pluricentric' supposed to have existed 'before 1500' and eventually disrupted by European conquest and colonial expansion.[21] Multipolarity here is understood in civiliza-tional terms that are inadequate to grasp today's challenges. Beyond this kind of argument, the concept of civilization has its own story, includ-ing, in the twentieth century, the contributions of figures such as Arnold Toynbee and Eric Voegelin. These thinkers cast a shadow over uses of the notion in contemporary debates on world history and politics. Yet, while these earlier visions had cataclysmic and mystical undertones, civilizational thought today tends to identify stable and even ontological units of conflict and comparison, giving it a distinctly reactionary cast.

Over twenty-five years after its publication, Samuel Huntington's *The Clash of Civilizations* continues to inspire dreams of civilizational renais-sances that have the propensity to turn quickly into nightmares. In this respect, as Ilya Budraitskis writes, 'the Putin regime has been Hunting-ton's star pupil'.[22] One has only to read a few pages from Aleksandr Dugin's *Theory of a Multipolar World* to get a sense of the ways in which the world is imagined in intellectual circles close to Putin. Known as an influential theorist of Eurasianism, a concept forged within the Russian émigré community after the October Revolution to designate the pecu-liarity of Russia and the so-called Russian world, Dugin is celebrated by the far right in Europe and beyond. Reading his theoretical account of multipolarity, one stumbles on sentences and even pages that echo postcolonial and decolonial criticism of the West: 'The elaboration of a

---

21   Walter Mignolo, 'On Pluriversality and Multipolar World: Decoloniality after Decolonization. Dewesternization after the Cold War', in Bernd Reiter (ed.), *Construct-ing the Pluriverse: The Geopolitics of Knowledge*, Durham, NC: Duke University Press, 2018, 90.

22   Ilya Budraitskis, *Dissidents among Dissidents: Ideology, Politics, and the Left in Post-Soviet Russia*, London: Verso, 2022, 10.

Theory of a Multipolar World,' he writes, 'must pass through the rejection of the very foundations of Western hegemony, and, accordingly, the IR theories built thereupon.'[23] Marxism and universalism in general are criticized as Eurocentric, while Huntington is explicitly praised for positing civilizations (plural) as 'actors' of politics and history. Starting from an 'ontological concept of civilization', which means claiming the 'ontological priority' of civilizations, Dugin integrates a panoply of aspects – from language to religion – to chart a map of the 'multipolar world' entirely predicated upon civilizations as foundational units.[24] Politics is completely subsumed under civilization, and as it is easy to see, for Dugin, Russia has a special role to play in this multipolar game.

In several essays, Dugin contends that 'Eurasia is the continent where everything is being decided'. His attention to India is telling. 'Multipolarity,' he writes, 'favors the sovereignty of big countries or civilization states, India being one of the most important constituents', while 'the spectacularly growing Indian identity, based on a system of values, is totally incompatible with Western liberalism'.[25] Such words clearly imply an endorsement of Narendra Modi's Hindutva regime and cast Dugin's multipolarity as a reactionary political project based on civilizational foundations and on the refusal of any kind of democracy or human rights as sheer Western ideology. If one considers that Modi himself has invoked the rhetoric of multipolarity, it is easy to understand why the notion has been at the centre of heated debates in India. Kavita Krishnan extends a critique of Dugin and Modi to those among the Indian and global left who have taken multipolarity as the main compass by which to understand world politics in the wake of Russia's aggression in Ukraine.[26] Krishnan has been, for many years, an activist and then a member of the Politburo of the Communist Party of India (Marxist–Leninist) Liberation, and her article must be read against the background of a polemical debate that led her to resign from the party's leadership due to divergences on a whole set of topics, including the Ukraine war. Krishnan considers multipolarity as the primary rhetoric shared

23   Aleksandr Dugin, *The Theory of a Multipolar World*, London: Aktos, 2020, 31–2.

24   Dugin, *Theory*, ch. 3 (45 for the quote).

25   Aleksandr Dugin, 'The Indian Moment of Multipolarity', *Seminar*, 2020, india-seminar.com.

26   Kavita Krishnan, 'Multipolarity, the Mantra of Authoritarianism', *India Forum*, 20 December 2022, theindiaforum.in.

by Putin and Xi Jinping, who, in early 2023, announced a Global Civilization Initiative.[27] She accuses many left thinkers and activists of supporting these leaders simply because of their hostility to the US, which leads them to neglect the crucial task of denouncing the social relations prevailing in Russia and China.

We are aware that the concept of multipolarity can invoke such connotations, and that – as Krishnan notes – the very language of polarities has a history in international relations that we do not necessarily endorse. We have already made clear our rejection of any civilizational understanding of the poles composing multipolarity, and we will revisit this point later in this introduction. For now, it is important to acknowledge the risk Krishnan identifies – that a geopolitical reading of the current conjuncture can obscure the social and political stakes underlying shifts in world politics. However, as we explain later in the book, our aim is to provide an analysis of such shifts that refuses to conceal the dynamics of social mobilization and class struggle that drive them. To offer a recent and pertinent example, we would never abandon our passionate support for the 'Woman, Life, Freedom' movement in Iran (which, significantly, adopts a Kurdish slogan) to take a position that celebrates the role of the country as part of an 'anti-American' pole in a multipolar world. The same principle applies to any other candidate that plays a similar role in such a world, no matter the pole with which they align. We reaffirm that, for us, multipolarity is neither a political slogan nor an ideal. It is, rather, a concept that helps us provide a description of the powerful shifts in the distribution of power and wealth that characterize the current shape of the world. This book is not a celebration of multipolarity; it is, rather, an attempt to disclose the contours of a new world, within which struggles for freedom and equality must be fought.

We do not know whether multipolarity can be contained, organized, and even transformed by a rules-based international order. What seems clear is that what has existed under that name since the end of the Second World War has corresponded to an architecture of world power led by the US, first in competition with the USSR and then, in the phrase of Samuel P. Huntington, as a 'lonely superpower'.[28] This is not to say

---

27 'Xi Proposes Global Civilization Initiative', *Xinhua*, 15 March 2023.

28 See Samuel P. Huntington, 'The Lonely Superpower', *Foreign Affairs* 78, no. 2 (March–April 1999), 35–49.

that the norms and principles encapsulated in the idea of an international order based on rules were operating for decades in the exclusive interest of the US and its allies, or that the UN (supposedly at the centre of this order) did not occasionally act also as a forum for anticolonial movements and for the settlement of controversies. Working in tandem with other agencies, including the Bretton Woods institutions (the International Monetary Fund, the World Bank, and since 1995 the World Trade Organization), the rules-based international order as we knew it after 1945 was, nonetheless, an effective framework for the articulation of US global hegemony and for the related development of capitalism. The multilateralism under US leadership that was pursued in the Clinton years was an attempt to reorganize the rules-based system according to the new scenario established by the end of the Cold War. In the wake of 9/11, that system was decidedly challenged by the unilateralism of the George W. Bush Jr administration: he famously declared in a press conference on 17 September 2001 that 'there are no rules'.[29] Remembering this statement indicates the rules-based order was in crisis long before Russia's invasion of Ukraine. A simple return to that order seems highly improbable today, even as the archives of its history may offer helpful insights for constructing a new international system.

As we anticipated earlier, our use of the concept of multipolarity leads us to be wary of the rhetoric of a New Cold War and of the related bipolar focus on the strategic competition between the US and China. To be sure, we devote much of our analysis to these two powers, with scattered mentions of other continental or imperial states, as we call them. But we do so in an attempt to go beyond the territorial boundaries of China and the US, underscoring the gap between the circuits of capital and power that constitute them and their national denominations, as well as the role of other states, international institutions, and corporations, both multinational and state-owned, that contribute to the composed assemblage of rule and governance of the contemporary world. As we explain in Chapter 4, a critical analysis of the rhetoric of *decoupling* and *friendshoring* highlights a persistent interdependence between China and the US, with their relations becoming a matter of political calculation. Perhaps more importantly, both states are immersed

---

29   See Andrew Hurrell, '"There Are No Rules" (George W. Bush): International Order after September 11', *International Relations* 16, no. 2 (2002), 185–204.

in fragmented processes of regional integration in which emerging economic and political powers may develop independent interests and initiate negotiations with uncertain ends. Latin America is a case in point. In Chapter 5, we analyse the shifting power relations in Latin America as symptoms of wider processes of transformation, charting an emerging map of power and wealth that guides our analysis of contemporary capitalism, as well as of China–US competition. In drawing this map, we never forget the disruption occasioned by Russia's invasion of Ukraine, which has concatenated with another set of disruptions brought about by the COVID-19 pandemic.

From pandemic to war

The pandemic is not over. As we write, deaths, hospitalizations, new variants, and the devastating effects of uneven vaccine distribution continue to wrack the world. Masks are off in many public spaces, China has relaxed its lockdown regime, and the World Health Organization has declared that COVID-19 is no longer a global health emergency. However, the risk of infection remains, no matter how far it is ignored in social life. Critics on the left have joined the chorus against lockdowns, even if, as Richard Seymour writes, most people made the judgement that 'suspending capitalism for a while . . . was a good thing'.[30] And the war in Ukraine has drawn public alarm and political resources away from pandemic concerns, regardless of case rates and reproduction ratios. Nonetheless, the virus remains a biological reality, which the world must coexist with for the foreseeable future, at least until something worse, or just more infectious, comes along. At this stage, we feel somewhat hesitant about making the pandemic a serious issue in this book. For two or three years, vast critical energies were expended on the analysis of COVID-19, and readers might be forgiven for feeling that all that was interesting to say has already been said by pundits glued to their keyboards and Zoom screens during the long tedious days of lockdown.

---

30 See Toby Green and Thomas Fazi, *The Covid Consensus: The Global Assault on Democracy and the Poor? A Critique from the Left*, London: Hurst, 2023; and Richard Seymour, 'Three Years On, There Is a New Generation of Lockdown Skeptics', *Guardian*, 23 March 2023.

But it is not the pandemic per se that concerns us in our analysis of contemporary capital and power. Rather, we are interested in the effects of the pandemic upon global processes and expanding patterns of multipolarization that were already in train before they were exacerbated by the virus, and which exist in continuity, rather than simply rupture, with the war regimes that have emerged in the pandemic's wake.

Why did a war that touches the centre of the world system explode just as the pandemic was reaching its long tail? Ida Dominijanni argues that the coronavirus outbreak exposed the impotence of established political bodies before biological processes that exceeded their control.[31] Like the catastrophe of climate change, which states and international organizations struggle to confront, the pandemic made evident the limits of constituted power. The Ukraine war, in this analysis, is a vengeful strike back against this helplessness and the injury it has brought. In the most reckless of ways, the war has reasserted the powers implicit in the traditional definition of the modern state, most notably sovereign powers attached to the capacity to wield violence and the control of territory. Although we place less emphasis on the symbolic dimensions of the war, Dominijanni's reading offers a means to co-locate the pandemic and Russia's invasion of Ukraine, recognizing their connection while noting the different kinds of crises they mark. Many have argued that the pandemic is an Anthropocenic event, a kind of dress rehearsal for a future conditioned by ecological change and the excesses of human life upon the planet.[32] In this view, the pandemic is less a crisis than a symptom of a permanently changed condition. Likewise, the Ukraine war marks a change, this time more geopolitical than Anthropocenic, although it is important not to forget the ecological dimensions of the conflict, which link not only to the devastation of the earth and atmosphere that results from fighting but also to energy politics. In geopolitical terms, the invasion of Ukraine has shifted the contours of the post–Cold War global order, in which US primacy enforced an internationalism based, in turn, on realist pragmatics and liberal doctrines. It is premature to pronounce the end of this order, which was always characterized

---

31   Ida Dominijanni, 'L'escalation delle parole', Centro per la Riforma dello Stato, 5 May 2022.

32   Bruno Latour, 'Is This a Dress Rehearsal?', *Critical Inquiry* 47, no. S2 (2021), S25–7.

by internal contradictions and chaos, while the war is still playing out on the ground. Nonetheless, Russia's actions, combined with China's ongoing challenge to US hegemony, intensify the centrifugal and multipolar tendencies at work in the world system at least since the 2007–8 financial crisis. At stake is the emergence of a new structure of global politics in which the dominance of a single power is clearly not accepted by all.

The notion of crisis is overused and carries narrative implications not always suited to the analysis of deep processes of change.[33] Nonetheless, we continue to use this term, recognizing its limits and qualifying its applicability. Although it is tempting and often necessary to substitute terms such as catastrophe or emergency, these concepts come with their own baggage and do not necessarily offer an exit from the analytical and descriptive quandaries at hand. In this optic, we can say that the pandemic and the Ukraine war embody two different kinds of globalization crisis, which have concatenated in important ways. The pandemic was clearly a health crisis, which was symptomatic of wider imbalances in the planetary ecosystem and triggered life support and mobility restriction measures that had critical impacts upon the circulatory and reproductive aspects of capitalism. The war, by contrast, marks a crisis of the world system, which reverberates not only through political relations as imagined in an international frame but also through economic and technological domains that cannot fully be contained by national interests or imperial rivalries. Together, these crises have contributed to the making of an unstable global conjuncture, in which the steady set of articulations that holds together the terrain on which change unfolds appears more up for grabs than in other historical moments. Disruption is the order of the day, and is certainly, if we think in terms of supply chains, one of the main elements of continuity between the pandemic and the war. In the former instance, lockdowns and the withdrawal of labour from workplaces led to a general paralysis of supply chains and production networks, and a consequent rethinking of logistical notions such as efficiency, resilience, and agility. In the case of war, supply chain disruptions were more geographically specific but affected sectors such as food and energy, which were considered essential parts of economies during the pandemic. Consequently, these disruptions had widespread effects and,

---

33   See Janet Roitman, *Anti-Crisis*, Durham, NC: Duke University Press, 2013.

compared to interruptions caused by lockdowns, were less responsive to political decisions about what to open up or close down.

Earlier, we quoted Richard Seymour on the wide public acceptance of 'suspending capitalism' during the pandemic. Although this is a nice piece of rhetoric directed against lockdown sceptics, we do not think that the coronavirus brought a stop to capitalism, even temporarily.[34] The notion of COVID capitalism proposed by Thomas Nail offers a way of registering how 'capitalism and the novel coronavirus alter and amplify each other'.[35] There are many dimensions to the mutations of capital occasioned by the pandemic, which we explore in Chapter 1. To anticipate our argument, we can mention the issues surrounding the production and distribution of vaccines, which raise not only questions of profit, innovation, and intellectual property, but also matters of global inequality and logistical organization, including the availability of cold chain infrastructures for vaccine transport and storage. Although Russia and China produced their own vaccines, these did not prove as effective as the mRNA vaccines, which, by the end of 2021, were available throughout the West. Despite contrary indications from the Biden administration, Western nations were unable to restrain pharmaceutical companies from exercising patent rights, which these firms argued were necessary due to a claimed link between innovation capacities and profit motives. The resulting situation left countries in the global South struggling to protect their populations. India, for instance, boasts a pharmaceutical industry that exports generic medicines throughout the world, but was only able to supply the less effective Astra Zeneca vaccine during the worst months of the pandemic. In the meantime, China was busy shipping vaccines to many parts of Asia, Africa, and Latin America, under the umbrella of its Health Silk Road programme. While it is possible to argue about the relative effectiveness of the United Nations' COVAX facility or to note that the World Trade Organization partially suspended COVID vaccine patents in 2022, the West's prioritization of profit over global health outcomes has surely affected the attitudes of many countries towards the Ukraine war.

---

34   See Sandro Mezzadra and Brett Neilson, 'The Capitalist Virus', *Politics* 44, no. 2 (2024), 188–202.

35   Thomas Nail, 'What Is Covid Capitalism?', *Distinktion: Journal of Social Theory* 23, nos 2–3 (2022), 327–41, 327.

An important feature of today's multipolarity is the extension of capitalism beyond any particular pole. The violent tensions that beset the world cannot be reduced to a conflict of different varieties of capitalism, not least because interconnections and junctions among poles remain crucial to the constitution of a variegated and unevenly developed global capitalism. If the circulation of vaccines in the pandemic highlighted certain features of the relations among capitalism and intellectual property rights, the Ukraine war has foregrounded the role of energy in shaping global political and economic relations. A distinct feature of the Russian war effort derives from the predominantly extractive form of capitalism that has evolved in that country: the need to keep selling energy to its enemies in order to fund its military campaign. This is just one logistical aspect of a multifaceted war that has also involved practices such as the targeting of supply lines and transportation networks, as well as difficulties with the timing and transport of Western arms provisions. However, the importance of energy interconnections to the war, including gas pipelines that pass from Russia through Ukraine to Western Europe, is a central feature. The restriction of energy supply by Russia (as much as its facilitation) has served as a geopolitical lever and bargaining chip, with the destruction of the Nord Stream pipelines connecting Russia to Germany remaining a clouded affair that in its own way signifies the relevance of energy to the war. The supply chain disruptions and price shocks that have resulted from these energy-related vacillations have had global ramifications, contributing to the re-emergence of inflation and concatenating with the logistical logjams introduced by the pandemic. Plainly, there are other challenges deriving from the war that have also contributed to these phenomena, including the halting of grain and neon exports from Ukraine, the latter being a key ingredient for the production of lasers used in making silicon chips, which are themselves at the heart of the technology war between China and the US.[36] But the inflationary effects of the war, felt unevenly across different global regions, are key, and receive careful consideration in this book.

Although there is a continuity between the inflationary effects produced by pandemic-induced supply shocks and those resulting from the

36   Sarah Schiffling and Nikolaos Valantasis Kanellos, 'Five Essential Commodities That Will Be Hit by the War in Ukraine', *The Conversation*, 25 February 2022.

war, their different regional impacts and economic causes, for instance in Europe and the US, need to be noted.[37] Nonetheless, the actions and policy responses of central banks in the face of these changes have displayed some similar features, having shifted from the stimulus packages and accommodative monetary policies of the COVID years to more restrictionary measures involving interest rate rises and the winding down of quantitative easing programs that were introduced with the 2007–8 economic crisis. Again, there are regional and even polar differences in this regard, with China maintaining quite a low inflation rate, for instance, while the Bank of Japan has made important moves on its bond yield policies, with potentially seismic effects for the economies of Australia and the Netherlands. In the US, the passing of the 2022 Inflation Reduction Act has important implications for the funding of the energy transition, reacting to perceived economic opportunities linked to climate change adaptation and mitigation, while also supporting new fossil fuel projects. This same Act foregrounds geopolitical and geoeconomic moves that seek to circumvent China's position in relevant energy transition supply chains, including ones in which it is presently dominant, such as those involving rare earth minerals, wind turbines, and photovoltaic panels. In these manoeuvres, the intertwining of capital's financial operations with its logistical and extractive aspects becomes evident. To make sense of these complex connections, we need to expand our analytical horizons beyond the confines of economic adjustments or policy shifts that pertain solely within single countries, continents, or regions (noting that these can be unstable denominations). Instead, we have to train our attention towards global spaces, processes, and junctures that intermesh and articulate the poles of the contemporary world, notwithstanding their centrifugal tendencies and the appearance of insularity. This approach entails an understanding of globalization that goes way beyond just trade and commerce, and an analytical focus that highlights the contradictory logics of capitalism and territorialism. In the next section, we attempt to advance this methodological line.

---

37   Isabella M. Weber, Jesus Lara Jeuregui, Lucas Teixeira, and Luiza Nassif Pires, 'Inflation in Times of Overlapping Emergencies: Systemically Significant Prices from an Input-Output Perspective', University of Massachusetts Amherst, Department of Economics Working Paper Series 2022-22, 2022.

(Geo)politics of capital

In this book we elaborate the analysis of contemporary capitalism that we started to articulate in *The Politics of Operations*.[38] Investigating the mutations of capital and capitalism through an examination of the operative logic that drives investments and processes of valorization in such domains as extraction, logistics, and finance, we flesh out in that book a shift in the composition of what we call, following Marx, 'aggregate capital' (*Gesamtkapital*). An expanded reading of the notion of extraction, beyond the literal reference to the world of oil, mining, and extensive agriculture, allows us to underscore the increasing relevance of specific *fractions* of capital – of capitalist actors that target and exploit processes of social cooperation from the outside, without directly organizing or coordinating the underlying productive activities. The prominence of such extractive dynamics, which include but are not limited to the instances of data extractivism discussed in Chapter 4, has significant implications for the composition of living labour and impinges on the very terrain of the antagonism between capital and labour. *The Rest and the West* takes this expanded notion of extraction as a background for an analysis that foregrounds the tensions, challenges, and processes of adaptation that surround the contemporary capitalist formation in a conjuncture of pandemic and war. As we explain in Chapter 2, reproduction and circulation are tested in particularly intense ways in such a conjuncture, by the pandemic no less than by the Ukraine war, which has strained the fabric of social reproduction in both warring countries and proved the issue of logistics once again strategic. Based on an analysis of the definition of *essential workers* during the pandemic in different parts of the world, we more generally contend that circulation and reproduction – crisscrossed and permeated as they are by multifarious extractive operations – play new roles in the workings of contemporary capitalism. They even provide us with an angle for grasping the persistently crucial although transformed position of production in processes of valorization and accumulation of capital.

---

38   See Sandro Mezzadra and Brett Neilson, *The Politics of Operations: Excavating Contemporary Capitalism*, Durham, NC: Duke University Press, 2019.

We are aware that this stylization of contemporary capitalism works at a quite abstract level. Nonetheless, we are convinced that to pursue more grounded investigations, such as those exploring infrastructures, platforms, and energy interconnections, we require what Marx refers to in the preface to *Capital*, volume 1, as 'the power of abstraction'. Questions of space and geography, homogeneity and heterogeneity, territorial boundaries and expanding frontiers of capital have concerned us since we wrote *Border as Method*.[39] In the present book, we continue to use the phrase *global capitalism*, although we also emphasize the processes of deep variegation that crisscross it. We resist the temptation to adopt conceptual nomenclatures, such as *varieties* of capitalism, or to ascribe a specific formation of capitalism to each of the poles that compose the contemporary multipolar world. This is because capitalism today is constituted by a set of global processes that simultaneously unify and diversify it due to the different ways in which they settle and intermingle with a wide array of political, historical, legal, and cultural differences. Our understanding of poles is far from a merely territorial one. As we argue in Chapter 3, the nexus between capitalism and 'territorialism', to use Arrighi's conceptual language, is today more problematic, marked by tensions and gaps, than in any previous age of the capitalist world system. Capital's production of space was never easy to superimpose on territorial borders, but in an age of proliferating logistical and infrastructural hubs, zones, and corridors, as well as digital networks, these contradictions have intensified to the point of rupture. We are confronted today with a disconnection of capitalism and territorialism that tests not only the national denomination of specific capitalist formations but also their subsumption within a number of clearly delimited and discrete poles.

Our focus on the processes that traverse and constitute global capitalism provides a way to go beyond any understanding of globalization unilaterally centred on trade flows and the relative degree of openness or closure of national economies. The global processes we investigate – in fields such as logistics, finance, digitalization, energy flows and infrastructures, or artificial intelligence – are in fact capable of exerting powerful transformative effects even in a protectionist international

---

39   Sandro Mezzadra and Brett Neilson, *Border as Method, or, the Multiplication of Labor*, Durham, NC: Duke University Press, 2013.

environment, although that environment is, of course, a crucial variable for shaping their form and the spaces they help to produce. Nonetheless, the global dimension is reproduced by those processes, which shape the operations of capital across different parts of the world and have therefore a deep impact on the life, joy, and travails of vast populations. Nowhere is this clearer than in the *operative spaces* that we analyse in Chapter 4 – the spaces where global processes are organized according to capitalist logics amid constant negotiations with a combination of powers, including states and other governmental actors. Investigating what we call, with a concept adapted from Michael Hardt and Antonio Negri's *Empire*, the 'mixed constitution' of operative spaces, we underscore both their constitutive role for processes of pole formation and the non-territorial logics at stake in their working. 'Non-territorial' here does not mean that territory is irrelevant, but rather signals a distance from the legal and political principle of territoriality that supposedly organizes the international world.

Operative spaces are deeply intertwined with, and indeed constitutive of, the processes underpinning pole formation. As we argue in the final section of this introduction, this destabilizes the very possibility of a territorial sealing or enclosure of poles as bounded, self-contained spatial units, in accordance with a traditional state-centred cartographic imagination. We wrote earlier that we take seriously the hegemonic crisis of the US, but we are wary of the prospect of a straightforward hegemonic transition, say from the US to China as the ostensible new global hegemon. Indeed, we would go so far as to suggest that the very language of hegemony may have become inadequate to grasp the turbulence, tensions, and conflicts that haunt the capitalist world system today. We know that the critique of hegemony has long been a touchstone of official Chinese rhetorical discourse, at least since the formulation of Mao's 'three worlds theory' in the early 1970s, which included the US and the USSR in the first world precisely due to their pursuit of hegemony.[40] While such critiques continue to be articulated today, we take a critical stance towards them, as we do towards any official state rhetoric. Nonetheless, we find interesting the argument of Qiao Liang, the Chinese military general and co-author with Wang

---

40 See Jiang An, 'Mao Zedong's "Three Worlds" Theory: Political Considerations and Value for the Times', *Social Sciences in China* 34, no. 1 (2013), 35–57.

Xiangsui of the celebrated book *Unrestricted Warfare*.[41] Underscoring the radical transformations in the calculation of space engendered by the rise of the internet and more generally by processes of digitalization, Qiao Liang plainly and abruptly contends that the age of hegemony and empire is over. The 'decentralization of power' towards the 'development of a multipolar world' appears to him an irreversible tendency, and this is why 'neither subjectively nor objectively China can become the new hegemonic power after the US'.[42]

It would be a relatively straightforward exercise to find Western and particularly US voices echoing Qiao Liang's position with different words, and struggling to find a new language and imaginary to grasp the current predicament at the level of international relations and the world system. Take for instance John Agnew's scepticism regarding the view of a '"regular" hegemonic succession' from the US to China, as well as his emphasis on the potential contribution of the latter to the 'pluralization' of the world system.[43] We duly take note of these voices, but we are far from reassured. As the Ukraine war and related proliferation of war regimes in different parts of the world including the Taiwan Strait demonstrate, the possibility of what we call a territorial simplification of international tensions is more acute today than ever. As we write this introduction, war is again at the centre of the scramble to control global spaces and processes. This deeply troubling situation compels us to rethink the vexed question of imperialism, which we undertake to do in Chapter 3. We speak ironically of imperialism as 'the lowest point of capitalism', to signal the profound gaps between the global processes that sustain capital's valorization and accumulation and the territorial logic that is always at stake in imperialism and wars, no matter how *hybrid*. To be clear, this does not mean that, by attributing imperialism to territorialism, we thereby obscure the nexus of capitalism and war. The opposite is the case, and the main stake of an analysis of imperialism today lies in a detailed analysis of how specific fractions of capital push towards what we just called the territorial simplification of international tensions, striking alliances with territorial power for the sake of

---

41   See Qiao Liang and Wang Xiangsui, *Unrestricted Warfare*, Beijing: PLA Literature and Arts Publishing House, February 1999.

42   Quiao Liang, *L'arco dell'impero*, Gorizia: Leg, 2021, 230, our translation.

43   John Agnew, *Hidden Geopolitics: Governance in a Globalized World*, London: Rowman and Littlefield, 2023, 89–90.

profit and disseminating regimes of war across economy and society. Struggling against such tendencies, against the war and the proliferation of regimes of war, is one of the most important tasks of the new internationalism we foreshadow in Chapter 5.

In discussing capitalism and territorialism, it is tempting to ascribe the former to the domain of economics, and the latter to the domain of politics. Many critical thinkers understand the differentiation between these two spheres as foundational for the functioning of capitalism, and neoliberalism is often charged with troubling and even blurring this boundary, prompting a process of colonization of the political by economic logics and rationalities.[44] In *The Politics of Operations*, we take a different view on this important question, charting and elucidating the directly political dimension of operations of capital, and describing the multifarious ways in which they impinge on the organization of society, the production of subjectivity, the government of conduct and even decision-making, with direct public consequences. This is an argument that we expand in the present book, focusing for instance on the governmental implications of capital's production of operative spaces. As we explain in Chapter 3, contemporary capitalism deploys forms of power that cannot be deemed simply *economic* since they concur in important ways to the political task of governing territories and populations. This may not be entirely new, but the intensity of such political effects of capital operations is indeed unprecedented. This is the reason why we reframe and employ the notion of political capitalism beyond established uses with respect to authoritarian states or to the issue of national security. We do this in order to grasp a set of features and tendencies within contemporary capitalism that are translated and expressed across heterogeneous configurations of power and money in different parts of the world. This particular conceptualization, along with what we wrote earlier about the increasing tensions and gaps between territorialism and capitalism, further complicates our understanding of multipolarity.

Capital remains for us, first and foremost, a social relation. Expanding on this memorable definition provided by Marx in *Capital*, volume 1, we investigate mutations of capital from the perspective of its antagonistic relationship with its main *other* – the subjective figure of living

44 See, for instance, Wendy Brown, *Undoing the Demos: Neoliberalism's Stealth Revolution*, Brooklyn: Zone Books, 2017.

labour. In Chapters 2 and 5, we carefully analyse the processes of diversification and multiplication that have effectively exploded the erstwhile
homogeneity of the industrial working class across diverse geographical
scales. The resulting imbrication of class and difference is for us a
crucial political issue today, and our discussion in this book is meant as
a contribution to ongoing critical debates revolving around concepts
such as the multitude, intersectional coalition, social reproduction,
wageless life, and circulation struggles. Feminist as well as antiracist
thought and activism provide us with key sources of inspiration in this
regard. Besides this, one of the goals of this book is to shed light on the
expanded reproduction of the antagonistic relations constitutive of
capital itself, within the broader framework of contemporary processes
of pole formation and multipolarity. In Chapter 5, we examine practices
of mobility and collective struggle that lead us to widen the concept and
scope of class struggle by fleshing out the multifarious and uneven ways
in which such antagonism crosses and contests emerging spaces of
capital well beyond the national scale. From this angle, class struggle
writ large enters the heterogeneous and mixed constitution of pole formation processes, further complicating the very notion of the pole. It is
to this question that we now turn to conclude this introduction.

What is a pole?

As we mentioned earlier, we are aware of the prevalent uses of the language of polarity in international relations, where it is commonly
employed to address and theorize the issue of the distribution of power
and 'capabilities' within a system deemed as international.[45] The discussion of stability, instability, and conflict-propensity of unipolar, bipolar,
and multipolar systems runs through the history of the discipline, with
purportedly realist thinkers usually deploying scepticism towards the
possibility of a stable multipolarity emerging. Issues of measure of the
degree of power concentration have also been tested in such discussions.
The Ukraine war has in many ways rehearsed, within Western policy
and intellectual circles, the controversy between realist and liberal

---

45   See Nina Graeger, Bertel Heurlin, Ole Waever, and Anders Wivel (eds), *Polarity
in International Relations: Past, Present, and Future*, Cham: Palgrave Macmillan, 2022.

scholars in international relations, with a proliferation of variants that have not really succeeded in challenging consolidated paradigms. In such controversies, states, great powers, and nations continue to be taken for granted as the fundamental units of analysis when it comes to the dynamics of world politics. Other factors are often considered, from economic might to cultural influence and so-called soft power, but exclusively from the perspective of their potential contribution to the sources and projection of political power at the level of the state. A pertinent exemplar is Carla Norrlof's *America's Global Advantage*, a book published in 2010 to demonstrate that we are living in 'an era of US hegemony, a unipolar moment, a Pax Americana, which has enabled Americans to enjoy the highest standard of living in human history'.[46] Norrlof affirms the stability of this 'unipolar moment', based on three key factors: the commercial power of the US, the status of the dollar as a global reserve currency, and unprecedented US military supremacy. Weapons and money, as Niccolò Machiavelli famously quipped, are indeed the basic sources of power. The crucial point is, however, that since the publication of *America's Global Advantage*, the US's position in the field of *money* (both regarding its commercial power and increasing processes of de-dollarization) has been steadily eroded by dynamics that do not originate within the bounded space of the US state itself, and that are largely independent of the involvement of any other single great power. Sure, *weapons* firmly remain on the side of the US, but *money* is also needed if they are to be useful.

Geopolitical approaches, which often intermingle with international relations, push this focus on the state even further, adding a deterministic accent with reference to the presumed laws of movement of landmasses and oceans. While natural factors definitely need to accounted for by a critical theory of politics in an age of climate change and ecological struggle, mainstream geopolitical approaches often refer to those factors to curtail the horizon of politics – and, indeed, to reduce it to issues of power, domination, and war. There is no space in these approaches for a politics of freedom, autonomy, and equality, for the forging of new projects of liberation. Luckily, the development of critical, radical, and Marxist geopolitics provides us with conceptual tools that enable an

---

46 Carla Norrlof, *America's Global Advantage: US Hegemony and International Cooperation*, Cambridge: Cambridge University Press, 2010, 2.

investigation of the shifts and tensions within the world system, paying attention both to the reorganization of relations of power and domination and to the opening of new spaces of struggle.[47] To do that, we need to explore what John Agnew calls 'the real world of potentially global but differentiated and fragmented spaces', which is very different from 'that of the world map with exclusively territorial states banging up against one another'.[48] In a way that may differ from Agnew's, who focuses his research on governance and 'hidden geopolitics', we aim in the following chapters to build a new compass for the political analysis of a world in which the actions and dynamics of states and even great powers are shaped by a panoply of other players, even as they remain key and often decisive actors. Capitalist logics and corporate endeavours figure prominently among these players, often serving to splinter territorial states into multiple zones, havens, enclaves, tech parks, duty-free districts, and hubs. As Quinn Slobodian writes in *Crack-Up Capitalism*, the world is becoming 'pockmarked, perforated, tattered and jiggered, ripped up and pin-pricked' due to capital's search for spaces freed of ordinary degrees of regulation.[49] The challenge is to understand how these fragmentary dynamics work in concert with global processes to create new and anomalous forms of territory that project their shadows not only on states but also on processes of pole formation.

It should be clear by now that our use of the concept of multipolarity in this book is far not only from any kind of propaganda in the current conjuncture of international turmoil and war but also from prevailing uses in international relations and geopolitics. Significantly, the classical language of polarity is increasingly challenged also within these disciplines, for instance by Richard Haass's diagnosis of the emergence of a 'nonpolar world'.[50] We have already explained that we are wary of any civilizational understanding of poles, although we note that China's Global Civilization Initiative launched by Xi Jinping in March 2023 speaks a language of inclusiveness and dialogue that, at least theoretically,

---

47   For an introduction, see Klaus Dodds, Merje Kuus, and Joanne Sharp (eds), *The Ashgate Research Companion to Critical Geopolitics*, London: Routledge, 2013.

48   Agnew, *Hidden Geopolitics*, 20.

49   Quinn Slobodian, *Crack-Up Capitalism: Market Radicals and the Dream of a World Without Democracy*, New York: Metropolitan Books, 2023, 8–9.

50   Richard Haass, 'The Age of Nonpolarity: What Will Follow US Dominance?', *Foreign Affairs* 87, no. 3 (2008), 44–56.

challenges any understanding of civilization as a bounded entity predicated on the sharing of given values and beliefs. It is also important to repeat that we take a critical stance towards an interpretation of poles in merely territorial terms, as if it were possible to project them neatly onto a world map, along with or instead of nation-states. Our analysis of *operative spaces* of capital in Chapter 4 highlights the emergence of heterogeneous spatial formations, such as infrastructural and logistical geographies, as well as the intertwining of digital and territorial logics in processes of platformization. These spaces play key roles in processes of pole formation but cannot be easily contained within any single pole. We are rather confronted with a process of nesting that we describe with the notion of a 'mixed constitution' of poles. Employing the conceptual language of Benjamin H. Bratton's *The Stack*, we can speak of a multiplicity of layers at stake in such constitution, although not in a top-to-bottom cascade, as is the case for Bratton.[51] Rather, in our understanding of pole formation, layers intersect, producing junctures and disjunctions, articulations, frictions, and even conflicts. States represent a first layer, accounting for power differentials and a whole set of social and economic dynamics that guide and influence their initiatives. However, these state-level dynamics are traversed by operative spaces; trade, financial and monetary dynamics; established forms of regionalism; supply chains; and global geographies of production, among other factors. We emphasize that this nested and mixed constitution of poles remains open to forms of territorial simplification and imperialism that may be exploited by nationalist and other reactionary movements.

Among the layers of pole formation, social struggles and movements play crucial although often elusive roles. In Chapter 5, we analyse instances of struggle that, from the Movement for Black Lives in the US in 2020 to the feminist mobilizations in Argentina beginning in 2015, work the boundaries of national formations, circulate and resonate within wider spaces, and at least foreshadow the emergence of a new scale of political action. We also refer to the scattered geography of contemporary migration, highlighting the often necropolitical violence that crisscrosses its management along multiple borders. At the same time, we show how people on the move engender the production of

---

51   See Benjamin H. Bratton, *The Stack: On Software and Sovereignty*, Cambridge, MA: MIT Press, 2015.

space across borders. While we follow Achille Mbembe in asking a set of questions regarding the conditions for such practices of mobility to become part (or a layer) of processes of pole formation, we also highlight that, in many parts of the world, migration shapes the composition of labour in circulation and reproduction, as well as related struggles.[52] We investigate one of the most powerful waves of struggle in recent years in Europe, the mass mobilizations in France against President Macron's pension reform, with reference to his state visit to China in April 2023 – and, of course, the other way around. The claim of the priority of life over labour that is one of simplest and most powerful claims of the French movement thus appears enmeshed within a dense fabric of geopolitical and international frictions, raising the question of Europe's position in the emerging multipolar world and of its relations with the US in the elusive construct of *the West*. This same perspective on social struggle and geopolitics also inspires our discussion of other relevant movements, including the anti-extradition protests of 2019–20 in Hong Kong, the protests against the Citizenship Amendment Act in India, and Indigenous struggles in different parts of the world.

The impact of struggles on geopolitical scenarios – their capacity to open new spaces for transformative political action – is particularly clear in the case of Latin America. Based on shared revolutionary traditions, the movements, struggles, and even insurrections that started in Latin America towards the end of the twentieth century gained momentum at the regional scale, providing the conditions for the emergence of progressive governments in many countries in the first long decade of the new century. In Chapter 5, we offer an analysis of the accomplishments, pitfalls, and failures characteristic of that conjuncture. More importantly, we register the continuity – although with new actors, issues, and languages – of social mobilizations beyond national boundaries in Latin America. And we ask whether the new progressive governments in the region will be able to take on the challenge of launching processes of integration and pole formation while maintaining an emancipatory character. As we emphasize, both the US and China are present in Latin America, and we believe that the point is not about substituting a historical dependence on the US with a full reliance on China (in other words,

52   Achille Mbembe, 'Les Africains doivent se purger du désir d'Europe', *Le Monde*, 10 February 2019.

playing the game of the New Cold War). At stake instead is the possibility of working towards the establishment of a regional autonomy that would allow a multiplication of resources to be appropriated and distributed under the pressure of struggles for social justice. This is a risky project, but not one that lacks realism. As we finish this introduction, we have carefully followed Brazil's President Lula's visit to Beijing in April 2023, following a visit to Washington in the previous month of February. Besides trade agreements and cooperation in the fields of science and technology, Lula has tackled, on the one hand, the issue of de-dollarization on the same day on which Dilma Rousseff (former president of Brazil and member of Lula's Workers' Party) took office as president of the new BRICS bank. If one considers that Lula is working on a common currency in Latin America, taking Argentina as the first partner (although Javier Milei's victory at the presidential election in 2023 has been a blow for such a project), it is clear that this is not an abstract issue for him. His statements on the urgent need of a peace politics with respect to the Ukraine war, taking China as a key partner, seem to be based on the other hand on an axis with Colombia's President Gustavo Petro (and probably with Mexico's president López Obrador). Lula and Petro have further entrenched their political position in the international arena with their readiness to denounce the slaughterous actions of Israel in Gaza as genocide.

Foreshadowed here is a multilayered regional politics in Latin America with global openings and negotiations. We do not want to overemphasize such a political model, which is contingent on unpredictable circumstances, including the stability of Lula's government in Brazil under the threat of an aggressive right, revealed to the world by the storming of federal government buildings in Brasilia on 8 January 2023. What interests us is not to forecast future developments but to emphasize the possibility of an innovative politics of regional integration in Latin America and beyond. Critical regionalism and even continentalism are among the strands of critical thinking that may spur reflections on this difficult but crucial task.[53] While we acknowledge the role that governments can play in pursuing it, our perspective is grounded in social struggles and movements, because we are convinced that a politics of liberation can only emerge from such roots.

---

53   See Mezzadra and Neilson, *Border as Method*, 51–9.

In this sense, in an emergent multipolar world, there is a need to think again the question of translation and communication between movements confronting heterogeneous contexts and challenges and speaking different languages to articulate the refusal of domination and exploitation. This is why we conclude the book with scattered reflections on the legacy of internationalism, as well as on the search for new tools to prompt what we call, paying homage to a book by Lisa Lowe, *continental intimacies* between struggles and movements in different parts of the world.[54]

---

54   See Lisa Lowe, *The Intimacies of Four Continents*, Durham, NC: Duke University Press, 2015.

1

Yet Another Crisis?

Mutations of capitalism

It should not have been a surprise. Warnings from international organizations, including the World Health Organization, were not lacking, while the experiences of HIV/AIDS, Ebola, SARS, and H1N1 were clear signs of the disruptive potential of new kinds of epidemics at the global level. Nevertheless, at the beginning of 2020, COVID-19 shook the world as something completely unexpected. A complex chain of hybridizations – of beings, spaces, and forms of life – spurred the start of the epidemic and its global spread. A *spillover* tested the boundary between the human domain and those of other animals (bats, pangolins), under radically altered environmental circumstances. A wet market supposedly worked as a contact zone between the countryside and a booming Chinese industrial metropolis, Wuhan, also known as the Chinese Detroit for its relevance to the automotive industry. The conduits of global mobility that connect Wuhan to the rest of China and to the world facilitated the virus's rapid circulation. Hybridization became infection, and scenes of death and lockdowns became the background of everyday life for populations around the world. Far from being smooth, the global spread of the virus reflected and intensified the unevenness and inequalities that characterize the contemporary world.[1]

---

1 See Esmé Berkhout et al., *The Inequality Virus: Bringing Together a World Torn Apart by Coronavirus through a Fair, Just and Sustainable Economy*, Oxford: Oxfam International, 2021.

In many regions, the pandemic hit racialized and subaltern populations in devastating ways: Native Americans and African Americans in the US, Indigenous people in Brazil, internal migrants and the poor in general in India. Governments' reactions to the pandemic were highly differentiated, ranging from the neo-Malthusian tones of Trump, Bolsonaro, Johnson, and the like, to more mixed approaches involving social control and welfarist rhetoric, as seen in the European Union, South Korea, and China.

Since the pandemic's onset, critical debates have reoriented perspectives on several important issues, from the meanings of (public) health to the status of science and its relationship with Big Pharma. Questions of surveillance and control also came to the forefront. In the following pages, we tackle some of these issues, but our aims are more specific, even beyond the need to connect the analysis of the pandemic with the disruptions occasioned by Russia's invasion of Ukraine. This is not a book on the COVID-19 virus or on the current geopolitical turmoil, although we take the pandemic and the war in Ukraine as necessary background and distinctive aspects of the time we are living through. At the centre of our work is the analysis of contemporary capitalism. We are interested in how capitalism is mutating in the current conjuncture, but also in the longer-term trends that drive such mutations. Our investigation is pursued from the viewpoint of what Marx called 'living labour'. In other words, the analysis we offer proceeds from the perspective of the exploited, dispossessed, and dominated people whose toil and labour continue to be at the root of the processes of capital valorization and accumulation, and whose struggles and movements provide the only basis to imagine a life beyond the rule of capital.

Crisis seems again to dominate public discourse and even critical studies. How many crises are we confronted with nowadays? We have had the pandemic crisis, sure, and the economic crises it unleashed in many parts of the world. But then there is the climate crisis, which confronts us with a completely different temporality and set of questions. Migration and refugee crises continue to flare up over and over again in various regions, including Europe, the Americas, and South Asia. Where we witnessed an amazing uprising and joyful convergence of struggles in the summer of 2020, in the Movement for Black Lives in the US and beyond, many observers discerned the contours of yet another race crisis. An energy crisis is always looming on the horizon, while even before Russia's invasion of Ukraine in February 2022, there was no shortage of international crises, from Afghanistan to Yemen and the Taiwan Strait (to say nothing of the many other examples that could be cited). 'Collapsology' seems an adequate research project for the present, and the analysis of cascading crises opens the space for discussion of the difference between 'conjunctural' and 'organic' crisis; Gramsci's words on the interregnum, where 'the old is dying and the new cannot be born' are continually quoted and discussed.[2] Even EU officials have been speaking of a 'polycrisis' over the last decade, combining the Eurozone crisis, the war in Ukraine since 2014, the 'refugee crisis', and Brexit.[3]

We do not deny the materiality and the often radical nature of the multiple 'crises' we have just mentioned. We contend that there is a need to investigate not only the dynamics of each crisis but also the multifarious and often unpredictable ways in which they interact. But we also want to ask whether the conceptual language of crisis is adequate to grasp the political challenges we confront today. At least since the publication of *Policing the Crisis* by Stuart Hall and his co-authors in 1978, we know that crisis management has become a form of governmentality that selectively targets specific populations.[4] Looking at the neoliberal dismantling of the welfare state as well as the financial convulsions of recent decades, the situation is not that different. In these instances, the impression is that crisis is understood not as a challenge to be overcome but rather as a state to be prolonged and reproduced in order to implement specific policies and measures. More generally, we are aware of the strategic relevance of the concept of crisis in the political lexicon of Western modernity.[5] While, in classical antiquity, the notion of crisis was closely linked to decision, in legal as well as the medical sense, what

---

2   Pablo Servinge and Raphaël Stevens, *How Everything Can Collapse: A Manual for Our Times*, Cambridge: Polity Press, 2020; Antonio Gramsci, 'State and Civil Society', in Quintin Hoare and Geoffrey Nowell Smith (eds), *Selections from the Prison Notebooks of Antonio Gramsci*, New York: International Publishers, 1971, 276.

3   See Jean Claude Juncker, 'Speech by President Jean-Claude Juncker at the Annual General Meeting of the Hellenic Federation of Enterprises', Athens, 21 June 2016.

4   Stuart Hall et al., *Policing the Crisis: Mugging, the State, and Law and Order*, London: Macmillan, 1978.

5   See Reinhart Koselleck, 'Krise', in Otto Brunner, Werner Konze, and Reinhart Koselleck (eds), *Geschichtliche Grundbegriffe: Historisches Lexikon zur politisch-sozialen Sprache in Deutschland*, vol. 3, Stuttgart: Klett-Cotta, 1982, 617–50.

characterizes modernity is the productivity of crisis precisely because it points to a predicament that must be overcome.[6] This is the root of the nexus between crisis and revolution that one can trace from the English Civil War of the seventeenth century to Thomas Paine and Vladimir Ilyich Lenin.

If, today, the productivity of crisis seems exhausted, the very ubiquity of the word crisis can be taken as a symptom of the concept's limitations. We will use the *word* crisis in the pages that follow to refer to specific dynamics and processes; but we will not employ the concept of crisis as a privileged epistemic angle to describe the current conjuncture, particularly as far as capitalism is concerned. In the wake of the outbreak of the pandemic, there were multiple crises in the workings of capitalism. Financial markets plunged, supply chains were disrupted, industrial sectors were paralysed. As we will analyse in Chapter 3, the war in Ukraine unleashed further critical dynamics – for instance in the energy sector, as well as more generally in the global circulation of commodities. We know that working people and the poor paid the highest price for those crises, an uncanny instantiation of Walter Benjamin's dictum that for the oppressed 'the "state of emergency" is not the exception but the rule'.[7] We will hark back to this point. However, instead of emphasizing the dimension of crisis, we find it more productive to focus on the trends that, constantly working through multiple crises, are driving the development of capitalism even in the framework of the pandemic and war. This is not to say that nothing new is happening. The opposite is true; powerful shifts and disruptions are occurring. But we need to make sense of them through a systematic analysis of the operations of capital that lie at the heart of the current capitalist formation. In this chapter, we focus on the impact of COVID-19. We tend to agree with Adam Tooze, who writes that 2020 (the year of the pandemic) 'is merely a moment in a process of escalation'. Multiple vectors of global change – 'environmental, economic, political, geopolitical' – continue to shape the workings of capitalism. 'Taken together,' Tooze writes, 'they form a dynamic

---

6 See Wendy Brown, 'Untimeliness and Punctuality: Critical Theory in Dark Times', in *Edgework: Critical Essays on Knowledge and Politics*, Princeton, NJ: Princeton University Press, 2005, 1–16.

7 Walter Benjamin, 'Theses on the Philosophy of History', in Hannah Arendt (ed.), *Illuminations*, New York: Schocken Books, 1969, 257.

parallelogram that makes de-escalation hard if not impossible to imagine. The great acceleration continues.[8]

Take the notion of neoliberalism, which has taken centre stage in critical debates over capitalism in the past decades. Even before the pandemic, in the wake of the financial crisis of 2007–8, it was clear that monetary politics and the new roles of central banks in the US and Europe as well as the giant stimulus plans in China were increasingly at odds with the supposed orthodoxy of neoliberalism. This is even more the case with the attempts of governments and central banks to cope with the economic and social implications of the pandemic. While the debt relief programmes of the European Central Bank ended up backing deficit spending of member states, the combination of fiscal and monetary policies in the US, even before Joe Biden's inauguration, pointed beyond the notion of self-regulating markets and depoliticization of central banks. We are convinced that we have reached a threshold as far as neoliberalism is concerned: that, as a system, as a coherent ideology and practice of government, this might be the end of an era. Is this a crisis of neoliberalism? It may well be. But as we have always been wary of simplistic reconstructions of neoliberalism (rolling back the state, privatizations, deregulation, and the like), we take a distance today from analyses that posit the logical implication of this crisis as the *return* of the state, that is, of Keynesianism and the welfare state. This caution is particularly necessary when such diagnoses do not consider, on the one hand, contemporary struggles (or lack thereof) on the terrain of social and economic policies and, on the other hand, the dramatic transformations of capitalism in the last decades. We may well be confronted today with a crisis of neoliberalism as a system, but its scattered elements recombine in new formations at the global level that was constitutive of neoliberalism since its inception.[9] New formations of neoliberalism and conservatism are emerging, while the specific form of neoliberal subjectivity epitomized by the notion of 'human capital' continues to shape recovery and stimulus programmes in many parts of the world.[10] At the

8   Adam Tooze, *Shutdown: How Covid Shook the World's Economy*, New York: Viking, 2021, 301.

9   See Quinn Slobodian, *Globalists: The End of Empire and the Birth of Neoliberalism*, Cambridge, MA: Harvard University Press, 2018.

10   See Melinda Cooper, *Family Values: Between Neoliberalism and the New Social Conservatism*, New York: Zone Books, 2017; and Wendy Brown, *In the Ruins of*

same time, the return of inflation and related changes in the monetary policies of central banks in 2022, in many ways related to the pandemic and war, may have unpredictable implications for the global financial landscape.

We repeat that our work focuses on capitalism. We are aware of the several critiques that a focus on capitalism attracts. Does such a focus imply that a number of crucial issues, ranging from race and gender to politics, culture, and environment, are obscured or at least subordinated to the analysis of purely economic dynamics? In our previous work, we criticize any economistic understanding of capitalism. Our point is that the logic of limitless accumulation of capital certainly has a rooting in the economic domain, but it constitutively spills over, shaping human life as a whole and, in particular, occupying the field of the production of subjectivity. Gender and race play crucial roles in that field, and while they both have histories that cannot be reduced to that of capital, they are violently synchronized within processes of class formation where they never figure as secondary factors. Politics and culture, in turn, are traversed and differentially tested and reorganized by capital, and the ensuing tensions, frictions, and clashes deserve a detailed investigation. Far from implying a narrow focus on a single domain of human action, capitalism invites a wide-ranging set of analyses that enable us to discern its place in the world, its disruptive effects, the violence that underlies its workings, the worlds and subjects it produces, and the struggles and desire for liberation that contest it.

Furthermore, we acknowledge that today we are confronted with a set of urgent problems that have usually been downplayed or even ignored by mainstream critiques of capitalism. Foremost among these is the issue of climate change and the discussion of the Anthropocene. 'The history of capitalism alone, as it has been told until now,' Dipesh Chakrabarty eloquently argues, 'is not enough for us to make sense of the human situation today.'[11] What is needed, he adds, is 'to think about aspects of the planet that humans normally just take for granted as they go about the business of their everyday life'. We do not have much

Neoliberalism: The Rise of Antidemocratic Politics in the West, New York: Columbia University Press, 2019.

11   Dipesh Chakrabarty, The Climate of History in a Planetary Age, Chicago: Chicago University Press, 2021, 4–5.

to object to in this statement. Nor do we ignore the peculiar issues of temporality, historicity, and even ontology raised by climate change. The point for us is not to claim that a critique of capitalism is sufficient for addressing that question; it is, rather, to establish that without a critique of capitalism climate change cannot be addressed in the present conjuncture. In his remarkable reading of *The Prince*, the late Louis Althusser credits Machiavelli with being 'the first theorist of the conjuncture'; he explains that to think in the conjuncture 'means, first of all, taking account of all the determinations, all the existing concrete *circumstances*, making an inventory, a detailed breakdown and comparison of them'.[12] For us, Althusser's statement provides a good provisional definition of the way we try to think in the conjuncture, taking also into account the contributions of Gramsci and Stuart Hall that we discussed briefly in the preface. As far as climate change is concerned, independently of the multifarious ways in which capitalist activities contribute to it (or to the pandemic, for that matter), there is a need to take stock of the fact that global capitalism (from finance to mining) will continue to be the frame within which every attempt to tackle climate change, every Green New Deal, will take place. In any case, although Chakrabarty writes that unlike in the crisis of capitalism, 'there are no lifeboats here for the rich and the privileged' amid climate change, this may be true for the fires in Australia or California, but not in general if one takes seriously the report on 'climate apartheid' released by the United Nations in 2019.[13] Class struggle is not suspended in the Anthropocene.

So, capitalism. Harking back to what we wrote above, it is clear that speaking of capitalism implies speaking of crisis. One can even say that capitalism *is* crisis, both with respect to the non-capitalist orders it disrupts to emerge as a hegemonic mode of production and with respect to its own workings. Speaking of the internal contradictions in the law of the tendential fall in the rate of profit, Karl Marx clearly posits in *Capital*, volume 3, the clash between contradictory forces as a defining feature of capitalism. He speaks of crises as the 'momentary, violent solutions for the existing contradictions, violent eruptions that

---

12 Louis Althusser, *Machiavelli and Us*, London: Verso, 1999, 18.
13 Chakrabarty, *The Climate of History*, 45; Philip Alston, *Climate Change and Poverty*, Geneva: United Nations, 2019, 12.

re-establish the disturbed balance for the time being.'[14] The intensity of the contradictions and clashes described by Marx accounts for the instability of the 'disturbed balance', making it dependent on the very factors that generate crises. From a different theoretical and political perspective, Joseph Schumpeter's notion of 'creative destruction' further underscores the elective affinity of capitalism and crisis. Focusing on the (Weberian) problem of innovation, he writes in *Capitalism, Socialism, Democracy* of a 'process of industrial mutation' that 'incessantly revolutionizes the economic structure *from within*, incessantly destroying the old one, incessantly creating a new one'. He adds that 'this process of Creative Destruction is the essential fact about capitalism. It is what capitalism consists in and what every capitalist concern has got to live in.'[15] It is easy to see that the destruction of the old and the creation of a new economic structure are not conceivable without multiple crises, of different intensity and scope.

This is not the place to provide a full-fledged discussion of the relation between capitalism and crisis, including the different theories of the cyclical dynamic of accumulation from Nikolai Kondratieff to Schumpeter himself and Giovanni Arrighi. For our purposes, the more important task is to stress the constitutive role of crisis within capitalism, which also casts a shadow over such concepts as recovery and development. Consistent with Schumpeter's notion of creative destruction, moments of crisis have often been junctures for the (more or less radical) reorganization of capitalism. In the age of industrial capitalism, recovery and development were specific projects of stabilization of the dynamics of capital accumulation, amid financial and commercial turbulences and above all under the constant threat of class struggle. We are convinced that, since the crisis of the mid-1970s, we have entered a new conjuncture in which the pace of crises has accelerated, and it became increasingly difficult to distinguish crisis from recovery and development. This is even more the case if one thinks of the new role of finance in the workings of capitalism and of the specific temporality that characterizes the dynamics of global financial markets. The economic

14   Karl Marx, *Capital*, vol. 3, trans. David Fernbach, London: Penguin Books, 1981, 357.

15   Joseph Schumpeter, *Capitalism, Socialism, Democracy*, London: Routledge, 2003, 83.

crisis of 2007–8 is a telling case in point. Initially a financial crisis spurred by the dynamics on the US real estate market, it ended up shaking the whole world economy, with a different temporality and different manifestations. To quote again from Adam Tooze, despite the stabilization programmes rolled out in 2012–13, 'the crisis was not in fact over'. What we face, Tooze writes in 2018, 'is not repetition, but mutation and metastasis'.[16] The effects of the 2007–8 crisis were still shaping economies and societies around the world when the pandemic hit. We will revisit this point later in the book.

For now, let us return to the COVID-19 virus and to the dynamics of its circulation. Viewed through the lens of the pandemic, the globe and the planet we inhabit appear markedly distracted. The shared experience of disease, viral circulation, and the search for remedy has once again highlighted the unity of the world. But as we have already mentioned, this unity manifests in highly heterogeneous ways, above all, exacerbating the devastating inequalities laid bare by the pandemic. Disputes surrounding patents and vaccines are integral to this global landscape. Moreover, many observers suggest that societies have become increasingly insular, fuelling once again rhetoric about the end of globalization – a sentiment only reinforced by Russia's invasion of Ukraine. But despite these frequent declarations, global dynamics such as logistical and financial processes appear more necessary than ever for the workings of capitalism. One aim of this book is to investigate emerging assemblages of power in a multiscalar perspective, a task that also provides us with an effective angle for analysing the new roles of the state in the current conjuncture. Moreover, this undertaking draws our attention to the tensions surrounding the mutations of what might be called the geopolitical framework of the capitalist world system. The ascent of China is spurring tumultuous transformations not only in international politics but also in the dynamics of world capitalism. In particular, China's changing position is opening new circuits of valorization – new spaces of capital indeed. This is a point that is often obscured in the discourse of a New Cold War and this obfuscation deserves a careful and detailed investigation. We will have more to say about this in Chapter 3.

---

16 Adam Tooze, *Crashed: How a Decade of Financial Crisis Changed the World*, New York: Viking, 2018, 19–20.

Rebordering the world

In many ways, the COVID-19 outbreak signalled a crisis of mobility. Although the virus spread through channels that enable the global extension of supply chains and the circulation of goods, the slowdown and in many cases standstill of logistical operations were among the immediate consequences of the pandemic. Indeed, the management of the pandemic entailed a reorganization of mobility, which affected movements of both people and things. International borders were selectively closed, with a reinforcement of the hygienic-sanitary components of border regimes, while internal boundaries proliferated even more than in the recent past, circumscribing worksites, productive zones, administrative territories, and even individual bodies and private homes.[17] Far from considering such bordering processes as fixed, we believe they must be confronted as part of a wider history of bordering and rebordering, which, alongside the extraction of wealth from the earth and patterns of social cooperation, provides a privileged lens on the mutations of capitalism.

Without doubt, the mobility crisis occasioned by the pandemic and related public health measures such as lockdowns had marked effects on the functioning of capitalism. In the wake of the outbreak, safety and navigation data generated by shipping vessels showed a double dip in world seaborne trade.[18] These downturns in February 2020 and April–May 2020 correlated to the initial lockdown in China, and then again to lockdowns in the rest of the world. Interestingly, these trade levels had recovered by October 2020, only to turn around again with the emergence of the Delta variant in 2021. There is much to be said about these disruptions, particularly with regard to the labour forces that absorbed their effects. In the world of shipping, the 'crew change crisis' left many

17   Martina Tazzioli and Maurice Stierl, '"We Closed the Ports to Protect Refugees": Hygienic Borders and the Deterrence Humanitarianism during Covid-19', *International Political Sociology* 15, no. 4 (2001), 539–58; Sandro Mezzadra, 'Testing Borders: COVID-19 and the Management of (Im)mobility', in Walter Baier, Eric Canepa, and Haris Golemis (eds), *Capitalism's Deadly Threat: Transform! Yearbook 2021*, London: Merlin Press, 2021, 246–55.

18   Pol Antràs, 'De-Globalisation? Global Value Chains in the Post-COVID-19 Age', Working Paper No. 28115, Cambridge, MA: National Bureau of Economic Research, 2020.

seafarers stranded on vessels, some for as long as twenty months, with others stuck at home without access to work.[19] Supply chain blockages or even just the decision of lead firms to cancel orders had devastating effects for workers further down supply chains, many of them located in the global South.[20] There were also sectors of capitalism that benefited from the pandemic, most prominently technology firms, e-commerce companies, and different kinds of delivery platforms. In all of these cases, there were reciprocal implications for workforces. The massive scaling up of warehouse industries, for instance, came with heightened risk of infection for those who were hired in. The same danger was faced by the predominantly migrant gig workers whose deliveries to urbanites in comfortable lockdown around the world were part of a more general platformization of the economy that we will discuss more thoroughly in Chapter 4.

That trade and even financial markets had significantly recovered by October 2020 was only partly the effect of central bank bailouts, which often involved the purchase of treasury bonds to prevent a bottoming out of the market for these currency-stabilizing assets. It is possible to trace other patterns of adjustment and reconstruction that attest capital's capacity to weather environmental and health catastrophes. In the world of supply chain capitalism, the shift from models of efficiency and leanness to ones of resilience and adaptation was a prominent feature of practice and debate. This change from *just in time* to *just in case* was particularly noticeable in supply chains for personal protective equipment and other goods necessary for the control of infectious disease that were in short supply at the beginning of the pandemic due to on-demand production strategies that had almost eliminated inventory. Supply chain analysts began to speak about going beyond resilience modelling, which they had been advocating for many years. In its place, they proposed strategies to advance viability or the design of supply chains with the ability not only to absorb and recover from negative events but also to react to positive changes and dynamically adjust

---

19   See Johanna Markkula, 'Containing Mobilities: Changing Time and Space of Maritime Labor', *Focaal – Journal of Global and Historical Anthropology* 89 (2021), 25–39.

20   See Mark Anner, 'Power Relations in Global Supply Chains and the Unequal Distribution of Costs during Crises: Abandoning Garment Suppliers and Workers during the COVID-19 Pandemic', *International Labor Review* 161, no. 1 (2022), 59–82.

utilizations and allocations in response to 'long term, severe global disruptions that affect all elements of supply chain ecosystems (i.e., business, society, nature, and economies)'.[21] If, as Deborah Cowen argues, the post–Second World War logistics revolution that ushered in globalized just-in-time production implied 'a shift from cost minimization *after production* to value added across *circulatory systems*', these changes signal further transformations in capital's operations.[22]

Stefano Harney and Fred Moten contend that logistics 'emerges as the science of loss prevention as much as the science of moving property through the emptiness'.[23] Grounded in their arguments about the emergence of commercial logistics in the Atlantic slave trade, this claim registers deep affinities between logistics and racial capitalism as well as between the control of the mobility of things and the forced migration of people. These likenesses resonate with the strategies of viability and loss prevention that emerged in the face of pandemic supply chain blockages. Many firms that sought to escape contractual obligations in the wake of shutdowns and disruptions resorted to legal claims citing force majeure, which required them to prove that interruptions to business as usual were the result of unforeseeable events.[24] This approach categorizes the pandemic with natural and human-generated events as diverse as financial crises, earthquakes, hurricanes, currency fluctuations, central bank decisions, civil riots, ship detainments, pricing index shifts, and state embargoes and sanctions.[25] However, force majeure also has a history in legal contestations surrounding slave rebellions and escapes. Consider the case of the 1841 *Creole* slave revolt, on which Frederick Douglass based his 1853 novella *The Heroic Slave*. During a journey from Norfolk, Virginia to New Orleans, slaves on

---

21   Dmitry Ivanov, 'Viable Supply Chain Model: Integrating Agility, Resilience and Sustainability Perspectives – Lessons from and Thinking beyond the COVID-19 Pandemic', *Annals of Operations Research* 319 (2022), 1414.

22   Deborah Cowen, *The Deadly Life of Logistics: Mapping Violence in Global Trade*, Minneapolis: University of Minnesota Press, 2014, 24.

23   Stefano Harney and Fred Moten, *All Incomplete*, Colchester: Minor Compositions, 2021, 17.

24   See Brett Neilson, 'Virologistics I: The Virus as Logistical "Force Majeure"', Centre on Migration, Policy and Society, University of Oxford, 18 April 2020.

25   Klaus Peter Berger and Daniel Behn, 'Force Majeure and Hardship in the Age of Corona: A Historical and Comparative Study', *McGill Journal of Dispute Resolution* 6, no. 4 (2019–20), 78–130.

board the *Creole* organized a mutiny. After directing the vessel to the Bahamas, 135 of them obtained freedom under laws that had outlawed slavery in the British Empire eight years earlier. The incident resulted in a diplomatic dispute between the US and Britain. In his letters on the matter, US Secretary of State Daniel Webster used the language of natural disaster to characterize the incident, deny the agency of the insurrectionists, and contend that the ship landed in the Bahamas under force majeure conditions that invalidated the application of local law.[26] In 1853, these arguments were upheld by the British-American Claims Commission, which, without revoking the liberty of the slaves, decided that the British government should compensate the slave owners with a payment of $30,300.[27] Such is the legal and logistical logic of loss prevention.

Harney and Moten's insights into how the racial dynamics of the Black Atlantic inform the development of commercial logistics are inspiring. However, for the purposes of our argument about loss prevention and the pandemic, we must understand these dynamics in relation to patterns of racialized and racist dominance, oppression, and labour extraction in other parts of the world. For example, how do we situate the transatlantic slave trade *vis-à-vis* indentured labour in the triangular trade between Britain, China, and India, or the forced labour of Indigenous populations under Latin America's *encomienda* system and myriad forms of settler colonialism? These are difficult questions addressed, for instance, in Lisa Lowe's landmark study *The Intimacies of Four Continents* and in historical scholarship that probes the limits of settler colonial studies.[28] We contend that similar questions should be asked of today's racial capitalism in its entanglement with forms of financial, logistical, and computational control. For us, the question of borders is pivotal to negotiating these relations. This is not simply because borders draw analytical and political attention to processes and struggles of

---

26   Carrie Hyde, 'The Climates of Liberty: Natural Rights in the *Creole* Case and "The Heroic Slave"', *American Literature* 85, no. 3 (2013), 475–504.

27   John Basset Moore, *History and Digest of the International Arbitrations to which the United States Has Been a Party*, Washington, DC: Government Printing Office, 1898, 417.

28   Lisa Lowe, *The Intimacies of Four Continents*, Durham, NC: Duke University Press, 2015. On the limits of settler colonial studies, see Jane Cary and Beth Silverstein, 'Thinking With and Beyond Settler Colonial Studies: New Histories After the Postcolonial', *Postcolonial Studies* 23, no. 1 (2020), 1–20.

migration, which are subject to distinct if heterogeneous forms of racialization. The investigation of borders poses fundamental questions about the changing role and form of the state, the restructuring of the world market, new geographies of development and production, and shifting power dynamics and subjectivities. The processes of rebordering occasioned by the pandemic make these relations even more challenging to trace.

In the wake of the capitalist globalization initiated in the late twentieth century, it has become common to observe that borders 'are no longer *at the border*'.[29] Saskia Sassen points to an 'actual and heuristic disaggregation of borders', or an unpacking of the multiple (legal, cultural, linguistic, social, and economic) components of the concept and institution of the border.[30] If, in the industrial and national phase of capitalism, the geopolitical boundary separating nation-states held together these components, acting as a kind of magnetic line, recent globalizing processes have tended to separate them out, displacing them often far from the literal border. How has the pandemic affected these arrangements? We have already described how border closures and mobility restrictions were among the first and most long-lasting of governmental responses to the outbreak. It is tempting to see these measures as a re-magnetization of the above-mentioned line, pulling together or at least closer the various border components disaggregated by globalizing practices of mobility, connection, and displacement. Claudia Aradau and Martina Tazzioli offer the discourse of rebordering as a frame to analyse the introduction of many restrictions to freedom of movement as an ostensible means to protect populations from COVID-19. As they argue, 'rebordering is not only about more borders: it is also about class-based and racialized access to mobility'.[31] Their point is that rebordering does not constitute a re-establishment of the geopolitical border between nation-states as a master signifier that calibrates and resets relations among other kinds of spatial boundaries, logistical seams, and social divisions. The multiplication, diversification, and enforcement of borders internal to the nation-state – including intimate bodily and

---

29 Étienne Balibar, 'The Borders of Europe', in *Politics and the Other Scene*, London: Verso, 2002, 89.

30 Saskia Sassen, *A Sociology of Globalization*, New York: W. W. Norton, 2007, 214.

31 Claudia Aradau and Martina Tazzioli, 'Covid-19 and Rebordering the World', *Radical Philosophy* 2, no. 10 (Summer 2021), 4.

sanitary borders, as well as the tightening of logics of regionalization and proliferation of offshore borders – belies such an understanding of the pandemic's effects. Extending Aradau and Tazzioli's arguments, we understand rebordering as a process catalysed, hastened, and complicated by the pandemic but well under way before the outbreak of COVID-19 and doomed to be tested further in the wake of Russia's invasion of Ukraine. From this perspective, rebordering is a reaction to conditions of hypermobility and Anthropocenic transformation that cannot be apprehended in separation from the conjunctural analysis of capitalism that we propose.

In his analysis of China's pandemic response, Xiang Biao draws a comparison with the governmental measures introduced to control the 2003 SARS outbreak. While in 2003 rural–urban migrants were the main targets of mobility control, COVID-19 outbreak measures applied to all residents, regardless of their migrant status. For Xiang Biao, this difference reflects the fact that Chinese society has become 'hypermobile': mobility, he writes, 'is no longer a special behaviour of migrant workers; instead, it is now an important part of ordinary social life'.[32] He relates this condition to the rise of service industries, the casualization of labour, and more general economic processes of 'logistification' that subordinate production to circulation. Importantly, while the pandemic brought lockdowns enforced through China's grid system of social management and the introduction of an individualized health code system, these were not the first rebordering exercises to match the rise of hypermobility. As Jean Christopher Mittelstaedt explains, the grid management system was piloted in 2004 and evolved over many years as a means of governing society–state relations by blurring the borders between the maintenance of social stability and service provision.[33] Involving spatial strategies of grid formation below the local government level, the building and updating of data platforms, and the recruitment of contracted local grid members to perform tasks such as information gathering, dispute resolution, and incident reporting, the

---

32 Xiang Biao, 'The Gyroscope-Like Economy: Hypermobility, Structural Imbalance and Pandemic Governance in China', *Inter-Asia Cultural Studies* 21, no. 4 (2020), 524.

33 Jean Christopher Mittelstaedt, 'The Grid Management System in Contemporary China: Grass-Roots Governance in Social Surveillance and Service Provision', *China Information* 36, no. 1 (2022), 3–22.

system was well in place before it was mobilized as a means of pandemic control. The 'social credit' system, introduced in 2016, is another governmental apparatus designed to manage the restless social change in China, primarily by 'protecting the social order of mobilities'.[34] Consisting of an array of interconnected and sometimes contradictory surveillance, ranking, reward, and evaluation mechanisms, the system has the capacity to impose penalties that restrict mobility (for example, by preventing the purchase of flights or high-speed rail tickets) for two main classes of violation: inappropriate behaviour during travel (including smoking or using fake documents) and financial transgressions (such as tax evasion, debt default, or delays in paying fines). Both the grid system and social credit system existed before the pandemic, showing how techniques and technologies of rebordering, while augmented by the outbreak, entwine with recent histories of social governance and logistification.

The situation in China has unique features deriving from the structure of the party-state and its relation to society, economy, and technology. Nonetheless, these patterns of rebordering have correlates elsewhere. Engin Isin and Evelyn Ruppert find the forms of power operative in pandemic tracking and tracing procedures to display 'the acceleration of strategies and technologies . . . that have emerged over the last forty years' in fields as diverse as 'finance, policing, crime, migration, borders, and education'.[35] Isin and Ruppert judge these forms of power to act upon the interstitial domain between bodies and populations, or to use the terminology they adopt from Michel Foucault, on an 'intermediary cluster of relations' that links disciplinary and regulatory forms of power. They find pandemic rebordering and mobility control not only to 'rely on technologies of machine learning, algorithms and visualization' but also to involve 'assemblages already in operation in several fields of commerce and government'.[36] Not by accident do Isin and Ruppert mention finance and logistics as fields in which the pandemic has removed 'legal, political and cultural limits' surrounding the governance of mobility and thus as areas in which there is scope for

---

34   Xiang, 'The Gyroscope-Like Economy', 524.

35   Engin Isin and Evelyn Ruppert, 'The Birth of Sensory Power: How a Pandemic Made It Visible', *Big Data and Society* 7, no. 2 (2020), 11.

36   Ibid., 9–10.

further development of monitoring and tracking technologies. Without giving geographical specificity to these observations, which are primarily developed in the context of the UK pandemic response, we can note that these thinkers too link rebordering to conditions of hypermobility, logistification, and capital accumulation.

As mentioned earlier, pandemic rebordering is also an Anthropocenic phenomenon. The shifts in spatial organization and mobility control ushered in by the outbreak need to be understood in relation to the unbalanced relationship between human animals and nature, which created the conditions for the virus to evolve and cross the zoonotic barrier. It is often noted that the pandemic brought an abatement in carbon emissions associated, for instance, with air travel. However, the wider question of climate-induced migration looms when assessing how planetary conditions mark the reorganization of mobility in the pandemic. Ingrid Boas and co-authors warn against grand predictions of mass climate migration from the global South to North. Such prognostications, they contend, reinforce a securitizing narrative that 'aims to keep climate migrants in their places of origin.'[37] In arguing that climate change precipitates a range of mobilities, they paint a picture that has some resonances with pandemic patterns of movement: 'Mobility commonly involves relatively short distances, meaning that people typically move within their country or region. Many may also face the problem of not being able to move to safety, while others do not want to move even when facing significant risk to their own well-being.'[38] To be sure, the pandemic has thrown up some novel mobility practices, including the massive and often deadly return of internal migrant workers in India to rural villages and an upswing in undirected or limbo mobility.[39] However, Boas and colleagues note that climate mobilities evolve in a context where 'movement and migration are inherent to the highly interconnected world we live in and a standard element of social life.'[40] They stress continuities with existing patterns, means, and motives for movement, rather than approaching climate mobility as an exceptional phenomenon that requires analysis in an exclusively Anthropocenic

37   Ingrid Boas et al., 'Climate Migration Myths', *Nature Climate Change* 9 (2019), 902.
38   Ibid., 902.
39   On the return of internal migrant workers in India, see Ranabir Samaddar, *A Pandemic and the Politics of Life*, New Delhi: Women Unlimited, 2021.
40   Boas et al., 'Climate Migration Myths', 902.

frame. For us, this continuity of climate mobilities with existing practices of movement and migration demonstrates the need for continued
attention to the interplay of capitalism and borders in the current
conjuncture.

The nexus of capitalism and borders is not simply an effect of the
qualities, gradations, and variegations of economic space that structure
and are produced by capital's operations. Marx famously described how
capital approaches 'every limit' as 'a barrier to be overcome'.[41] However,
borders are not merely negative enablers of capital's need for expansion.
They also have their productive dimensions, which is to say, they make
worlds. A single border implies and relies on its relations with other
borders to generate its powers of connection and division, exclusion and
inclusion. Moreover, the '*world-configuring function*' of borders crosses
and complicates the making of the world market, which, as Marx wrote
in the sentence preceding the one quoted above, 'is directly given in the
concept of capital itself'.[42] From the enclosures of 'so-called primitive
accumulation' to the emergence of the modern territorial state, the territorial division of the world under modern imperialism, and the
constitution of the 'free' wage labourer in contradistinction to myriad
forms of 'harnessed' labour, borders and bordering have played a central
role in capital's development and negotiation of crises.[43]

The same is true in the context of the pandemic and its aftermath.
The reorganization of mobility for both people and things brought by
the pandemic is more complex and uneven than the narrative of national
confinement, as real as it was for many people, suggests. The temporal
pattern of waiting, which is already embedded in migration, seemed to
dominate in the COVID years, as both formal and informal spaces of
confinement proliferated. Nevertheless, under the appearance of standstill, tensions between mobility and control continued to play out. While
the hardening and multiplication of borders foreshadowed new disciplinary techniques and legal apparatuses, practices of mobility, and
struggles of migration continued to reorganize themselves. New forms

---

41   Karl Marx, *Grundrisse: Foundations of the Critique of Political Economy*, trans.
Ben Fowkes, London: Penguin Books, 1973, 408.

42   Étienne Balibar, 'What Is a Border?', in *Politics and the Other Scene*, London:
Verso, 79; Marx, *Grundrisse*, 408.

43   On harnessed labour, see Yann Moulier Boutang, *De l'esclavage au salariat:
économie historique du salariat bride*, Paris: Puf, 1998.

of migrant mobility opened routes and struggles for regularization intensified, while a micropolitics of care and solidarity provided help from within migrant communities to people on the move. Refugees, asylum seekers, and other irregular migrants continued to challenge borders, which, after all, remained largely closed to them before the pandemic. The absence of safe transit routes pushed many to make journeys more perilous than they would have otherwise undertaken, risking infection and straying beyond zones of rescue or humanitarian assistance. These and other shifts in mobility and bordering played out in a field of mutating capitalist operations and dynamics that continued to shape the legal and political constitution of labour markets and the production of labour power as a commodity. To make this observation is not to subordinate human mobilities to movements of capital but to recognize how the compulsion to move often emerges under a pressure that compels many, above all the poor, to commodify the 'mental and physical capabilities' contained in their bodies.[44] In the context of the pandemic, such an analysis cannot be deepened without sustained attention to the category of 'essential labour'.

Pandemic labour

We learn something about contemporary capitalism by noting that the pandemic crisis at first resulted from a labour-supply shock due to lockdowns. Regardless of arguments that maintain that financial speculation and the 'asset economy' have replaced the extraction of surplus value from labour as the main source of value in capitalism, the pandemic showed that labour still plays a crucial role in sustaining the circulation and accumulation of capital.[45] Finance undoubtedly provides an abstract point of synchronization for the operations of contemporary capital and processes of financialization continue to impinge on daily life, as we shall discuss when we come to analyse the performance of financial markets during the pandemic. But it was the absence of

---

44 Karl Marx, *Capital*, vol. 1, trans. Ben Fowkes, New York: Vintage Books, 1977, 270.

45 For an argument foregrounding financial speculation as the main source of value generation in capitalism, see Lisa Adkins, *The Time of Money*, Stanford, CA: Stanford University Press, 2018.

workers from many sites of production and circulation that resulted in
the dips in global economic activity that corresponded with lockdowns.
Labour shortages continued to haunt the so-called recovery as late as
the fall of 2021, particularly in the US, where an unprecedented number
of workers voluntarily quit their jobs in the wake of the experience with
COVID. 'The Great Resignation', to quote the title of a timely Wikipedia
entry, also known as 'the Big Quit', has been aptly described by Robert
Reich as 'an unofficial general strike'. 'For the first time in years,' Reich
writes in a post of 22 October 2021, 'American workers have enough
bargaining leverage to demand better working conditions and higher
wages – and are refusing to work until they get them.'[46] This refusal to
work also took the form of official strikes, which multiplied in October
2021 (dubbed Striketober), in manufacturing, filmmaking, healthcare,
and the food industry, as well as in other sectors. This was an important
aspect of social and labour struggles during the pandemic, which also
sheds light on the ambiguity, and indeed on the disciplinary dimension
of the notion of *essential labour*, to which we now turn.

In the wake of the COVID-19 outbreak, the essential worker emerged
as a figure attracting hollow praise and experiencing heightened vulnerability. At once indispensable and expendable, essential workers were
those condemned to keep society ticking under circumstances of lockdown or restricted mobility in which the social itself had been narrowed
to the supply chain. With precedents in the classification of industrial
workers in wartime, Cold War national security planning, and occupation lists for countries seeking to attract skilled migrants, the concept of
essential labour introduced a new social classification and economic
division.[47] Essential workers were those who could not withdraw into
the safety of electronically mediated home-based labour, whose livelihoods depended on continued circulation and possible exposure to
infection but whose jobs were deemed necessary for the reproduction of
capital and society. To be sure, the classification was different across
countries or even within different subnational states or regions. A

---

46   Robert Reich, 'Don't Believe Corporate America's "Labor Shortage" Bullshit. This
Is an Unofficial General Strike', *Robert Reich* (blog), 22 October 2021, robertreich.org.

47   Peter Dewey, 'Military Recruiting and the British Labour Force during the First
World War', *Historical Journal* 27, no. 1 (1984), 199–223; Andrew Lakoff, '"The Supply
Chain Must Continue": Becoming Essential in the Pandemic Emergency', *Items*, Social
Science Research Council, 5 November 2020, items.ssrc.org.

constant, though, in many parts of the world, was its association with jobs predominantly performed by migrant workers or feminized labour, demonstrating that the raced and gendered aspects of essential work were among its defining features.

Essential workers had distinct experiences depending on the context and on the ways in which the pandemic was managed. Take India, where a large part of the workforce operates in the informal sector and where the 'shock and awe' about the lockdown in March 2020 paved the way not only for the plight of internal migrants, as mentioned above, but also for reforms that increased the vulnerability and insecurity of millions of workers, in particular those belonging to minorities.[48] Essential workers were immersed in such processes in India and had to negotiate the ensuing deadlocks, pain, and deprivation. Or consider the case of Mozambique, another country in which informal labour is prolific, especially in the agricultural sector. As Sara Stevano, Rosimina Ali, and Merle Jamieson argue, the category of essential work struggles 'to account for diverse and intersecting working lives' in this context.[49] In Mozambique, many workers perform both essential and non-essential work, making it difficult to fix the notion of essential work to particular bodies or subjects. Furthermore, the exclusion of informal work, particularly unpaid reproductive labour, from essential work reveals 'a productivist and Western bias', making the concept 'ill-suited and inconsequential' in low-income peripheral economies.[50]

It is important to keep in mind the materiality of different contexts and the limits this variation places upon the essential work classification. However, it is also necessary to stress the common traits of the figure of 'essential workers' in the pandemic. This is because that figure conveys to us an image of the composition of labour in contemporary capitalism that will matter well beyond the conjuncture we are living through. We need to ask, therefore, who *are* the essential workers? In the

48 See Manish K. Jha and Ajeet Kumar Pankaj, 'Insecurity and Fear Travel as Labour Travels in the Time of Pandemic', in Ranabir Samaddar (ed.), *Borders of an Epidemic: Covid-19 and Migrant Workers*, Kolkata: Calcutta Research Group, 2020, 56–65; Deepak K. Mishra, 'Migrant Labour during the Pandemic: A Political Economy Perspective', *Indian Economic Journal* 69, no. 3 (2021), 410–24.

49 Sara Stevano, Rosimina Ali, and Merle Jamieson, 'Essential for What? A Global Social Reproduction View on the Re-organisation of Work during the COVID-19 Pandemic', *Canadian Journal of Development Studies* 42, nos 1–2 (2021), 189.

50 Ibid., 190, 192.

US, the Cybersecurity and Infrastructure Security Agency (CISA) within the Department of Homeland Security stated in December 2020 that: 'The industries that essential workers support represent, but are not limited to, medical and healthcare, telecommunications, information technology systems, defense, food and agriculture, transportation and logistics, energy, water and wastewater, and law enforcement.'[51]

This list is wide, and in a way quite generic. Nevertheless, it is possible to discern a focus on what Andrew Lakoff aptly calls 'the systems underpinning social and economic life' and on the need to secure 'the continuous flow of resources through a set of vital, vulnerable systems.'[52] As Lakoff demonstrates, such a focus has a history in the US, where the notion of 'essential critical infrastructure workers' emerged from a broader national security framework at the beginning of the Cold War. This military imprinting of the notion of essential workers registers more generally an important genealogical aspect of the government of emergency that characterizes the pandemic conjuncture.[53] After all, modern logistics, which figures prominently in CISA's list has, among other historical roots, military origins. The fantasy of a continuous and smooth flow that characterizes contemporary logistics seems to encapsulate the rationality that led the US and other governments to define what was meant by 'essential workers'. At stake is an extensive notion of infrastructures, which includes both traditional and digital infrastructures as well as what we might call biopolitical infrastructures of health and care. During the pandemic, essential workers were often compelled to risk contagion and even death to provide services (from electricity to food) that allowed other people to work from home. Teleworking, Lakoff comments, 'was put in place to reduce vulnerability at the level of the system'. But it soon 'generated a novel form of risk at the level of individuals and communities – the risk of being classified as essential.'[54]

---

51   Cybersecurity and Infrastructure Security Agency, *Advisory Memorandum on Identification of Essential Critical Workers during COVID-19 Response*, Washington, DC: Department of Homeland Security, 2020, 1.

52   Lakoff, '"The Supply Chain Must Continue"', para. 7.

53   See Stephen J. Collier and Andrew Lakoff, *The Government of Emergency: Vital Systems, Expertise, and the Politics of Security*, Princeton, NJ: Princeton University Press, 2021.

54   Lakoff, '"The Supply Chain Must Continue"', para. 14.

The notion of essential workers is particularly relevant for this book. The pandemic emergency exposed something about what is understood as normality in contemporary capitalism. The shifting and stretching of the notion of infrastructure, as well as the emergence of a new 'infrastructure space' have, for several years, been at the centre of critical architectural, social, and geographical studies.[55] The role of logistics in the workings of capitalism today has likewise nurtured challenging strands of research and theory.[56] Figures of labour revolving around infrastructures and logistics have consequently taken centre stage in many political attempts to grasp the composition of contemporary living labour.[57] Infrastructures and logistics are not synonymous. Nevertheless, they share an elective affinity with the sphere of circulation. While infrastructures lay the conditions that enable flows of commodities, signs, resources, and people, logistics organizes those flows according to calibrated protocols and standards. We will revisit in future chapters the issue of supply chains and their multiple disruptions in the pandemic. For now, we note that such disruptions demonstrate once again the strategic position occupied by logistics in the fabric of contemporary capitalism. The fact that logistical workers were deemed essential by many governments reflects this position and raises important questions regarding the more general status of circulation today.

Traditionally associated with material networks for transportation, distribution, or communication, the meaning of infrastructures has expanded over recent years because of the necessary integration of the digital dimension. The notion of 'infrastructures of care' has emerged in architecture as well as in research on public health systems (it is worth remembering that the original version of Joe Biden's infrastructure plan included in 2021 significant chapters on care and welfare). In the face of the pandemic, medical and healthcare workers were obviously acknowledged as essential workers, and, in many parts of the world, praising them as heroes was the miserable compensation for their dire working conditions and for continuous exposure to the risk of contagion. Medicine and healthcare are important aspects of what we can call in more

---

55   See, for instance, Keller Easterling, *Extrastatecraft: The Power of Infrastructure Space*, London: Verso, 2014.

56   See, for instance, Cowen, *The Deadly Life*.

57   See, for instance, Kim Moody, *On New Terrain: How Capital Is Reshaping the Battleground of Class War*, Chicago: Haymarket Books, 2017.

general terms social reproduction. While established systems of reproduction and the gender relations sustaining them were tested by the
pandemic (just think of homes during lockdown and the difficult
balance between work and caring for children), social reproduction as
such emerged even more clearly as the foundation of social and economic life – as both a condition and an operative space for contemporary
capital. This was clear, for instance, in so-called popular economies in
Latin America, where workers deemed essential were directly linked to
reproduction and feminized.[58] More generally, the pandemic foregrounded the centrality of care labour. Domestic and care work was
widely recognized as essential, but, in many parts of the world, it faced
what Kritika Pandey, Rhacel Salazar Parreñas, and Gianne Sheena Sabio
call 'the contradiction of being simultaneously essential and expendable',
due to the lack of protection, rights, and even betterment of labour
conditions during the pandemic.[59]

'Nearly half of all essential workers', we read in an interesting paper
on 'care penalties' in the US, 'are employed in care services (education,
healthcare, and social service industries), and almost three-fourths of all
essential care workers are women.'[60] This is another circumstance that
informs our analysis of the composition of contemporary living labour.
One of the main theses of this book is that circulation and reproduction,
the two domains that figure most prominently in the definition of
'essential workers' in the pandemic conjuncture, play new roles in the
workings of contemporary capitalism. We can even say that they tend to
guide processes of valorization and accumulation of capital, subordi-
nating production to their temporality, spatial arrangements, and
rationality. We will develop this point in the next chapter. For now, we
want to be absolutely clear about the fact that such a theoretical hypothesis does not imply any underestimation of production, and, in
particular, of manufacturing and industrial activities as well as of labour
struggles in these domains. Although there is a need to test and rethink

---

58   See Verónica Gago, *Feminist International: How to Change Everything*, London:
Verso, 2020.

59   Kritika Pandey, Rhacel Salazar Parreñas, and Gianne Sheena, 'Essential and
Expendable: Migrant Domestic Workers and the COVID-19 Pandemic', *American
Behavioral Scientist* 65, no. 10 (2021), 1288.

60   Nancy Folbre, Leila Gautham, and Kristin Smith, 'Essential Workers and Care
Penalties in the United States', *Feminist Economics* 27, nos 1–2 (2021), 178.

the very notion of production, we are fully aware of its persistent relevance. After all, industrial occupations in sectors such as food processing, semiconductor fabrication, and the pharmaceutical industry were also deemed essential during the pandemic. What interests us are new emerging relations among circulation, reproduction, and production – and even more importantly, the potential and actual articulation of struggles across these domains as a basis for a new politics of liberation.

We know that Marx made lapidary statements regarding the relation between production and circulation. In the 1857 introduction to the *Grundrisse*, he writes that circulation is 'merely a specific moment of exchange' and that due to the relation between exchange and consumption, which 'appears as a moment of production', circulation is 'obviously also included as a moment within the latter'.[61] Or take what Marx writes in *Capital*, volume 3: 'It is not in the process of circulation that capital exists as capital in its real movement but only in the process of production, the process of exploiting labour-power'.[62] The next chapter will explore Marx's works in greater depth, but it is clear that the previously discussed relationship between circulation and production in contemporary capitalism necessitates a conceptual revision and perhaps even the formulation of a new *Tableau économique*. We work in that direction with an awareness that critical thinkers have provided new lenses in recent years through which to rethink the notion of circulation. Michel Foucault's engagement with the topic, most notably in the course he held at the Collège de France in 1977–8, 'Security, Territory, Population', famously led him to stress the need 'of organizing circulation, eliminating its dangerous elements, making a division between good and bad circulation, and maximizing the good circulation by diminishing the bad'.[63] This approach to circulation has had an impact on critical research on borders and migration management, which are important topics in this book. From a different angle, Joshua Clover has introduced the category of 'circulation struggles' to register the increasing reliance of capital on circulation for its very survival; we welcome this notion, although we do not limit its manifestations to 'the riot, the blockade,

---

61   Marx, *Grundrisse*, 98–9.

62   Marx, *Capital*, vol. 3, 464.

63   Michel Foucault, *Security, Territory, Population: Lectures at the Collège de France, 1977–1978*, Houndmills: Palgrave Macmillan, 2007, 34.

the occupation, and at the far horizon, the commune'.[64] As we will show later, circulation struggles are also characterized by strikes, be they in logistical warehouses, in ports, or in metropolitan spaces. What is needed here is a political reading of circulation, capable of reconstructing the social cooperation that enables it and the material fault lines that cross and divide such cooperation.

The next chapter poses a set of questions regarding the relations, connections, and disconnections among circulation and reproduction. The latter notion bears a stratification of meanings that we investigate in a separate although related manner. Any analysis of reproduction within a Marxist framework must acknowledge the relevance of Rosa Luxemburg's 1913 book *The Accumulation of Capital*. Taking as her main methodical lens Marx's notion of 'social aggregate capital' (*Gesamtkapital*), Luxemburg is, indeed, the first major Marxist thinker to propose a systematic analysis of capitalism from the point of view of its reproduction. She takes from Marx the distinction between 'simple' and 'expanded' reproduction, and delves into the conditions that enable the dynamic, expansive movement that makes up the historical peculiarity of the capitalist mode of production – going beyond the mere 'repetition, renewal of the process of production'.[65] For Luxemburg, the main difference between expanded and simple reproduction lies in the fact that 'in the latter the capitalist class and its hangers-on consume the entire surplus value, whereas in the former a part of the surplus value is set aside from the personal consumption of its owners, not for the purpose of hoarding, but in order to increase the active capital – i.e., for capitalization'.[66] As discussed in the next chapter, such an incremental and expansive process relies on a whole set of conditions that cannot be limited to the economic domain in a strict sense. This is because capital, as understood by Marx, is a social relation whose reproduction concurrently involves the reproduction of specific forms of subjectivity – succinctly put, the reproduction of capitalists and wage labourers.

Today, the question of subjectivity is crucial for any discussion of reproduction, especially in the light of feminist debates that became

---

64 Joshua Clover, *Riot. Strike. Riot: The New Era of Uprisings*, London: Verso, 31.

65 Rosa Luxemburg, *The Accumulation of Capital*, trans. Agnes Schwarzschild, London: Routledge, 2003, 3.

66 Ibid., 84.

prominent in the 1970s. The strand of radical feminism that worked on the issue of the reproduction of labour power emphasized the strategic relevance of a huge amount of historically feminized labour that had previously been unacknowledged from an economic or political point of view. Activists and scholars such as Mariarosa Dalla Costa, Selma James, Silvia Federici, and Alisa Del Re, often associated with autonomist Marxism, and the transnational campaign 'Wages for Housework', are particularly relevant in this respect. However, they are far from being the sole proponents who have pursued this line of thought and politics.[67] These days, discussions of the reproduction of labour power as a societal and multi-dimensional process must address the constitutive role played by race, a question that did not figure prominently in those early debates. Nonetheless, the question of race has always been crucial. Tithi Bhattacharya asks: 'If workers' labor produces all the wealth in society, who then produces the worker?'[68] Following the thread of this question, social reproduction theory today explores the manifold and heterogeneous ways in which society as a whole is created and reproduced, investigating the figures of human labour and activity that enable such a process. Social reproduction is materially permeated by an intertwining of exploitation and oppression, to use the terms of intersectionality theory, and as we saw in our earlier discussion of the composition of 'essential care workers' in the US during the pandemic, it continues to be shaped by the majoritarian presence and engagement of female (and often racialized) labour.

Above all, what feminism teaches us is that the reproduction of capital is the reproduction of life. A similar point is made by a thinker whose writings are today the main reference for debates on biopolitics: namely Michel Foucault. Think of Foucault's famous statement in *Discipline and Punish* regarding the need to analyse together, in order to grasp the historical emergence and actual workings of capitalism, the 'accumulation of capital' and the 'accumulation of men'.[69] Overlooking

---

67   See Louise Toupin, *Wages for Housework: A History of an International Feminist Movement, 1972–77*, London: Pluto Press, 2018.

68   Tithi Bhattacharya, 'Introduction: Mapping Social Reproduction Theory', in Tithi Bhattacharya (ed.), *Social Reproduction Theory: Remapping Class, Recentering Oppression*, London: Pluto Press, 2017, 1.

69   Michel Foucault, *Discipline and Punish: The Birth of the Prison*, New York: Vintage Books, 1995, 221.

the gender-insensitive use of the word 'men' (*hommes*), what Foucault has in mind is the constitutive role played by a whole set of disciplinary techniques to make 'the cumulative multiplicity of men useful' for capital: in other words, to turn labour power – once it has been violently produced as a commodity – into a 'productive force'.[70] The need to foster an accumulation of humans doomed to be exploited by capital and to enable its accumulation continues to haunt contemporary capitalism, although it takes forms that are far removed from those described by Foucault when he discusses the dawn of industrialization. Taking this need seriously means articulating an analysis of capitalism that is not limited to the economic domain, and that above all gives centre stage to the messy and even dirty sphere of social reproduction. In this sphere, let us repeat, life is always at stake. And as we look at the prominent role played by social reproduction in contemporary capitalism through the angle of the pandemic, we have to be aware of the multiple ways in which life has been tested, manipulated, torn apart, and reconstituted in the face of COVID-19. Notions such as biopolitics and bioeconomics, with their implications for the analysis of power, need to be tested and reframed, while *biocapital* – understood as capital invested in the development of postgenomic drugs and biotechnologies – has emerged as one of the winners of the pandemic conjuncture.[71] It is to this conjuncture that we now turn, to assess what is really new in it amid myriad claims for the return of the ghosts of the past.

Returns?

In *Ghosts of My Life*, Mark Fisher links the sense that there is no alternative to capitalism to what he calls, echoing a phrase from Franco 'Bifo' Berardi, 'the slow cancellation of the future'.[72] Notable for its register that shifts between philosophy, cultural analysis, and accounts of his own mental suffering, Fisher's writing brilliantly captures the 'closed

---

70 Ibid. See also Pierre Macherey, 'Le Suject productif: De Foucault à Marx', in *Le Sujet des norms*, Paris: Éditions Amsterdam, 2014, 149–212.

71 Kaushik Sunder Rajan, *Biocapital: The Constitution of Genomic Life*, Durham, NC: Duke University Press, 2006.

72 Mark Fisher, *Ghosts of My Life: Writings of Depression, Hauntology and Lost Futures*, Winchester: Zero Books, 2014, 13.

horizons' of the present while refusing political resignation.[73] The book's invocation of the 'disappearance of the future' is all the more powerful when read in the wake of Fisher's 2017 suicide.[74] One can only imagine how Fisher would have negotiated the lockdowns and heavy digitalization of social life that accompanied the pandemic. If four decades of neoliberalism brought a gradually declining sense of futurity and an 'extraordinary accommodation towards the past', the pandemic seems to have fast-forwarded these tendencies.[75] Confronted with death, extinction, and exhaustion on a global scale, society itself appeared to retreat. The sense of the future as expansion, acceleration, and liberation became bankrupt, and echoes of the past seemed to return with vengeance. Time and again, we heard that the pandemic exacerbated processes of renationalization or recoil that set back, or even reversed, decades of globalization, development, and growth. How are we to understand these assertions, which often make recourse to cyclical versions of history, without the subtlety or incisiveness of Fisher's analysis? This is a question we have to ask also against the background of the war in Ukraine and the related spread of war regimes across world regions and continents, which confront us with a different and more threatening rhetoric of the return of the state.

Let us begin with the concept of renationalization, because claims for the hastening of this process were rife during the pandemic and corresponded to an important element of experience for many people around the world. We have already noted that border closures were among the first and most consistent of governmental responses to the emergence of COVID-19. Although the virus triggered a reorganization of mobility across many different domains of economy and society, lockdowns and travel restrictions meant that confinement to national and even subnational spaces was a reality for citizens and denizens in many countries. It is easy to see why these measures compounded a sense of renationalization, particularly in light of the increased access to international mobility that had become a familiar, although unevenly distributed, element of social life over recent decades. The supply chain disruptions occasioned by the pandemic added to this impression, insofar as a

---

73   Ibid., 29.
74   Ibid., 22.
75   Ibid., 19.

standard response to them was the heightened call for reshoring of industries and greater national autonomy in the manufacture of goods and provision of services. Amplifying existing renationalizing trends associated with migration control and populist politics, these dynamics contributed to a growing consensus that nationalism and the nation-state had struck back against globalizing tendencies in train since the 1990s.[76]

Indeed, it was in the 1990s that critical thinkers forged the concept of renationalization to explain the disjunctive workings of globalization. In 1996, Saskia Sassen used the term to distinguish processes of denationalization affecting economic institutions and spaces within nation-states from the renationalizing of politics that was providing one of the main contexts for migration policy and practice.[77] Sassen extended her discussion in *Territory, Authority, Rights*, a book that concentrated on how economic globalization was accomplished through the internal denationalization of the state but also explored how such processes could coexist with virulent nationalisms.[78] In this perspective, renationalizing dynamics, which find prevalent expression in border hardening, are not an undoing of globalization but part of its uneven and multivalent effects. More recently, use of the term has attempted to invert this perspective. Already before the pandemic, commentators were deploying the notion to explain phenomena as diverse as the China–US trade wars or the blocking of international borders to migrants in Europe's Schengen zone. Although it described empirical processes that were doubtless

76   On renationalization and migration control, see Manuela Bojadžijev and Sandro Mezzadra, '"Refugee Crisis" or Crisis of European Migration Policies', *Focaal Blog*, 12 November 2015, focaalblog.com; Bernd Kasparek and Matthias Schmidt-Sembdner, 'Renationalization and Spaces of Migration: The European Border Regime after 2015', in Katharyne Mitchell, Reece Jones, and Jennifer L. Fluri (eds), *Handbook on Critical Geographies of Migration*, Cheltenham: Edward Elgar, 2019, 206–18. On renationalization and populist politics, see Anna Klimbovskaia and Jonathan Diab, *Populist Movements: A Driving Force behind Recent Renationalization Trends*, Policy Brief, Balsillie School of International Affairs, Waterloo, Canada, September 2015; Anne Jenichen and Ulrike Liebert, *Europeanisation and Renationalisation: Learning from Crises for Innovation and Development*, Opladen: Verlag Barbara Budrich, 2019.

77   Saskia Sassen, 'Beyond Sovereignty: Immigration Policy Making Today', *Social Justice* 23, no. 3 (1996), 9–20.

78   Saskia Sassen, *Territory, Authority, Rights: From Medieval to Global Assemblages*, Princeton, NJ: Princeton University Press, 2006, esp. ch. 4.

reshaping the world, this approach cast renationalization as an almost ideological concept. Protagonists used the notion to position these changes as evidence of an onset of deglobalization, reducing geopolitical tensions to rivalries of statecraft and, in some instances, even positing the desirable reversal of a transnationalism sustained by supposed elites and a return to essential and meaningful anchors of national identity. The pandemic seemed to confirm this narrative, as the global circulation of people and things became a conduit of disease, and governments, rightly or wrongly, deemed border closures necessary public health measures. With most people neatly shut away in national spaces, it appeared that renationalization had finally overwhelmed denationalizing processes, and globalization could safely be identified as a historical blip, the fantasy of businesspeople and intellectuals who emerged from the 1990s with a mission to celebrate travel, openness, and hybridity as indisputable goods.

Notwithstanding the highly rhetorical nature of much debate in this area, the dynamics of renationalization have attracted serious intellectual analysis that relates this supposed abeyance of globalization to a claim for a political turn away from neoliberalism, at least in North Atlantic societies. Paolo Gerbaudo's *The Great Recoil: Politics After the Pandemic and Populism* mobilizes the model of the Polanyi cycle and the Hegelian concept of *Erinnerung* to argue for a re-embedding of the economy in the state.[79] Focusing on the need for states to assert sovereignty, protection, and control, Gerbaudo applies his analysis not only to populist movements and governments on the right but also to leftist political projects such as those associated with Bernie Sanders and Jeremy Corbyn. He argues that the pandemic has 'uncovered some key weaknesses of the populist right – its nefarious demeaning of science, irresponsible management of healthcare and prioritisation of business interests over citizen's welfare'. To seize this strategic opportunity, however, the left needs to adopt 'a democratic patriotism; a reassertion of belonging and commitment to the democratic political communities of which each one of us is a member, as a jumping-off point towards an authentically universalist politics'.[80] For Gerbaudo, only 'by adopting

---

79   Paolo Gerbaudo, *The Great Recoil: Politics after the Pandemic and Populism*, London: Verso, 2021.
80   Ibid., 28.

the vantage point of nation and locality will it be possible to develop a progressive politics responding to the crisis of identity that the era of neoliberal globalisation has left in its wake.'[81]

There are many versions of this argument, which is prevalent among thinkers working in the post-Brexit UK context. Using Foucauldian nomenclature, for instance, William Davies contends that 'resurgent nationalism and protectionism' have led to 'the revenge of sovereignty on government'.[82] Doubtless, it is possible to argue about whether neo-liberalism has driven renationalization or the extent to which neoliberal thought and policies can coexist with nationalism. However, Gerbaudo's argument is useful for its links to Karl Polanyi and G. W. F. Hegel, which join it to cyclical versions of history that have a deeper precedent in Giambattista Vico's concept of *ricorso*. Rather than understanding rena-tionalization to exist in permanent and unresolved tension with denationalization, Gerbaudo views it as a dialectical movement, and, in particular, as that part of the dialectic that Hegel calls *Erinnerung* or 'the moment when the Spirit withdraws into itself and becomes self-absorbed, after recoiling from its outer existence'.[83] There is much to be said about this application of dialectical thought, or rather a certain moment of the dialectic, to claims for deglobalization. Suffice it to say that the concepts of recoil or renationalization may not be able to flesh out trends in the development of capitalism that recombine elements of the past within a completely new conjuncture.

Before coming to the empirical detail of renationalization, it is worth engaging with the concept of *Erinnerung*, which Gerbaudo uses to specify his discussion of recoil and which has particular relevance for situating renationalization with respect to questions of future and past. The category of *Erinnerung* plays a role in different parts of Hegel's philosophical system, including those pertaining to phenomenology, logic, anthropology, psychology, history, and aesthetics. There is dispute over the role of the concept at the level of the system itself. Ernst Bloch famously understands *Erinnerung* to be at the root of the closed charac-ter of Hegel's system because it internalizes the past in the present and

81   Ibid., 251.
82   William Davies, 'The Revenge of Sovereignty on Government? The Release of Neoliberal Politics from Economics Post-2008', *Theory, Culture and Society* 38. no. 6 (2021), 95–118.
83   Gerbaudo, *The Great Recoil*, 16.

disregards the future.[84] Among those who contest this interpretation is Herbert Marcuse, who argues that the category provides the ontological possibility for Hegel's theory of history by specifying the reflexive structure of self-consciousness.[85] Valentina Ricci and Federico Sanguinetti contend that, although *Erinnerung* has neither unitary meaning nor a stable conceptual function in Hegel's philosophy, it has a 'dynamic structure' that brings 'continuity' to different parts of the system by 'mediating between the different forms of interiority and exteriority, or subjectivity and objectivity'.[86] This interpretation joins that of Thamar Rossi Leidi, who argues that the concept of *Erinnerung* furnishes a *Weltanschauung* or guiding notion for Hegel's philosophical system.[87] In any case, the centrality of the notion to Hegel's thought has been noted for some time, including by Jacques Derrida, who understands it as the crucial moment in the dynamic of *Aufhebung* or the process by which the contradiction between two contrasting ideas or things is resolved. For Derrida, this resolution of metaphysical opposites conceals a necessary suppression – necessary in order that the privileged member of an opposition subsumes the other as its truth and meaning, thereby interiorizing it: in this way, he comprehends *Erinnerung* as 'a movement of idealization' that 'produces signs, interiorizes them in elevating, suppressing, and conserving the sensory exterior'.[88]

We do not blindly affirm this insight of Derrida, which has implications for his wider reading of Hegel and the Western metaphysical tradition. Nor do we correlate too readily the philosophical concept of *Erinnerung* with contemporary dynamics of renationalization, just because one author adopts it as an explanatory device. For us, the workings of *Erinnerung* are not totalizing, elevating, or comprehensive but rather *differential*, because the violence of idealization, suppression, and

---

84   Ernst Bloch, *Subjekt-Objekt. Erläuterungen zu Hegel*, Frankfurt am Main: Suhrkamp, 1962.

85   Herbert Marcuse, *Hegel's Ontology and the Theory of Historicity*, Cambridge, MA: MIT Press, 1987.

86   Valentina Ricci and Federico Sanguinetti, 'Introduction', in Valentina Ricci and Federico Sanguinetti (eds), *Hegel on Recollection: Essays on the Concept of Erinnerung in Hegel's System*, Newcastle upon Tyne: Cambridge Scholars Publishing, 2013, xxiv.

87   Thamar Rossi Leidi, *Hegels Begriff der Erinnerung. Subjektivität, Logik, Geschichte*, Frankfurt am Main: Peter Lang, 2009.

88   Jacques Derrida, 'White Mythology: Metaphor in the Text of Philosophy', in *Margins of Philosophy*, Sussex: Harvester Press, 1982, 226.

exteriorization can just as easily apply to efforts of integration, inclusion, or even welcoming. The concept of differential inclusion, developed within wide discussion and political practice surrounding borders and migration, offers a means of describing and analysing how inclusion in a sphere or realm can be subject to varying degrees of subordination, violence, discrimination, and segmentation. The concept has a multiform genealogy, including within feminist thought, where it can specify empirical dynamics of discrimination and animate theoretical critiques of the totalizing tendencies of masculine philosophical inquiry – see, for example, Carla Lonzi's *Sputiamo su Hegel*.[89] Approaching *Erinnerung* as a differential, partial, or failed process throws light on its application in discussions of renationalization. This approach draws attention to the dynamics of bordering or the need to 'rethink political processes and conflicts *on the border* between inclusion and exclusion'.[90] Such a perspective contrasts the Hegelian dynamics of *Erinnerung*, which have an essentializing logic insofar as the category of essence in Hegel's *Science of Logic* sustains itself by means of *interiorizing* its determinations.[91]

Framed in this way, the discussion on renationalization opens to less polarizing horizons. It becomes possible to explain how certain market movements or economic processes have been subject to renationalizing dynamics, while others continue to exhibit high degrees of interconnectedness. Consider the so-called decoupling of technology markets in China and the US – a topic of relevance to the thesis of a new Cold War that we discuss in the next section as well as in later chapters of the book. Since 2016, there has been a tendency for separation in this once highly integrated sector, with the politics surrounding semiconductors, 5G networks, and artificial intelligence playing prominent roles. This tendency was intensified in 2022, in the new conjuncture of war. In other economic spheres, there is still a high degree of mutual interest and exposure – for instance in capital markets, which remain tightly integrated despite the high-profile delisting of some Chinese

---

89   Carla Lonzi, *Sputiamo su Hegel: La donna clitoridea e la donna vaginale*, Milano: Scritti di Rivolta Femminile, 1974.

90   Sandro Mezzadra and Brett Neilson, 'Between Inclusion and Exclusion: On the Topology of Global Space and Borders', *Theory, Culture and Society* 29, nos 4–5 (2012), 58–75.

91   See Georg Wilhelm Friedrich Hegel, *The Science of Logic*, trans. George di Giovanni, Cambridge: Cambridge University Press, 2010, 337.

technology companies from the New York Stock Exchange and Beijing's decision to stop tech firms such as Ant Financial from making public offerings in US capital markets. In this perspective, the dynamics of renationalization seem to accord an uneven and partial logic of *Erinnerung*, which applies to certain sectors or activities while others continue to enmesh in denationalizing ways. Rather than obeying a dialectical or circular logic, renationalization proceeds as Sassen describes, although more pronounced than in previous decades.[92] To recognize this predicament is not to disavow the insights of dialectical thought, particularly those that follow Marx in positing the subsumption of society under capital. Rather, it is to affirm the power of a constitutive process not bound to a centralized authority or state and open to forms of political creativity capable of producing radical alternatives to capitalism.

Such alternatives reach beyond the logic of re-embedding or the swing of Polanyi's 'double movement', which posits the return of social protection in the face of market expansion. Writers such as Gerbaudo imagine that a progressive politics of re-embedding might emerge in the wake of the pandemic – a hope that finds sustenance in the various stimulus packages and welfare initiatives that central banks and governments launched with the emergence of COVID-19. Seen from the perspective of triumphant platformization, however, the pandemic introduces a kind of reverse embedding – not the undoing of the market society but the creation of a 'society market' in which human relationality itself becomes a source of economic value.[93] It is also necessary to take stock of the view of thinkers such as Melinda Cooper, who emphasizes the conservative nature of Polanyi's organic vision of society and community, or Nancy Fraser, who focuses on 'boundary struggles' over social reproduction, nature, and debt that do not unfold along the lines of the marketization/protection dyad.[94]

Whatever the perils of Polanyi's vision, the pandemic has highlighted the continued power of states, whether they have acted to

---

92   Sassen, *Territory, Authority, Rights*, ch. 4.

93   On the society market, see Xiang Biao, 'On Human Relatedness and the "Society Market"', Concept Note 2, 'Mediating Economic Life: Relation, Operation, Experimentation' workshop, Max Planck Institute for Social Anthropology, Berlin, 19 November 2021.

94   Cooper, *Family Values*; Nancy Fraser, 'Contradictions of Capital and Care', *New Left Review* 100 (2016), 99–117.

protect life through public health and other measures or pursued neo-Malthusian dreams of herd immunity. This renewed prominence of the state, however, offers no guarantee that renationalization can aid a state-based politics that addresses the social inequalities that have resulted from the global proliferation of neoliberal forms of capitalism. Such arguments fail to account sufficiently for state transformation, or how forces of capital have changed the state in recent decades by destabilizing its unity, range of action, and even the homogeneous figure of the people that underlies calls for popular sovereignty. Moving beyond modern state theories, such as those of Max Weber or Carl Schmitt, requires 'a more "positive" description (positive in analytical terms) of what states are actually doing today without presuming to know already what the state is or might be'.[95] Such an approach entails acknowledging that states may lack the capacity to take back control or to return to an era when the national economy was constituted as an integrated and governable entity. An analysis of the fiscal-monetary and welfare measures introduced by many states in response to the pandemic reveals a departure from neoliberal orthodoxies concerning the permissible extent of government interventions. But such an analysis should not ignore the fact that these responses to the pandemic crisis were shaped by multiple neoliberal legacies, including the overwhelming role of finance, the weakening of welfare systems, dramatic inequalities, and the persistent influence of notions such as human capital in the governing of rescue programmes.

As we noted earlier, the pandemic has entailed the multiplication of borders internal to the nation-state. It is important to understand how this factor relates to logics of renationalization and is not separate or opposed to them. Renationalization, in other words, implies not only the control of international borders but also the division of nations from within. In many cases, the pandemic brought formal border closures within nation-states. Consider the case of Australia's internal states and territories, which repeatedly closed their borders to populations from elsewhere in the country. In this instance, state and territory governments exercised statutory and legal powers that were less evident

---

95 Sandro Mezzadra and Brett Neilson, *The Politics of Operations: Excavating Contemporary Capitalism*, Durham, NC: Duke University Press, 2019, 224.

before the pandemic.[96] In Australia's urban lockdowns too, different local government areas were subject to uneven mobility restrictions, reinforcing longstanding social divisions.[97] Even in countries where internal and urban borders were not subject to formal closure, there was a multiplication and hardening of spatial and social boundaries, including those surrounding workplaces, domestic spaces, and individual bodies. The situation is much more profound than that registered by the trite observation that populist politics has exacerbated social divisions and turned countries such as the US and the UK into divided nations. COVID-19 exacerbated the sexualization, racialization, and economization of social boundaries and inequalities entrenched by the neoliberal turn of capitalism in recent decades. Renationalization, in this perspective, not only hives nations off from each other but also explodes them from within.

Nationalists, then, beware renationalization! If you bought into the narrative that globalization was eroding the nation from without, something worse could be growing in the bosom where you thought you could take refuge. Indeed, the notion of a globalization that transforms the nation from outside not only falls prey to taking the nation, as opposed to the city or the region, as the primary unit of globalization, but also fails to register the partial character of so-called global operations or processes that manifest themselves inside, between, and across nations. To observe that renationalization might fracture nations as much as heal them is not to claim that the state form inherited from modernity cannot ride out the crisis, as it has ridden out many before, or even provide a basis for a popular sovereignty that might begin to redress widening social divisions. If hallowed constitutionalisms have survived the pandemic, it is not only because they embody a logic of immunization, which, as European philosophers argue, aims to protect life. It is also because their founders built them as self-sustaining systems only by staring in wilful ignorance at the differentiation, fragmentation, and unevenness of the political and legal systems that comprised colonialism.

---

96 Andrew Burridge, 'Australia's State Border Closures under COVID-19: Materialities and Futures', paper presented at 'The "Worldmaking" Power of Borders and Contemporary Politics', Swinburne University and Griffith University, 15 October 2021.

97 Kurt Iveson and Alistair Sisson, 'Transmission and Territory: Urban Bordering during COVID-19', *Political Geography* 104, published online June 2023.

A scenario in which the making of states accompanies the splintering of nations is no novelty to historians of colonialism. Partha Chatterjee argues that anticolonial nationalism in Africa and Asia was based not on identity but on its difference from the nationalism propagated by the West and the constitutional forms of the colonial state.[98] The post-colonial critique of the transition from empire to nation-state is by now well established and requires recognition of colonial power's mutually constitutive relation with micro-polities, regions, and political spaces of odd, fragmented shape. As Lauren Benton writes of the formation of the colonial state, 'no matter how essential in its imagining or how widely recognized by statesmen and political thinkers, the nation continued to sit beside or partially constitute other configurations of political community: commune, town, empire, confederation, network of alliances, politically composite region, or international order'.[99] To note this diversity of categories of political community and its vexed relation to anticolonial struggles is not to argue that it offers a ready repertoire of alternatives that might somehow be marshalled to counter the exclusions, differential inclusions, and sovereign prerogatives that flared with the pandemic. While it is important to acknowledge resonances between today's border struggles and decolonial or decolonizing politics in the manner of thinkers like Walter Mignolo or Harsha Walia, these affinities do not stack up in a one-on-one fashion to chart an exit from renationalizing dynamics. Nonetheless, affirming the worldmaking power of borders means at least entertaining the possibility that they may be subject to processes of proliferation, mutation, and fragmentation that do not merely reinforce the nation-state system, the view of the state as the only meaningful anchor for society in turbulent times, or the geopolitical spectre of a new Cold War. For this reason, the archives of anticolonial resistance offer a rich resource for minds and bodies that seek to outlive the anxieties of pandemic renationalization.

---

98   Partha Chatterjee, *The Nation and Its Fragments: Colonial and Postcolonial Histories*, New York: Columbia University Press, 1993.

99   Lauren Benton, 'Afterword: The Space of Political Community and the Space of Authority', *Global Intellectual History* 3, no. 2 (2018), 259.

Extractive entanglements

A crucial domain in which archives of anticolonial resistance continue to nurture social struggles and mobilizations is the sphere of extraction. The history of modern colonialism has been strictly linked to a diverse array of extractive ventures and related processes of dispossession. Across numerous regions, this history has continued in new forms in postcolonial times, lending an anticolonial tenor to resistance against extractive projects, where Indigenous people are often at the forefront. Such resistance has become increasingly important over recent decades in which there has been a dramatic intensification of extractive activities. In Latin America, heated debates on 'neo-extractivism' surrounded the political cycle of new 'progressive governments' in the early 2000s. Since then, extraction has spurred a series of innovative research projects in fields such as cultural studies, critical geography, and political theory.[100]

Extraction is a form of economic activity that structurally needs an *outside* – such as the earth's surface, or the depths of the oceans – to pursue its operations. The sense that such an outside is free for the taking is the reason why extractive economic activity is often opposed to production, which generates profit from unpaid surplus labour. Writing of mining in *Capital*, volume 3, Marx associates extraction with rent and monopoly, underscoring the 'palpable and complete passivity displayed by the owner' of mines, 'whose activity consists simply in exploiting advances in social development'.[101] Although Marx grasps persistent features of extractive activities, today this 'passivity' of the owner (usually big transnational corporations) appears in a quite different shape. In recent decades, mining has become a crucial field of experimentation for new technologies of prospecting and excavation, including the digitalization and robotization of the whole economic process. Such an intertwining of social knowledge, machines, and the dirty world of mining was accelerated by the pandemic and the related emphasis on

---

100   See, for instance, Laura Junka-Aikio and Catalina Cortes-Severino, 'Cultural Studies of Extraction', *Cultural Studies* 31, nos 2–3 (2017), 175–84; Mezzadra and Neilson, *The Politics of Operations*; Martin Arboleda, *The Planetary Mine: Territories of Extraction under Late Capitalism*, London: Verso, 2020.

101   Marx, *Capital*, vol. 3, 908.

the ecological transition. Of relevance for our current discussion is the recognition that the rationality and materiality of extraction are far from being simply *national*, a point that was one of the key considerations in the aforementioned Latin American debates. 'The immanent dynamics that underpin the spaces of extraction', writes Martín Arboleda in his *Planetary Mine*, 'are global in content and national only in form.'[102] Facing extraction, the state touches upon radical limits to its action, and the (colonial) ghosts of foreign powers, be it the US and the West, or China, continue to haunt public and critical debates – with capital looming behind any national denomination.

The literal extraction of materials from the earth's surface and biosphere plays paramount roles in social and political life in many parts of the world and is certainly an important aspect of the global workings of capitalism. As we just mentioned, this is not going to change in the near future. Two of the main trends we can discern in the current conjuncture – the further digitalization of life and labour, and the green transition – will rather have the effect of intensifying extractive activities. Think of the so-called lithium triangle in Latin America (Chile, Argentina, and Bolivia), where an expected boom, with demand far outstripping supply at the global level, has turned into a 'lithium buzz', with new extractive projects and the intensification of mining activities.[103] Lithium is now considered a *transition mineral*, along with cobalt, nickel, copper, and rare earth elements that are needed to spur processes of decarbonization and digitalization. An easily predicted boom and even glut in the extraction of these minerals will open up new spaces for capitalist operations, while it can provide a chance for a socialist government, such as the one in Bolivia, to innovate its developmental policies.[104]

While it is important to pay attention to the dynamics of literal extraction, and to the circuits of valorization and accumulation of capital they enable and support, in our previous work we joined a series of critical thinkers arguing for the need to take an expanded notion of extraction as a conceptual thread for analysing the operations of contemporary capital and the composition of what we call, following Marx,

102   Arboleda, *The Planetary Mine*, 26.

103   Donald V. Kingsbury, 'Lithium's Buzz: Extractivism between Booms in Argentina, Bolivia and Chile', *Cultural Studies* 37, no. 4 (2023), 580–604.

104   Michael Hardt and Sandro Mezzadra, *Bolivia Beyond the Impasse*, Brooklyn, NY: Common Notions, 2023.

global aggregate capital.[105] To put it briefly, we insist on the fact that a relation with multiple *outsides* (the defining feature of extraction) con-stitutively characterizes today the operations of capital in several domains of economic activity, including those of logistics and finance. A good case in point is digital platforms, whose extractive nature is widely acknowledged and whose operations have become further entrenched in social and economic life during the pandemic due to their ability to manage the mobility crisis, as mentioned above.[106] We will hark back to digital platforms in Chapter 4, investigating their hetero-geneity and providing a detailed analysis of their operations. For now, suffice it to say that their extractive nature refers, on the one hand, to data that are produced by social interaction, and on the other hand, to an algorithmic management of labour and life that aims at extracting capacities and value from social cooperation. Moreover, there is a global dimension to the operations of digital platforms, notwithstanding the important differences characterizing them in different parts of the world.[107] The spread of the extractive logics embodied by platforms is in any case another factor that places severe limits on the regulative action of the state. This does not mean that such limits cannot be managed, or even overcome, but this requires a good deal of political innovation, well beyond the figure and historical experience of the welfare state – of the 'Left's social protectionism', as Gerbaudo has it – that continues to haunt contemporary debates.[108]

We have already mentioned finance in the context of an expanded notion of extraction. The extractive nature of financial operations has been stressed by several thinkers over recent years.[109] What matters more for us is finance's dependence on circuits of future labour and

---

105   Mezzadra and Neilson, *The Politics of Operations.*

106   On the extractive operations of platforms, see Nick Srnicek, *Platform Capital-ism,* Cambridge: Polity Press, 2017, 29.

107   Mark Davis and Jian Xiao, 'De-Westernizing Platform Studies: History and Logics of Chinese and U.S. Platforms', *International Journal of Communication* 15 (2021), 103–22.

108   Gerbaudo, *The Great Recoil,* 212.

109   See, for instance, Saskia Sassen, 'A Savage Sorting of Winners and Losers: Contemporary Versions of Primitive Accumulation', *Globalizations* 7, nos 1–2 (2010), 23–50, and Saskia Sassen, *Expulsions: Brutality and Complexity in the Global Economy,* Cambridge, MA: Harvard University Press, 2017. See also Michael Hardt and Antonio Negri, *Assembly,* New York: Oxford University Press, 2017, ch. 10.

social cooperation that it does not directly organize but nonetheless figure as significant sources of value. The spread of finance across the fabric of social life – the financialization of daily life, to quote the title of an important book by Randy Martin – corresponds therefore to the spread of an extractive logic, as indebted populations and poor people across the world have had to learn all too well in recent decades.[110] Despite the multiple discourses on global blowback and deglobalization that characterize the current conjuncture, it does not seem that the grip of finance on societies and economies is going to decline in the near future. On the contrary, processes of financialization, which, since the beginning, were at the heart of globalization, have accelerated in the wake of the pandemic, in forms that we will analyse in the next chapter. An important factor here is the role played by financial markets in the funding and composition of stimulus packages and recovery plans to address the economic and social disruption brought about by the pandemic. As we have already pointed out, those plans undeniably signal a shift from orthodox neoliberal monetary policies and they potentially open new spaces of contention and struggle around social policies and reproduction. They also provide one of the main material bases for discourses celebrating the return of sovereignty and the nation-state.

From the latter point of view, the situation is far from being crystal clear and straightforward. Despite the renewed interest in Keynesian and post-Keynesian economics, also spurred by so-called modern monetary theory's criticism of the obsession with debt and of the 'deficit myth', the national denomination of stimulus packages and recovery plans must be handled with care even in countries such as the UK, Australia, and the US, where unlike in the European Union the initiative was not directly taken by supranational institutions like the European Commission and the European Central Bank.[111] As Adam Tooze demonstrates, processes of financialization are far from reversed or even slowed down by those impressive monetary measures. 'The supportive cooperation between central banks and treasuries in the common struggles against the coronavirus,' he writes, 'was . . . no more than an

---

110   Randy Martin, *Financialization of Daily Life*, Philadelphia: Temple University Press, 2002.

111   On modern monetary theory, see Stephanie Kelton, *The Deficit Myth: Modern Monetary Theory and the Birth of the People's Economy*, New York: Public Affairs, 2020.

incidental side effect of their frantic and clumsy efforts to manage the economy by way of financial markets.' This meant, in practice, 'under-writing the high-risk investment strategies of hedge funds and other similar investment vehicles'. The 'roundabout mechanism' between one branch of the government, the central bank, and another one, the treasury, with the former buying the debt issued by the latter, ended up consolidating the entanglement of the state in the meshes and in the extractive logics of global financial market.[112]

While this has been true at least for the West in the first two years after the outbreak of the pandemic, the ascent of China did not appear to be hindered by the spread of a virus that started in one of its metro-poles. On the contrary, the 'zero-COVID' policy that began with the lockdown of the entire city of Wuhan and that was contested and even-tually dismissed in late 2022 initially appeared to be successful and was celebrated by the Communist Party of China as a demonstration of technical and logistical superiority to the West – and in particular to the US, which surpassed one million COVID-19 deaths in May 2022. Through the Health Silk Road, part of its Belt and Road Initiative, China began a new age of diplomacy aiming to consolidate a global network of relations through medical aid and consultation. Seen through the nar-rative of a new Cold War between the US and China, 2020 was not a bad year for the latter, which had seemingly demonstrated responsiveness and effectiveness in dealing with COVID-19. Regardless of the polemics surrounding the issue of the origin of the virus, however, the conjunc-ture shifted quite abruptly in the following two years. On the one hand, repeated lockdowns and the internal effects of supply chain disruptions brought about a significant slowdown of economic development in the country. On the other, Russia's invasion of Ukraine tested Chinese foreign politics and raised a series of challenges regarding alliances as well as the tense relation between the strategy of projection of China's economic power and geopolitical dynamics.

We will discuss the new scenarios opened by the Ukraine war in detail in Chapter 3. For now, we want to stress that we have always been wary of the rhetoric of a new Cold War. Although there is, obviously, a fierce strategic competition between China and the US in the fields of technology, national business interests, and markets for minerals and

---

112   Tooze, *Shutdown*, 148–9, 144–5.

other commodities, we find misleading the implicit parallel with the Soviet–US tensions that emerged in the wake of the Second World War. While the Soviet Union was a mighty military power with a system of alliances that China lacks today, it never exercised anything like the economic power of contemporary China. This economic power generates a dense web of relations among China and countries that belong to Western military alliances, from Australia to Germany, and is at the root of systems of entanglement that appear resilient in the face of the rhetoric and politics of so-called decoupling, reshoring, and friendshoring, which only escalated after Russia's invasion of Ukraine. Moreover, while developments along the China–US axis are reshaping the capitalist world system, it is reductive to see the current transition only in this light. We are confronted today with a more diffuse distribution of economic and political power, which is reflected by an emergent multipolarity. As we argue in Chapters 3 and 4, coming to grips with such multipolarity means combining an analysis of logics of power that revolve around a traditional understanding of territoriality with an investigation of other rules-based systems, encompassing elements such as zoning technologies, communication infrastructures, and international industrial standards. This opens new perspectives on the state, which even in the case of China 'is neither a unified whole, nor a collection of broken pieces', and has clear implications for the analysis of military tensions and potential conflicts.[113]

Criticizing the narrative of a new Cold War does not imply rejecting any scenario of rising military tensions and even war between China and the US. Although that narrative can easily become a self-fulfilling prophecy when handled by influential political actors in the West as well as the East, Russia's invasion of Ukraine shows the instability and even fragility of the contemporary international system. For a moment, the escalation to a full-fledged war of the military clashes that had begun in 2014 displaced the bipolar frame of a new Cold War through the initiative of Russia, which had seemed confined to the status of a regional power. At the same time, the war intensified tensions between the US, which has promoted and led the Western intervention to support Ukraine, and China, caught in a relationship of diplomatic cooperation

---

113   Lee Jones and Shahar Hameiri, *Fractured China: How State Transformation Is Shaping China's Rise*, Cambridge: Cambridge University Press, 2021, 14.

with Russia. More generally, the Ukraine war has spurred a kind of crystallization of lines of antagonism, which became apparent with China's military exercises across the Taiwan Strait in August 2022, while processes of militarization and regimes of war spread across the world, most evidently in the Middle East. Russia's invasion of Ukraine demonstrates that the multipolar distribution of power within the capitalist world system is crisscrossed by dynamics that can lead to a simplification of conflict lines and even to an entrenchment of military confrontation along territorial lines.

From an economic point of view, the effects of the Ukraine war impinged on the disruptions and new dynamics brought about by the pandemic, in some cases multiplying them while in others adding new challenges and developments. Supply chain disruptions, for instance, affected the export and circulation of grain, with Ukraine and Russia supplying 30 per cent of globally traded wheat. The short supply of grain led to an exacerbation of food crises in different parts of the world, including the Greater Horn of Africa, the Middle East, and North Africa. A new logistical geography emerged to sustain the military endeavour and mobilization of the warring parties, including the supply of weapons from the West to Ukraine, while private actors took on key roles in this geography – from the Wagner Group to Elon Musk's Starlink satellite constellation that became an integral part of Ukraine's military and civil response to Russia's invasion. These developments are part of a longer-term process of privatization of warfare, which became clear with the infamous involvement of Blackwater in the US invasion of Iraq in 2003.[114] Nonetheless, the operations of SpaceX, Musk's company, are also in line – although on a different scale – with the processes of digitalization and platformization of capitalism that we have discussed with respect to the pandemic. While their impact on warfare deserves a closer analysis, Starlink was key to neutralizing Russia's attempt to cut off Ukraine from digital space. Western sanctions, multiplied and hardened since 24 February 2022, have a different aim – to cut off Russia from access to markets, financial circuits, and technology. Energy markets have been torn and tested by sanctions, new eastward routes of supply of Russian oil and gas towards India and China have been

---

114 See, for instance, Peter Warren Singer, *Corporate Warriors: The Rise of the Privatized Military Industry*, Ithaca, NY: Cornell University Press, 2011.

opened, the Russian Central Bank has raised interest rates to shield the rouble, and new bank communication systems have been tested in the wake of the country's exclusion from the Swift system.

Regardless of the debate surrounding the effectiveness of sanctions, it is undeniable that they further contribute to a fracturing of global space that was already under way due to the pandemic. It is important to stress that few countries outside the US and the European Union have implemented sanctions against Russia. From the Gulf states to Turkey (a key NATO member), from Israel to the so-called BRICS and most emerging countries, there was scant support for sanctions against Russia, which does not mean that its invasion of Ukraine was backed. At the United Nations many members, including India, Brazil, and South Africa, abstained during critical votes regarding the Ukraine war.[115] This abstinence – more recently mirrored by US and Western vetoes at the Security Council against the condemnation of Israel's war on Gaza – may be taken as an instantiation of the processes encapsulated by the title of this book, *The Rest and the West*. While it is important to note that such opposition has been used in the wake of the invasion of Ukraine for the sake of propaganda by Russian leaders like Putin and Lavrov, we will show later in the book that lines of conflict and cooperation in the present world are much more complicated than suggested by a simplistic reading of the phrase 'the Rest and the West'.

For now, it is more important to look at continuities between the pandemic and the war. The geopolitics of vaccines is important in this respect. This is an issue that raises many questions, ranging from patent and production regimes to vaccine nationalism, and to the transformation of vaccines into a political tool instead of considering them a global common.[116] We return to some of these concerns later in the book. What matters here is that Chinese vaccines, although they turned out to be less effective than Western RNA ones, were widely supplied since late 2020 to countries in Latin America, Africa, and Asia, while despite launching the ambitious UN-backed Covax project, the West did not

---

115   See Francesco Strazzari, *Frontiera Ucraina: Guerra, geopolitiche e ordine internazionale*, Bologna: il Mulino, 2022, 201–3.

116   See, for instance, Biljana Vankovska, 'Geopolitics of Vaccines: War by Other Means?', *БЕЗБЕДНОСНИ ДИЈАЛОЗИ/Security Dialogues* 12, no. 2 (2021), 41–56.

show any will to curb the power of pharmaceutical corporations and ended up being perceived in many parts of the world as promoting a 'vaccine apartheid'.[117] As Francesco Strazzari explains, this was at the root of a 'trauma' that may have prompted further disillusionment with the US and the West, particularly in Africa, contributing to a lack of support for Ukraine in the wake of Russia's invasion.[118]

Another combined effect of the pandemic and war is the rise of inflation, which started in 2021 in the US and Europe. Spurred by diverse circumstances, including the impact of the stimulus packages discussed earlier in this chapter as well as other measures taken by governments to respond to the pandemic, inflation was accelerated by a surge in energy prices that began in autumn 2021, foreshadowing the war. Economists explain that the causes of inflation differ in the US, where it is mainly driven by the dynamics of demand, and Europe, where energy supply shocks generate what is called *cost-push* inflation. Regardless of these differences, central banks have reacted to this return of inflation by increasing interest rates, putting an end to the expansionary monetary politics prevailing since the crisis of 2007–8, and raising a whole set of issues regarding the possible fracture of markets due to tensions between monetary politics and financial stability. This change of scenario deserves careful investigation that remains attentive to the frictions between the US and Europe that were already apparent with respect to the Inflation Reduction Act adopted by the Biden administration. At the same time, the position of the US dollar is shifting in the world monetary system, where its 'exorbitant privilege' is increasingly being placed under duress by the combined effect of de-dollarization efforts and central bank digital currencies.[119] And this process has accelerated in an age of pandemic and war.

While opinions differ regarding inflation and the related tightening of monetary politics, two-thirds of twenty-two senior economists surveyed by the World Economic Forum in January 2023 warned of 'global

---

117   See Katerini Tagmatarchi Storeng, Antoine de Bengy Puyvallée and Felix Stein, 'COVAX and the Rise of the "Super Public Private Partnership" for Global Health', *Global Public Health* 18, no. 1 (2023).

118   Strazzari, *Frontiera Ucraina*, 203.

119   Zoltan Pozsar, 'Great Power Conflicts Puts the Dollar's Exorbitant Privilege Under Threat', *Financial Times*, 30 January 2023.

recession danger'.[120] Nonetheless, the dynamics of inflation are quite heterogeneous at the global level: high in Latin America (with a peak in Argentina) and elsewhere in the world (for instance in Turkey and Sudan), but generally low in East Asia, with the average inflation rate in China remaining at around 2 per cent in 2022. Despite the financial turmoil engendered by the nation's second largest developer Evergrande's default on its debt in December 2021 and by the tightening of state and party control on tech companies including Alibaba and Tencent, Chinese financial markets remain relatively stable. Efforts to manage the effects of financialization through the opening of two separate stock markets denominated in RMB and foreign currencies respectively are playing a key role in the country's navigation through an age of pandemic and war. This is not to say that China is moving towards the future with happy and even glorious prospects, while the West is haunted by the ghost of recession. That is not at all the case, as we will show later in the book. The turbulent and centrifugal multipolar world we inhabit provides other criteria to assess the challenges faced by powers such as China and the US. To acknowledge this is to pull the prospect of a new Cold War down from the realm of grand strategy and into the more mundane spheres of logistics, finance, and extraction that structure contemporary processes of circulation and reproduction, unfold within natural environmental limits, and cannot be sustained in separation from the all-too-human world of labour and exploitation. While this chapter has focused on the pandemic and on the related shifts engendered in all these factors, Russia's invasion of Ukraine and the threat of expanding war following Israel's violent actions in Gaza has further complicated the global landscape. Before analysing the new scenarios brought about by war in more detail, the workings of circulation and reproduction demand scrutiny, given their relevance for the contemporary operations of capital we have highlighted against the background of the pandemic. It is to this task that we now turn.

---

120 'Economists Warn of Global Recession Danger Ahead of World Economic Forum at Davos – As It Happened', *Guardian*, 17 January 2023.

2

Turning Production Over

Logistics and care

How do the geopolitical fractures that have opened in the pandemic's wake relate to the mutations of capitalism caused by the virus? We think that current wars are driven by conflicts for control of the spaces of globalization, and that there is a link between them and the growing significance of circulation and reproduction in contemporary capitalism. To put the argument briefly, the capacity of nation-states to organize production and regulate competition between fractions of capital has declined in importance relative to their ability to orchestrate flows and coordinate supply chains at transnational scales. Consequently, interstate competition has begun to revolve more heavily around logistical and financial operations, as evidenced by China's Belt and Road Initiative, Russia's control of energy flows, or US influence asserted through the dollar-based financial system. To note this tendency is not to discount the role of ideological, historical, or strategic factors in generating discord among states. Nor is it to forget the wars that states have waged against decentred transnational networks such as Al-Qaeda, which were the prevalent mode of conflict in the early years of the twenty-first century. However, the growing incapacity of states to guarantee the reproduction and turnover of capital at the national level has led them to seek advantage by strengthening their control over transnational circulatory processes. States have thus come into conflict over the geopolitical and geoeconomic factors that organize globalization. At the same time, the challenges faced by states in controlling the reproduction of capital has affected their ability to frame the reproduction and socialization of labour power, for instance through internal governance measures or welfare provision. Obviously, there is a great deal of variation among states on these matters. But a general crisis of social reproduction has accompanied recent processes of state transformation, with implications for gender relations and household economies as well as racial politics. This crisis of social reproduction and its relation to the circulation of capital and commodities became painfully evident during the pandemic, as states struggled to care for populations and to cope with supply chain disruptions resulting from the withdrawal of labour from workplaces. In a country like Ukraine, processes of militarization under way since 2014 and foreshadowing a regime of war have intertwined with austerity measures and the pandemic. This situation has had significant implications for the social reproduction of working-class communities and related gender dynamics of reproductive labour.[1]

We have already discussed how the figure of the essential worker provides a kind of cipher that registers this intersection of circulatory and reproductive processes. Although agricultural and pharmaceutical production continued under even the most stringent lockdowns, most essential jobs were either in industries necessary for the circulation of goods and services, including logistics, energy, food distribution, and communications, or sectors that contribute to the reproduction of labour and life, such as healthcare, education, and housing. In some instances, circulatory and reproductive tasks combined in unprecedented ways. Consider the gig worker who transports food ordered via an app to an urbanite in comfortable lockdown: usually, this kind of platform worker is considered to perform a logistical task, carrying out the work of last-mile delivery. Under lockdown conditions, in which the shut-in customer comes to rely on app-ordered provisions, this worker also performs a form of reproductive labour. There is much to say about how digital platforms have affected labour relations and processes in sectors usually understood to be part of the circulatory or reproductive economies. But the crossover of tasks performed by the platform delivery worker suggests the need to examine the intersection of two areas

---

1   See Olena Lyubchenko, 'On the Frontier of Whiteness? Expropriation, War, and Social Reproduction in Ukraine', *LeftEast*, 30 April 2022, lefteast.org.

of critical debate that have heretofore been held separate, namely discussions of logistical labour and analyses of care work.

Let us briefly review the debates in each of these areas before considering how they might work together. Logistics has multiple genealogies, which commentators associate variously with Napoleonic military campaigns, the transatlantic slave trade, or the advent of the steamship.[2] Not until the period of the so-called logistics revolution, beginning in the 1960s, did it emerge as a distinct knowledge field, replete with professional associations, degree programmes, specialized software routines, and the like. Initially addressed to lowering the costs of transportation and making processes of physical distribution more efficient, logistical techniques and technologies evolved to the point where they began to alter the spatial and managerial ordering of capitalist circulation. At stake was the reorganization of production at the global scale, the emergence of supply chains that stretched across national borders and regional spaces, and the computerization of business operations. No longer a matter of cost minimization after surplus value had been extracted in the process of production, logistics became central to profit making and the organization of extractive industries, not least because it eased the possibility for firms to search across the world for cheap labour rates, tax breaks, favourable environmental regulations, and other conditions advantageous for capitalist production. These changes altered the constitution of global space, through the emergence of sites such as economic zones and corridors, logistical hubs, and containerized shipping ports. Furthermore, logistics shifted production processes in the service economies and digital industries, assisting the birth of the platform economy and acquiring relevance far beyond the transportation and communication sectors. In this light, it can be understood as 'a distinctive realm of movement (both material and financial) that expands the capacity of capital to reproduce itself'.[3]

---

2   See respectively Martin van Creveld, *Supplying War: Logistics from Wallenstein to Patton*, Cambridge: Cambridge University Press, 1977; Stephen Matthias Harney, Niccolò Cuppini, and Mattia Frapporti, 'Logistics Genealogies: A Dialogue with Stefano Harney', *Social Text* 36, no. 3 (2018), 95–110; and Liam Campling and Alejandro Colás, *Capitalism and the Sea: The Maritime Factor in the Making of the Modern World*, London: Verso, 2021.

3   Charmaine Chua, 'Logistics', in Svenja Bromberg, Sara Farris, Beverley Skeggs, and Alberto Toscano (eds), *The Sage Handbook of Marxism*, Thousand Oaks, CA: Sage, 2021, vol. 3, 1455.

The connection between logistics and capital reproduction is often reduced to the question of turnover time. However, logistics has a wider grip on contemporary processes of circulation and production than such an emphasis suggests. Critical logistics scholars stress the fantastical element of logistical worldviews, particularly their commitment to smoothing out spaces for circulation and creating uninterrupted arcs of movement. This has led to an emphasis on concepts and techniques of interoperability, which aim to ensure faultless communication across systems and the compatibility of material infrastructures, often through the introduction and diffusion of standards. The breakdown of interoperability has become a focus of theory and method for critical logistics studies. In highlighting blockages, disruptions, and choke points, critical logistics scholars not only upend myths of logistical seamlessness but also explore the labour conflicts, social inequalities, cultural translations, and shifts in use of digital and analogue technologies that tend to occur at these critical junctures.[4] What Ned Rossiter calls 'logistical nightmares' become central to understanding 'the force of contingency, disruption, and failure' in logistical systems.[5] In this way, the fantasy essential to the reproduction of logistical power gives way to a grounded account of the material conditions, forms of life, and practices of social cooperation necessary to support the circulation processes and turnover time reductions that contemporary logistics seeks to accomplish.

That logistics cannot live up to its sustaining fantasies does not mean it is without effects. The bearing of logistics upon circulation and turnover time has implications for capital reproduction, stretching supply chains across global spaces in ways that tend to privilege efficiency above resilience, as became evident during the pandemic. Beyond easing circulation for capital reproduction, logistics contributes to the wider reproduction of labour and life. Deborah Cowen writes that 'logistics is not just about circulating *stuff* but sustaining life'.[6] In this perspective, logistics actively produces environments and subjectivities, including those of workers and labour forces, through techniques of

---

4   Jake Alimahomed-Wilson and Immanuel Ness, *Choke Points: Logistics Workers Disrupting the Global Supply Chain*, London: Pluto, 2018.

5   Ned Rossiter, *Infrastructure, Software, Labour: A Media Theory of Logistical Nightmares*, London: Routledge, 2016, 190.

6   Deborah Cowen, *The Deadly Life of Logistics: Mapping Violence in the Global Trade*, Minneapolis: University of Minnesota Press, 2014, 3.

measurement, coordination, and optimization. At stake is not only the reliance of populations on logistical processes for the supply of goods and services, including the most basic provisions, but also the role of logistical labour in recasting 'the relationship between *making and moving*'.[7] From the masculinized work of 'heavy lifting' to the feminized tasks of data entry and processing, logistical labour stokes the engines of physical distribution and the digital economy. Even the most automated logistical systems require labour power inputs, if only through the abstraction and agglomeration of human actions, living knowledge, and intelligence in the datasets used to train these systems. But the dependence of logistics on such inputs does not reverse its capacity to shape labour processes and relations. Logistics separates workforces across global spaces, incorporates different labour modalities into supply chains, introduces real-time labour-monitoring technologies, and undermines work conditions and possibilities for organizing. With uneven effects at the global scale, the result is the general precarization of logistical labour, coupled with patterns of racialization rooted in the targeting of economically vulnerable communities. Despite this situation, logistics workers can position themselves strategically, especially if they occupy choke points where labour actions can ricochet up and down supply chains – although see the work of Charmaine Chua and Kai Bosworth on the ambiguity of blockades as a political tactic.[8] In this sense, logistics workers are essential workers *par excellence*, at once undervalued and indispensable.

A similar claim can be made for care workers, whose feminized labour practices have dominated the debate on social reproduction for at least half a century. While care can be understood as an ontological category, as in the Heideggerian concept of *Sorge*, or as an ethical orientation, as in the work of Joan Tronto, the debate on care work has focused on practices of care being constitutive for the reproduction of labour and life.[9] Early 1970s feminist interventions, such as the writings of Mariarosa Dalla Costa and Selma James, emphasized the unpaid nature of women's domestic work and demanded wage

---

7 Ibid., 103.

8 Charmaine Chua and Kai Bosworth, 'Beyond the Chokepoint: Blockades as Social Struggle', *Antipode* 55, no. 5 (September 2023), 1301–20.

9 See Joan Tronto, *Moral Boundaries: A Political Argument for an Ethic of Care*, London: Routledge, 1993.

payments as a starting point for a struggle that would address how reproductive labour underpins capitalism at large.[10] Muddying the distinction between production and reproduction, this perspective was contested by feminists who argued that reproductive labour outside of the wage relation is incommensurable with capitalist value production. These thinkers maintained that unpaid domestic work had use value only, and not exchange value.[11] To a large extent, this division in understanding reproductive labour continues to structure debates in the field. The work of Silvia Federici, who contributed to the initial wages for housework movement, is probably the most important instance of a sustained argument that 'every articulation of the reproduction of labor power has been turned into an immediate point of accumulation.'[12] Federici emphasizes the need for workers to take control of the material conditions of social reproduction, which she understands to extend beyond unpaid domestic work and to encompass various forms of informal, unwaged, and unfree labour. Her writings have influenced feminist thinkers as diverse as Kathi Weeks, who joins this perspective to the campaign for a universal basic income, and Verónica Gago, whose writings on topics such as housing, financialization, and resource extraction in Latin America are important for the Ni Una Menos movement we discuss in Chapter 5.[13] Gago positions social reproduction as 'fundamental to current forms of exploitation and value extraction, and also constitutive of the precarious and restrictive condition of collective sustenance.'[14] By contrast, thinkers who maintain that reproductive labour is not organized in accordance with capitalist value production hold that such work produces material, emotional, and intellectual qualities that cannot be reduced to abstract labour.

---

10   Mariarosa Dalla Costa and Selma James, *The Power of Women and the Subversion of the Community*, Bristol: Falling Wall Press, 1972.

11   See, for instance, Paul Smith, *Domestic Work and Marx's Theory of Value*, London: Routledge, 1978; and Lise Vogel, *Marx and the Oppression of Women: Towards a Unitary Theory*, New Brunswick, NJ: Rutgers University Press, 1983.

12   Silvia Federici, *Revolution at Point Zero: Housework, Reproduction and Feminist Struggle*, Oakland, CA: PM Press, 2012, 102.

13   See Kathi Weeks, *The Problem with Work: Feminism, Marxism, Antiwork Politics, and Postwork Imaginaries*, Durham, NC: Duke University Press, 2011.

14   Verónica Gago, *Feminist International: How to Change Everything*, London: Verso, 2020, 13.

Emphasizing the differences between these strains of thought and politics on social reproduction can obscure commonalities between them. Arguments from thinkers such as Cristina Morini, who separate the capitalist production of value from practices of measure, suggest ways of recasting the reproductive labour debate.[15] If the value of reproductive labour cannot be derived from the temporal unity of measure, there is scope for integrating arguments for its direct role in capitalist accumulation with ones that question its compatibility with abstract labour. In any case, both modes of analysis have expanded their range of discussion beyond unpaid domestic work to encompass other forms of reproductive labour, for instance in education, health, cleaning, and in some versions sex work.[16] There has been recognition that social reproduction takes place beyond the patriarchal family, for instance on the slave plantation, in the hospital, school, and prison, or in the work of caring for the natural environment. Additionally, there is acknowledgement that previously feminized qualities and competencies of reproductive labour, associated primarily with affective and communicational capacities, are now requisite proficiencies in the service industries and crucial to negotiating the shifting boundaries between work and life under regimes of labour precarity. Shared across the debate is a commitment to interrogating the nexus of reproductive labour and social oppression – particularly gender oppression, but also race oppression or discrimination based on sexuality and disability, understood in an intersectional frame.[17] The question of how social oppression crosses capitalist accumulation needs to begin with the recognition that labour power is an embodied capacity, inseparable from raced and gendered qualities. Such a realization not only questions the perspective in which race, gender, colonial, or sexual relations are secondary with respect to class struggle but also problematizes a merely economistic understanding of capitalism. The emphasis on embodiment enables an approach that highlights the role of situated bodies in the labour of social reproduction. As such, it opens the possibility to

---

15   See Cristina Morini, *Vite lavorate. Corpi, valore, resistenze al disamore*, Rome: Manifestolibri, 2022.

16   See Leopoldina Fortunati, *The Arcane of Reproduction*, New York: Autonomedia, 1995.

17   See Ashley J. Bohrer, *Marxism and Intersectionality: Race, Gender, Class, and Sexuality Under Contemporary Capitalism*, Bielefeld: Transcript, 2019.

interrogate the spatial division of reproductive labour that is an important factor under globalized conditions in which migrants from poorer
parts of the world perform a great deal of care work, especially in the
global North. In this way, the debate on reproductive labour crosses that
on logistics.[18]

The notion of the global care chain, introduced by Arlie Hochschild
over two decades ago, describes a pattern of women from the global
South leaving their families to travel to wealthier parts of the world to
perform care work in well-off families. These women, in turn, hire
poorer women or recruit family members to perform reproductive
labour in their own households, creating a 'series of personal links
between people across the globe based on the paid or unpaid work of
caring'.[19] As many studies have documented, global care chains have
been stretched close to breaking point in the years since Hochschild
introduced the concept, creating so-called reproductive vacuums in
sending countries and subjecting migrant care workers to extreme conditions of exploitation, threats to personal safety, and social entrapment
in domestic spaces. The production of these conditions relates to the
rearrangement of social reproduction under financialized capitalism,
which has externalized care work onto families and communities while
also diminishing their capacity to perform it. As Nancy Fraser explains,
the result is 'a dualized organization of social reproduction, commodi-
fied for those who can pay for it, privatized for those who cannot'. More
deeply, the situation shows how 'capitalism's orientation to unlimited
accumulation tends to destabilize the very processes of social reproduction on which it relies'.[20] At stake is not simply a crisis of care, but the
ability of the capitalist system to reproduce itself under conditions in
which social reproductive functions are pushed to the point where they
can no longer support the reproduction of capital. The turn to global
care chains is an attempt to plug this gap, but, as evident in our

18   See Sara Ferguson and David McNally, 'Precarious Migrants: Gender, Race,
and the Social Reproduction of a Global Working Class', *Socialist Register* 51 (2015),
1–23.

19   Arlie Hochschild, 'Global Care Chains and Emotional Surplus Value', in Will
Hutton and Anthony Giddens (eds), *On the Edge: Living with Global Capitalism*, London: Jonathan Cape, 2000, 131.

20   Nancy Fraser, 'Contradictions of Capital and Care', *New Left Review* 100 (2016),
104 and 100.

discussion of logistics and circulation, such efforts of coordination cannot be successful in the absence of the living labour, material conditions, and practices of social cooperation that underlie efforts to coordinate and synchronize the movement of people and things.

Indeed, it is possible to view the prevalence of logistics as part of capital's attempt to save itself from a crisis of reproduction. Circulation, in this sense, provides a condition of possibility for reproduction, but the opposite is also true because there can be no circulation of capital without social reproduction. These two processes – circulation and reproduction – are crucial to rethinking the role of production in contemporary capitalism, not because their analytical distinctness means that they can be prized apart from production in practice, but because their dynamics tend to drive possibilities for production. In the industrial and national phase of capitalism, the inverse appeared to be the case, and production seemed to impel processes of circulation and reproduction. It is not a case of a diminution in production processes, which we know are increasing in many parts of the world; nor is it a matter of production somehow becoming secondary to circulation and reproduction in an analytical or ontological sense. We see these practices as existing in 'differentiated unity', as Stuart Hall writes in his analysis of Marx's 1857 Introduction to the *Grundrisse*; by this, as we will show more in detail in the next section, Hall means that 'different terms or relations or movements or circuits . . . form a "complex unity"' which 'requires them to preserve *their difference*: a difference . . . which is not subsumed into some "higher" but more "essential" synthesis involving the loss of concrete specificity'.[21] In other words, production, circulation, and reproduction are not involved in a zero-sum game, where the augmentation of one means a lessening of the others. To say that circulation and reproduction tend to drive production is merely to observe that they increasingly set and condition the circumstances in which production occurs: the first by linking the turnover of capital to the physical movement of commodities, people, and information within chain or network-like structures; the second by furnishing (or failing to furnish) the social resources, care, knowledge, and labouring bodies necessary for capital circulation and accumulation. These are the

---

21   Stuart Hall, 'Marx's Notes on Method: A "Reading" of the "1857 Introduction"', *Cultural Studies* 17, no. 2 (2003), 127.

concrete and conceptual parameters within which production must be rethought today.

To suggest that logistical techniques and technologies provide capital with a kind of fix – an attempt to counteract its own destruction of the conditions necessary for its reproduction – is to observe that the movement of bodies and goods can offer some delay or respite in a process of entropy. Migration and border policies that seek strategically to augment national labour supplies provide an instance of such logistical calculation. So does the stretching of supply chains across global vistas, searching for cheap labour costs, lax safety and taxation regimes, or various other externalities linked to gender oppression, coloniality, and so on. Likewise, the movement of informal care workers into a country where labour market and welfare conditions militate against potential wage earners performing household work provides a way of staving off a crisis of reproduction, or at least of passing it on to somewhere else in the world. All these strategies, and there are many more, mean that states have dwindling control over the total stock of capital, the aggregate capital, circulating within and across their borders. The traditional position of the modern state as a regulator of capital circulation and of competition among various fractions of capital, whether through regimes of planning, taxation, welfare, central banking, or labour arbitration, is diminished. In other words, states are less and less able to supply the conditions for social reproduction or to position themselves as effective managers of aggregate capital. This is not to say that states have fully lost control over aggregate economic forces, or that the degree of control that different states exercise over their economies or sectors of their economies is not highly uneven. It would be naïve, to say the least, to claim that the People's Republic of China maintains a similar degree of control over its economy as say a state such as Greece or Sri Lanka. However, tight control over the circulation of capital does not necessarily set the conditions for flourishing relations of social reproduction, and indeed such control can diminish both the collective and individual resources available for these ends. Either way, the circumstances described above compel states to reach out and seek to control patterns of flow and circulation at transnational and extranational scales – a situation that, in turn, drives competition among states for the ability to shape the spaces of globalization. These are the dynamics we see at work in the eruption of current conflicts, whether deemed overt warfare or colder contests, and the escalating prevalence of regimes of war. But before turning to analyse these conflicts and their governance, we need a stronger account of the role of circulation and reproduction in the operations of capital, starting with a discussion of their positions in Marx's critique of political economy.

Surfacing grounds

As we anticipated in the previous chapter, Marx often emphasizes that the 'real movement of capital' takes place in the process of production and not in the process of circulation. This is a cornerstone of the critique of political economy, one behind which there are also clear political reasons. In the *Grundrisse*, Marx asks: 'can the existing relations of production and the relations of distribution that correspond to them be revolutionized by a change in the instrument of circulation, in the organization of circulation?' And, furthermore, 'can such a transforma-tion of circulation be undertaken without touching the existing relations of production and the social relations which rest on them?'[22] Here Marx is referring to a book on bank reform by Alfred Darimon, but his wider target is the whole set of socialist theories of the nineteenth century, and most notably the work of Pierre-Joseph Proudhon, which aimed at restoring through such measures as free credit 'a pure, deployed, and abundant circulation' – in other words, a circulation predicated upon equality.[23] Facing such theories and political proposals, Marx main-tained that circulation (and money, its instrument) in a capitalist society is necessarily grounded in the class relations and antagonisms that structure the realm of production and continuously reproduce it. The dream of a circulation based on equivalence and equality is therefore unattainable, and corresponds to the 'necessary illusion' of the inde-pendence from capital of the system of exchange of equivalents establishing the wage relation.[24]

---

22   Karl Marx, *Grundrisse: Foundations of the Critique of Political Economy*, trans. Martin Nicolaus, London: Penguin, 1973, 122.

23   Antonio Negri, *Marx beyond Marx: Lessons on the* Grundrisse, Brooklyn, NY, and London: Autonomedia and Pluto, 1991, 26.

24   Marx, *Grundrisse*, 509.

This reference to a 'necessary illusion', which means to an illusion that is generated by the very working of the capitalist mode of production, leads to some of the most memorable pages ever written by Marx. In *Capital*, volume 1, in the section dedicated to 'The Transformation of Money into Capital', we read that circulation (the realm analysed in the previous chapters of the book) 'creates no value'.[25] This is the apex of a compelling theoretical demonstration that leads Marx to stage a dramatic shift of the plane of analysis, inviting his readers – so as to unveil the 'secret' of the making of surplus value – to leave the 'noisy' sphere of circulation, 'where everything takes place on the surface and in full view of everyone', and to descend into the 'hidden abode of production'.[26] Dante Alighieri's description of the descent into Hell in *The Divine Comedy* is clearly taken by Marx as a literary blueprint here, adding dramatic tones, intensity, and effectiveness to the passage. We know what happens in the 'hidden abode of production'. Labour power, the commodity that was purchased by the owner of money in the sphere of circulation through a seeming exchange of equivalents, is 'consumed' here in forms that follow a completely different logic – the logic of valorization of capital that requires the 'tanning' of the owner of labour power, now transformed into a worker.

Again, Marx's analysis is deeply political, in both the concepts and language that he mobilizes. 'The sphere of circulation or commodity exchange,' he famously writes, 'within whose boundaries the sale and purchase of labour-power goes on, is in fact a very Eden of the innate Rights of man. It is the exclusive realm of Freedom, Equality, Property, and Bentham.'[27] We are again close to the semantic of illusion, although it is important to trace it back to Marx's reference to a 'necessary illusion' in the *Grundrisse* to understand the constitutive role played not only by circulation but also by the legal arrangements that sustain it for the working of the capitalist mode of production.[28] Anyway, there is no doubt that circulation appears here completely subordinated to production, as a surface whose very operative logic obscures the real ground of the capitalist mode of production and allows political economy to

---

25   Karl Marx, *Capital*, vol. 1, trans. Ben Fowkes, New York: Vintage Books, 1977, 266.
26   Ibid., 279.
27   Ibid., 1, 280.
28   See for instance Katharina Pistor, *The Code of Capital: How the Law Creates Wealth and Inequality*, Princeton, NJ: Princeton University Press, 2019.

proceed without coming to grips with the deeply political question of the making of surplus value, which means of exploitation.

Our investigation into the new roles of circulation in contemporary capitalism is inspired neither by a fascination with Proudhon nor by a yearning for a return to the 'Eden of the innate Rights of man'. On the contrary, we are convinced that what Marx calls the 'hidden abode of production' overlaps today's sphere of circulation. This is a situation that challenges the very possibility of relegating circulation to a subordinated position and requires a new understanding of its relationship with production, whose status and nature are also profoundly transformed. Circulation may well continue to be considered the *surface* of the capitalist mode of production, although the role played for instance by black box algorithms and artificial intelligence in organizing logistical circuits challenge the idea that it takes place 'in full view of everyone', to recall Marx's words. In any case, our guess is that in the critical analysis of that surface, the 'secret' of the making of surplus value is often fully evident before our eyes.

To forge conceptual tools that allow us to analyse this new role of circulation, it may be helpful to go further in the analysis of Marx's work by looking at how he makes sense of the articulation between circulation and production. The *Grundrisse* is an important reference in this respect, starting with the renowned 1857 Introduction. The opening sentence of this text, which has spurred lively discussions in Marxism, stresses once again the methodical and theoretical primacy of production. 'The object before us,' Marx writes, 'to begin with, *material production*.'[29] After analysing its relationship with consumption, Marx turns to discuss 'distribution', which 'steps between the producers and the products, hence between production and consumption, to determine in accordance with social laws what the producer's share will be in the world of products'.[30] The polemical target of these pages is no less than David Ricardo, highly respected by Marx and nevertheless criticized for assuming distribution as the main object of political economy. It is, rather, production that commands over distribution as well as over circulation, defined here as 'exchange regarded in its totality'. Marx writes that, far from being 'identical', production, distribution, exchange,

---

29   Marx, *Grundrisse*, 83.
30   Ibid., 94.

and consumption form 'distinctions within a unity', while it is production that 'predominates' not only over itself, but 'over the other moments
as well', although it may be well determined by the other moments in its
extent, pace, and quality.[31]

To describe the working of this differentiated unity, which is also a
dialectical 'totality', Marx employs the notion of 'mutual interaction'
(*Wechselwirkung*), doomed to play a role in the development of German
classical sociology, and most notably in the work of Georg Simmel. As
we mentioned above, Stuart Hall has called attention, in his brilliant
reading of the 1857 Introduction, to the way in which Marx attempts to
grasp, with and against Hegel, the tricky and elusive nature of the
'mutual interaction' between the different moments that compose the
complex unity at hand. Following the thread provided by the notion of
mutual interaction, he emphasizes the specificity of an 'internal connection', according to which 'production not only proceeds to its own
completion but is *itself reproduced again through consumption*' – and, we
can add, through distribution, exchange, and circulation.[32] Hall's reference to reproduction is clearly important, as well as his insistence on the
peculiar operative logic of the 'internal connection', which must not be
confused with other identity relations as 'immediate identity' and
'mutual dependence'. We are confronted, here, with the formulation of a
method that Marx deploys with great effectiveness in the *Grundrisse*.
Among the many instances we could provide, consider the following
passage, where Marx distinguishes the circulation of money and the
circulation of capital. While the former is given in advance, in the latter
'capital expands itself and its path, and the speed or slowness of its circulation itself forms one of its intrinsic moments'. Capital, Marx
continues, 'becomes qualitatively altered in circulation and the totality
of the moments of its circulation are themselves the moments of its
production – its reproduction as well as its new production'.[33]

The nexus between circulation and reproduction of capital is key to
Marx's as well as to our argument in this book. Before discussing it in
more detail, however, we need to insist on the issue of circulation and to
flesh out at least some aspects of Marx's investigation in *Capital*, volume 2.

---

31   Ibid., 98–9.
32   Hall, 'Marx's Notes on Method', 124.
33   Marx, *Grundrisse*, 516.

In *The Limits to Capital* (originally published in 1982) – a book that played an important role in emphasizing the relevance of Marx, and in politicizing his arguments – David Harvey insists on what he calls the 'process definition of capital'. Such a definition implies that 'we can define as "capitalist" any economic agent who puts money and use value into circulation in order to make more money'.[34] This is at the root of a specific capitalist form of circulation, which includes different moments, starting from the distinction and connection between circulation of money and circulation of commodities (*money capital* and *commodity capital*), and differentially involves the distinct components of capital, as Marx's conceptual differentiation between 'fixed' and 'circulating capital' clearly demonstrates. Even more important for us is that taking circulation as a privileged point of observation, capital appears as 'a movement, a circulatory process through different stages, which itself in turn includes three forms of the circulatory process'. Hence, Marx adds, it 'can only be grasped as a movement and not as a static thing'.[35] If one takes a closer look at the 'three forms of the circulatory process', production is the second moment, after the purchase of labour power and the means of production, and before the sale of the produced commodities on the market. There is no need to go into a discussion of the vexed and complicated question of the realization of surplus value in the third moment. What is important is to stress the unity of production and circulation in Marx's analysis. 'The total process,' he writes, 'presents itself as the unity of the process of production and the process of circulation; the production process is the mediator of the circulation process, and vice versa.'[36]

In *Capital*, volume 2, Marx introduces another notion to grasp the 'circuit of capital' as a systematic and periodic process: that of *turnover*, whose duration 'is given by the sum of its production time and its circulation time'.[37] While the process of circulation of capital is predicated upon the spatial coordinates provided by 'the existence of the market as a world market', capital's circulation time is a limit to its production time, hence to its 'valorization process'.[38] Therefore, Marx gives importance

34 David Harvey, *The Limits to Capital*, London: Verso, new edn, 2006, 21.
35 Karl Marx, *Capital*, vol. 2, trans. David Fernbach, London: Penguin, 1978, 185.
36 Ibid., 180.
37 Ibid., 235.
38 Ibid., 190 and 203–4.

to the transport industry, writing lines that inspire many studies of logistics today. That industry, he contends, 'forms on the one hand an independent branch of production', while on the other hand 'it is distinguished by its appearance as the continuation of a production process *within* the circulation process and *for* the circulation process'.[39] This blurring of the boundary between circulation and production anticipates the current formation of capital's valorization and accumulation, where circulation can no longer be considered as a mere 'limit', since it plays crucial roles in the generation of value, in steering economic processes, and in forging standards and protocols that penetrate and reshape the world of production. It is important to note that, in speaking of the circuit of capital as a whole, Marx writes that capital must be understood as '*industrial capital*, industrial here in the sense that it encompasses every branch of production that is pursued on a capitalist basis'.[40] This reminds us of the fact that Marx developed his critique of political economy in a specific historical conjuncture, characterized at least in Western Europe by capitalism becoming industrial. While his work remains in many ways a fundamental source of inspiration, updates and even theoretical innovations are needed to relaunch the spirit of Marx's critique in the face of radically different conditions. To borrow from the title of a book by François Quesnay that Marx used as one of his main references for *Capital*, volume 2, a new *Tableau économique* is now needed.[41]

Quesnay's analogy between the economic system and blood circulation inspired Marx's conjectures on the question of capital's reproduction, beyond his general critique of physiocracy's focus on the primacy of agriculture. Predicated on the distinction between 'simple' and 'expanded' reproduction, the 'reproduction schemes' elaborated in *Capital*, volume 2, figure among the most original and influential contributions made by Marx to economic theory. From Tugan-Baranowski to Lenin and Luxemburg, from Keynes to Leontief, Marxist and bourgeois thinkers have harked back to these schemes to tackle complex issues of economic politics and planning, while the question of the sustainability of the

---

39   Ibid., 229.
40   Ibid., 133.
41   See also Michael Hardt and Antonio Negri, *Commonwealth*, Cambridge, MA: Harvard University Press, 2009, 285–90.

capitalist mode of production was always in the background of these debates. Important for our investigation is acknowledging the expansive character of the reproduction process in a capitalist economy, which means its structural link with the 'self-valorization of capital' – with *accumulation*. Combining production and circulation, reproduction organizes and articulates their 'mutual interaction', to remember the notion employed by Marx in the introduction to the *Grundrisse*. In this process, the capitalist mode of production never remains the same. Even in simple reproduction, Marx writes, 'the mere repetition of the process of production . . . imposes on the process certain new characteristics, or rather, causes the disappearance of some apparent characteristics possessed by the process in isolation'.[42] This is even more the case once we consider reproduction on an expanded scale, which coincides with accumulation and is therefore characteristic of the capitalist mode of production.

While Marx's theory of reproduction of capital takes the process of production as its presupposition and describes its mediation and artic- ulation with the process of circulation, its implications are far from being limited to the realm of economy. This is because what is repro- duced with capital is the capitalist mode of production as a whole. The antagonism between labour and capital intersects with the process of reproduction in all its moments, which is to say that the expanded reproduction of capital necessarily implies the expanded reproduction (as well as a set of mutations) of that antagonism. Marx makes this point repeatedly, stressing what we can term the subjective sides of reproduction. When we consider the capitalist process of production as 'a total, connected process, i.e., a process of reproduction', he writes, it is clear that it 'produces not only commodities, not only surplus value, but it also produces and reproduces the capital relation itself; on the one hand the capitalist, on the other the wage-labourer'.[43] Reproduc- tion of capital, we could comment, is at the same time reproduction of a split field of subjectivity – of the two antagonistic figures that consti- tute the capital relation. The conditions of such expanded reproduction necessarily include social processes and dynamics that take place

---

42   Marx, *Capital*, vol. 1, 712. For a genealogy of the concept of reproduction, see Étienne Balibar, 'Reproductions', *Rethinking Marxism* 34, no. 2 (2002), 142–61.
43   Marx, *Capital*, vol. 1, 724.

outside of the 'hidden abode of production'. Marx himself seems to be aware of this when he writes that 'this incessant reproduction, this perpetuation of the worker is the absolutely necessary condition for capitalist reproduction'.[44]

This reference to the reproduction of the worker opens a new field of analysis that Marx himself did not really explore. At stake here is the production of labour power as a commodity, which means the production of individuals compelled to sell their labour power on the market to reproduce their lives. Such production implies 'procreation' of new proletarians, but once they are born, the production of labour power consists in their 'reproduction', or 'maintenance'. In labour, Marx writes, 'a definite quantity of human muscle, brain, etc. is expended, and these things have to be replaced'.[45] This mention of muscle and brain is just a short-hand formula for a whole set of processes, practices, and conditions that surround and enable the production and reproduction of labour power as a commodity, on whose existence the capitalist mode of production is predicated for Marx. However, after mentioning this issue, he does not provide any analysis of the tensions and conflicts that characterize the process of reproduction of labour power. Such an analysis would have complicated and widened the understanding of the very antagonism between labour and capital as well as the notion of the working class. As Marx's use of the word *procreation* makes clear, we are confronted here with the constitutive role of women in the production and reproduction of labour power. Reproductive labour as such is historically constituted as female labour, and, as we discussed in the previous section, the critique of Marx's blindness in this respect was one of the main points of departure for Marxist feminism, particularly in the 1970s in Europe and in the US. Writing in 1979, Alisa Del Re was speaking on behalf of many when she noted that labour power 'is a *special commodity*' and 'behind its existence there is someone who continuously produces and reproduces it: women'.[46] We will return to this issue later in this chapter.

---

44   Ibid., 716.
45   Ibid., 274–5.
46   Lucia Chistè, Alisa Del Re, and Edvige Forti, *Oltre il lavoro domestico. Il lavoro delle donne tra produzione e riproduzione*, Milano: Feltrinelli, 1979, 10.

Circulate, circulate

'Circulation sweats money from every pore,' writes Marx in a memorable phrase from *Capital*, volume 1.[47] The formulation is notable because it not only registers the relation between the circulation of capital and the exchange of money, with the former driving and necessitating the latter, but also reminds the reader of the bodily roots of the circulation metaphor, which derives from William Harvey's 1628 discoveries regarding blood flow. In 1651, Thomas Hobbes described the circulation of money through the social body as the 'Sanguification of the Common-wealth'.[48] Charles Davenant wrote in 1698 that trade and money are 'like blood and serum, which though different juices, yet run through the same veins mingled together'.[49] As Michel Foucault explains in *The Order of Things*, it was in the late seventeenth and eighteenth centuries that the metaphor of circulation assumed a central role in economic thought, influencing and structuring the debates between mercantilists and physiocrats.[50] If, in standard histories of political economy, it is the work of Adam Smith and David Ricardo that displaces this emphasis on circulation and substitutes a focus on production, it is in Marx's critique of political economy that the category of production comes into its own, providing, as we have discussed in the previous section of this chapter, the motor of the economy and a structuring device for social relations and historical development. As we have argued, Marx's emphasis on production need not obscure processes of circulation and reproduction, which are not only implied by production but also back it up by supplying the conduits and necessary conditions for its functioning. We do not see it as an accident that today debates in political economy have swerved towards the critical analysis of circulation and social reproduction. Indeed, we understand

---

47   Marx, *Capital*, vol. 1, 208.

48   Thomas Hobbes, *Leviathan*, ed. Crawford B. Macpherson, London: Penguin, 1968, 300.

49   Charles Davenant, 'Discourses on the Public Revenue and on the Trade of England', 1698, in Sir Charles Whitworth (ed.), *The Political and Commercial Works of That Celebrated Writer Charles D'Avenant*, vol. 1, London, 1771, 350.

50   Michel Foucault, *The Order of Things: An Archaeology of the Human Sciences*, London: Routledge, 1989.

the current forms of these processes, as well as the reactions of nation-states to them, as central to contemporary geopolitical and geoeconomic conflicts.

Among contemporary accounts, as we mentioned in the previous chapter, Foucault's understanding of circulation as a form of liberal or free movement which raises the need for governance and security is doubtless the most influential. In his lectures of 1977–8, published as *Security, Territory, Population*, Foucault traces the emergence of 'the economy' as an object of governance, emphasizing the role of the physiocrats in creating principles of economic governance that aim to support circulation in ways consistent with freedom and security. He characterizes circulation 'in the very broad sense of movement, exchange, and contact, as a form of dispersion, and also as a form of distribution'.[51] The emphasis on movement and distribution here chimes with his interest in the prevention of food scarcities and epidemics, and, more generally, with his focus on the emergence of the population as a statistically knowable entity amenable to a liberal governance distinct from sovereign power and prohibitive law. Foucault contends that something more than the 'entry of human existence into the abstract world of the commodity' is at stake in the rise of liberal market society, and that this *something* is an art of government 'whose basic aim is the organization of relations between a population and the production of commodities'.[52] Already in this approach there is an indication that the relation between the Foucauldian and Marxian concepts of circulation is more complex than suggested by Foucault's descriptions of Marx as 'our Machiavelli', by which he means that the importance of Marx's thought lies not in its substantive content but in how it galvanizes thinkers who argue for or against it.[53]

We will not rehearse the complex debate about Foucault's relation to Marx, which was shaped by his rejection of doctrinaire varieties of Marxism and has been discussed in detail by many other thinkers.[54]

---

51   Michel Foucault, *Security, Territory, Population: Lectures at the Collège de France, 1977–1978*, Houndmills: Palgrave Macmillan, 2007, 92.

52   Ibid., 440.

53   Ibid., 320.

54   See, for instance, Didier Eribon, *Michel Foucault*, Cambridge, MA: Harvard University Press, 1991; Étienne Balibar, 'Foucault and Marx: The Question of Nominalism', in Timothy J. Armstrong (ed.), *Michel Foucault: Philosopher*, New York:

Suffice to mention that Foucault's writings, at various points, cross the question of the circulation of capital and the production of labour power as a commodity. As we mentioned in the previous chapter, in *Discipline and Punish* Foucault contrasts the 'accumulation of capital' with the 'accumulation of men', stressing not 'the growth of an apparatus of production' but the rise of a 'disciplinary power, whose general formulas, techniques of submitting forces and bodies . . . could be operated in the most diverse political regimes, apparatuses or institutions'. He offers the 'projection of military methods onto industrial organization' as an 'example' of this 'unitary technique by which the body is reduced as a "political" force'.[55] Yet, as one of us has argued, the military frame in which Foucault conceives of disciplinary power bears traces of a Marxian understanding of class struggle and the production of labour power as a commodity insofar as the collective subjects engaged in such struggle are constituted through it rather than existing prior to such an engagement.[56] This perspective becomes particularly evident in *The Punitive Society*, where Foucault's attention to refusal, contestation, and subjective resistance provides an angle on proletarianisation that exceeds Marx's emphasis on struggles at the point of production.[57] Likewise in a 1976 lecture entitled 'Meshes of Power', Foucault finds in Marx's writings 'several elements . . . for the analysis of power in its positive mechanisms'.[58] Without discussing this lecture in detail, we can note that it provides an important perspective on Foucault's forging of the concept

Harvester Wheatsheaf, 1992, 38–56; Roberto Nigro, 'Foucault, Reader and Critic of Marx', in Jacques Bidet and Stathis Kouvelakis (eds), *Critical Companion to Contemporary Marxism*, Leiden: Brill, 2008, 647–62; Rudy M. Leonelli (ed.), *Foucault-Marx. Paralleli e paradossi*, Milan: Bulzoni, 2010; Christian Laval, Luca Paltrinieri, and Ferhat Taylan (eds), *Marx and Foucault: Lectures, Usages, Confrontations*, Paris: La Découverte, 2015; and Antonio Negri, *Marx and Foucault: Essays*, Cambridge: Polity Press, 2017.

55   Michel Foucault, *Discipline and Punish: The Birth of the Prison*, New York: Vintage, 1995, 221.

56   See Sandro Mezzadra, 'Class Struggle, Labor Power, and the Politics of the Body: Marxian Threads in the Work of Michel Foucault', *Zinbun* (Institute for Research in Humanities Kyoto University) 50 (2020): 57–69.

57   See Michel Foucault, *The Punitive Society: Lectures at the Collège de France 1972-1973*, New York: Palgrave MacMillan, 2015.

58   Michel Foucault, 'The Meshes of Power', in Jeremy W. Crampton and Stuart Elden (eds), *Space, Knowledge and Power: Foucault and Geography*, Aldershot: Ashgate, 2007, 156.

of governmentality, suggesting that Marx's account of the history of political economy and the circulation of capital lurks behind his own discussion of liberal circulation.[59]

Interestingly, Foucault's claim that the rise of circulation as an object of liberal governance involves something more than entry into 'the abstract world of the commodity' highlights an important aspect of Marx's own theorization of the circulation of capital.[60] Deborah Cowen notes how 'Marx's discussion of the circuits of capital is largely abstracted from its material forms.'[61] While commodities must circulate and have their value realized on the market before the social labour expended in their production can be recognized, this circulation can 'take place without their physical movement . . . a house that is sold from A to B circulates as a commodity, but it does not get up and walk.'[62] At stake here is the difference between the Marxian categories of circulation and distribution, which we have already discussed. Distribution is an important moment in the realization of circulation, insofar as it involves the physical transport of commodities, including labour power and money, or the transmission of commodities that take the form of messages or signals, an increasingly prominent form of distribution in societies awash with media and digital technologies. This last example makes clear an important difference between the physical distribution of already produced commodities and modes of circulation supported by current logistical practices. In the first instance, surplus value is added in the production process, with distribution providing a drag in terms of both time and cost. In the latter instance, 'the continuation of a production process *within* the circulation process and *for* the circulation process', which we discussed in the previous section of this chapter, occurs.[63] The point becomes clearer if we consider the operation of logistical supply chains, which make circulation part of the production process, with materials, personnel, and knowledge moving in complex patterns of coordination from site to site as commodities are assembled,

---

59 For a more detailed discussion of Foucault's lecture, see Sandro Mezzadra and Brett Neilson, *Border as Method, or, the Multiplication of Labor*, Durham, NC: Duke University Press, 2013, 192–4.

60 Foucault, *Security, Territory, Population*, 440.

61 Cowen, *The Deadly Life*, 101.

62 Marx, *Capital*, vol. 2, 226.

63 Ibid., 229.

branded, and shipped to consumers in what Peter Drucker called in 1969 'the whole process of business'.[64]

The relation between the abstract circulation of capital and the material circuits of production and distribution can never be fully foreclosed or predetermined. As a rule, capital impels an acceleration in physical production and distribution to maximize value production by decreasing turnover time. Today, some of the most striking instances of such acceleration are found in the worlds of financial trading and the digital economy. High-frequency financial trading makes use of data centres, fibre optic cables, and other items of digital infrastructure to execute trades at the speed of light.[65] Yet even this does not accede to a pure capital abstraction that escapes physical distribution: arbitrage in high-frequency trading depends on the time taken for data to travel through cables between differently located financial markets. Although it is a more complex proposition to trace the physical movement of finance capital than that of manufactured commodities, such an effort is necessary to understand how finance provides an abstract point of synchronization for the multiple, spatially dispersed operations of capital. The tendency of capital to 'annihilate . . . space with time', as Marx famously puts it in the *Grundrisse* – 'to reduce to a minimum the time spent in motion from one place to another' – is never complete.[66] Speeding up the abstract circulation of capital need not entail an acceleration in physical distribution. In the world of container shipping, for instance, energy costs and economies of scale mandate the use of bigger vessels that travel at slower speeds to reduce turnover time. Such *slow steaming* attests to the ongoing relation between the production of space and the circulation of capital. Although goods can be bought and sold multiple times while they are in motion, or even while they sit in a warehouse, the moment of physical distribution remains crucial to capital's striving for 'an even greater extension of the market', which, as we know, occurs on the world horizon.

---

64   See Peter Drucker, 'Physical Distribution: The Frontier of Modern Management', in Donald D. Bowersox, Bernard J. La Londe, and Edward W. Smkyay (eds), *Readings in Physical Distribution Management*, New York: Collier MacMillan, 1969, 3–8.

65   Donald MacKenzie, *Trading at the Speed of Light: How Ultrafast Algorithms Are Transforming Financial Markets*, Princeton, NJ: Princeton University Press, 2021.

66   Marx, *Grundrisse*, 539.

In contemporary logistical processes, circulation appears as something other than 'a *natural barrier* to the realization of labour time'. Accordingly, this situation has implications for the production of subjectivity. Marx notes that 'if labour time is regarded not as the working day of the individual worker, but as the indefinite working day of an indefinite number of workers, then all *relations of population* come in'.[67] Here, as in Foucault, the relation of circulation to population becomes critical. For Marx, however, it is not liberal practices of governance that are at stake; or rather, such practices are relevant only insofar as they provide legal and economic codes that paper over 'the hidden abode of production', which, as we have earlier argued, crisscrosses the realm of circulation today. What distinguishes capital 'from all previous stages of production' is the positioning of 'the free, unobstructed, progressive and universal development of the forces of production' as 'the presupposition of society and hence of its reproduction'.[68] Here, Marx comes close to diagnosing what contemporary thinkers such as Nancy Fraser identify as a crisis of reproduction; but for him, the situation is predicated not on the relations between the economic system and its background conditions of possibility but on capital's internal push 'toward dissolution', which makes it 'a mere point of transition'.[69] The problem of how capital persists in the face of such declared transitoriness – of its survival beyond historical shocks, internally generated crises, and decimation of populations and natural environments – is often answered in terms of circulation. At least the possibility for capital to reproduce itself without surplus labour extraction provides a basis for explaining its persistence regardless of its tendency to erode the conditions for social reproduction.

For Gayatri Spivak, who offers an early articulation of the problems with claims for value production beyond the labour relation, such a possibility arises with the advent of 'micro-electronic capitalism'.[70] Spivak offers a reading of Marx's account of the circulation of capital that emphasizes the relationships among the various phases through

67   Ibid., 539–40.
68   Ibid., 540.
69   Ibid. See Nancy Fraser, 'Behind Marx's Hidden Abode', *New Left Review* 86 (2014), 55–72.
70   Gayatri Chakravorty Spivak, 'Scattered Considerations on the Question of Value', *Diacritics*, Winter 1985, 82.

which capital moves. She cites enthusiastically Marx's claim from *A Contribution to the Critique of Political Economy*: 'An ounce of gold, no matter how one may twist and turn it, in any way you like, will never weigh ten ounces. But here in the process of circulation one ounce does indeed amount to ten ounces.'[71] At stake is what Spivak calls the textuality of value: the fact that circulation bestows value upon money 'equivalent to the amount of gold it contains multiplied by its number of moves', but that outside of this process money would be 'a simple natural object'.[72] How to account for the seemingly magical transformation by which money becomes capital? In the *Grundrisse*, Marx contends that time is important: 'the nature of capital presupposes that it travels through the different phases of circulation not as it does in the mind, where one concept turns into the next at the speed of thought, in no time, but rather as situations which are separate in time.'[73] Spivak asks if the circulation time of capital has been 'sublated to the speed of Mind (and more) in telecommunication'. And, consequently, whether the labour theory of value has receded before an electrified financial system that brackets time as a 'vehicle of change' and assigns value as a *differential* that cannot be taken as 'representing labor, even if "labor" is taken only to imply "as objectified in the commodity"'.[74] Spivak's answer to these questions is complex. On the one hand, she recognizes how the financial production of money by means of money questions the 'mechanics of limiting the definition of value to the physical embodiment of abstract labor time'.[75] On the other hand, she writes that 'even as circulation time attains the apparent instantaneity of thought (and more), the continuity of production ensured by that attainment of apparent coincidence must be broken up by capital: its means of doing so is to keep the labor reserves in the comprador countries outside of this instantaneity'. As a result: 'Any critique of the labor theory of value, pointing at the unfeasibility of the theory under post-industrialism, or as a calculus of economic indicators, ignores the dark presence of the

71   Karl Marx, *A Contribution to the Critique of Political Economy*, in Karl Marx and Friedrich Engels, *Collected Works*, vol. 29, New York: International Publishers, 1988, 343.

72   Spivak, 'Scattered Considerations', 82.

73   Marx, *Grundrisse*, 548.

74   Spivak, 'Scattered Considerations', 87 and 77.

75   Ibid., 90.

Third World'.[76] Once again, space takes revenge on its annihilation by time, demonstrating how the circulation of capital necessarily passes through the physical embodiment of labour power, even as that embodiment eludes the artificial measure of abstract labour time.

If Spivak's argument is an artefact of the 1980s, written prior to the 1987 Black Monday financial crash, Benjamin Lee and Edward LiPuma's 2002 article 'Cultures of Circulation: The Imaginations of Modernity' points to 'a major transformation over the last twenty years in the relations between finance capital and labor'.[77] Written amid the market booms and busts of the turn of the twenty-first century, the piece focuses on the rise of financial derivatives, instruments for which, in the minds of the authors, 'Marx's analysis affords no place'.[78] Derivatives are financial instruments that derive monetary value from underlying assets, such as stocks, bonds, commodities, or currencies, which individuals buy the right to trade by a specified date. Introduced as a means to hedge risk, especially for floating currency trades after the fall of the Bretton Woods agreement in 1973, Lee and LiPuma assert that 'derivatives have now become speculative instruments that circulate in their own universe'.[79] For them, 'the structure of derivatives creates a break with the classic relationship between finance capital and value proposed by Marx', sparking 'a dynamic of constant expansion, in which labor's place is taken by risk'.[80] They thus posit a shift, analogous to that between gift economies and commodity societies, from 'Marx's production-based dynamic of self-reflexivity, time, and labor' to 'a circulation-based capitalism' that 'harnesses technology for the extraction and manipulation of data that can then be converted into quantifiable measures of risk'.[81] Furthermore, the derivative provides the blueprint for the wider social reimagination of collective agency and the making of circulation as 'a cultural process with its own forms of abstraction, evaluation, and constraint, which are created by the specific types of circulating forms and the interpretive communities built around

---

76   Ibid., 84.
77   Benjamin Lee and Edward LiPuma, 'Cultures of Circulation: The Imaginations of Modernity', *Public Culture* 14, no. 1 (2002), 203.
78   Ibid., 205.
79   Ibid., 204.
80   Ibid., 207.
81   Ibid., 205 and 210.

them'.[82] Lee and LiPuma present an unabashedly globalizing vision in which capitalism has definitively reinvented itself, giving rise to 'a unified cosmopolitan culture of unimpeded circulation'.[83]

To what extent does this vision participate in the obscuration of labour in the global periphery of which Spivak speaks? Did the sub-prime crisis of 2007–8 pierce and crumble the self-sustaining universe of derivative circulation? What does the fact that the pandemic crisis was driven by the withdrawal of labour from worksites and productive zones tell us about the role of financial speculation in contemporary capitalism? How do we relate the processes of data extraction of which Lee and LiPuma write to the forced removal of raw materials and other goods from the earth's surface and biosphere, which has become such a central environmental issue in the time of the Anthropocene? What is the relation among these extractive dynamics and the processes of exploitation that have become evident in the growing precarity of work and life? And what about the impact of current wars on the working of financial markets? These are questions to which we turn later in this book, but to do so, we must relate the momentous developments in the world of finance over the past four decades to a phenomenon Lee and LiPuma never mention, but whose importance we have signalled earlier in the chapter – namely, social reproduction. Only by situating circulation with respect to reproduction, we claim, can we square its relation to the world of production, which has never gone away but whose relation to the wider operations of capital and capitalism has undergone deep transformation.

A coercive law

As we mentioned in the previous chapter, Rosa Luxemburg's *Accumulation of Capital* continues to be an inspiring work for anybody interested in a systematic study of capital's reproduction. From the beginning of her investigation, Luxemburg focuses on the nexus and articulation between circulation and production; as she writes, 'comprising not only production but also circulation (the process of exchange), reproduction

---

82   Ibid., 192.
83   Ibid., 210.

unites these two elements'.[84] At stake in reproduction are therefore, to hark back to two notions we drew from Marx and Stuart Hall, the 'mutual interaction' and 'internal connection' between production and circulation. We will come back in the concluding section of this chapter to this important issue. Before doing that, it is worth discussing a further point taken from Luxemburg's work. 'Expanded reproduction', she explains, is not invented by capital. It has, rather, characterized 'since time immemorial' every form of society 'that displayed economic and cultural progress'.[85] What makes up the specificity of the expanded reproduction of capital is the drive to accumulation and the production of surplus value that constitutes the basic economic and societal rule in the capitalist mode of production. This point leads Luxemburg to emphasize the logical and historical compulsions that guide and circumscribe the reproduction of capital, while, at the same time, forcing it to expand at an accelerating pace and to overcome any limit. The capitalist mode of production, she writes, does 'more than awaken in the capitalist this thirst for surplus value whereby he is impelled to cease-less expansion of reproduction. Expansion becomes in truth a coercive law, an economic condition of existence for the individual capitalist.'[86]

Luxemburg, interestingly, discusses the gaps and tensions between social capital as a whole and the individual capitalist, demonstrating that to expand reproduction the latter depends 'upon factors and events beyond his control, materializing, as it were, behind his back'.[87] None-theless, the coercive law of accumulation crisscrosses the entire field of the reproduction of capital and one can say that it takes even more compelling forms in contemporary capitalism. This has important implications also for ecological issues in our time, regardless of whether one chooses the term Anthropocene or Capitalocene to define the current geological predicament of the earth. Ecological thinking opens new angles on the reproduction of capital, stressing the constitutive relationship between economic processes and the material environment. Since the early 1970s, Marx's reproduction schemes were criticized by ecological economists such as Nicholas Georgescu-Roegen, precisely

---

84   Rosa Luxemburg, *The Accumulation of Capital*, trans. Agnes Schwarzschild, New York: Routledge, 2013, 6.

85   Ibid., 12.

86   Ibid., 12.

87   Ibid., 17.

because they did not take stock of that relation, treating the economy as a self-referential system. This criticism is not entirely accurate since Marx's analysis of the reproduction of capital explicitly recognizes its reliance on natural conditions, although it does not deal with situations in which shortages of natural resources engender crises of reproduction.[88] The blossoming of ecological Marxism, at least since the contributions of James O' Connor, introduced the concept of a 'second contradiction' of capitalism (briefly put, that between capital and the environment).[89] This perspective further widens the scope of Marx's analysis of reproduction, positioning the ecological question (as well as the related issue of 'social metabolism') as a general backdrop of that analysis.[90]

That the reproduction of capital violently impinges on the earth is one of the most striking manifestations of the coercive law of expansion and limitless accumulation highlighted by Luxemburg. We have learned to see what Jason Moore calls 'the ceaseless transformation of Earth systems at every scale' as a key aspect of capital's accumulation and expanded reproduction.[91] From this angle, what Marx famously terms 'the so-called primitive accumulation of capital' is indeed a continuous and neverending process of appropriation, exploitation, and depletion of resources posited as a 'free gift'. Nonetheless, we agree with Moore that such a process should not be considered simply in terms of looting and plunder, since it has its creative and transformative sides (without giving a positive value to such words).[92] Both historically and in the present, the expanded reproduction of capital has produced its own world, the world we all inhabit. In recent decades, the nihilistic and destructive dimensions of this world production have emerged in full light under labels such as *climate change* and *global warming*. In the wake of Hiroshima, Günther Anders spoke of a 'Promethean shame' to

---

88 See Paul Burkett, 'Marx's Reproduction Schemes and the Environment', *Ecological Economics* 49 (2004), 457–67.

89 See James O' Connor, 'Capitalism, Nature, Socialism: A Theoretical Introduction', *Capitalism, Nature, Socialism* 1, no. 1 (1988), 11–38.

90 John Bellamy Foster and Paul Burkett, *Marx and the Earth: An Anti-critique*, Leiden: Brill, 2016.

91 Jason W. Moore, 'The Capitalocene, Part I: On the Nature and Origins of Our Ecological Crisis', *Journal of Peasant Studies* 44, no. 3 (2017), 8.

92 Jason W. Moore, 'The Capitalocene, Part II: Accumulation by Appropriation and the Centrality of Unpaid Work/Energy', *Journal of Peasant Studies* 45, no. 2 (2018), 265.

designate the human condition in such a world, characterized by the
inability to imagine the implications of what has been produced.[93] In a
time in which the threat of nuclear warfare is again becoming acute, it
may be helpful to recall that image.

An interesting aspect of Jason Moore's critical notion of the Capitalocene is that it invites us to consider together capital's appropriation of
nature as a key aspect of its expanded reproduction and the appropriation of unpaid labour that enables and intersects with the wage relation.
Moore draws from this dialectic of 'paid and unpaid work' the need to
analyse capitalism in terms of 'shifting configurations of exploitation
and appropriation' – or, one could say, *dispossession*, to cite the influential work of David Harvey.[94] We discuss Harvey's work in our earlier
writings, stressing the relevance of processes of dispossession in capitalism but at the same time calling attention to the peculiarity and new
character of exploitation today.[95] What interests us here is, rather,
Moore's emphasis on the formal parallel between the appropriation of
nature, which creates a key condition for the expanded reproduction of
capital, and unpaid labour, which as we mentioned above enables the
production and reproduction of labour power as a *special commodity*. A
convergence between an ecological and a feminist critique of capitalism
emerges here, anchored in the domain of reproduction. Moore makes
an important point when he stresses, following the lead of Marxist
feminists, that neither nature nor unpaid work are 'out there', as given.
They are, rather, actively produced 'through complex, patterned relations, re/production and accumulation'.[96] Today, it is precisely looking
at the intersection of the combined although separate spheres of the
production and reproduction of nature (as an exploitable web of
resources and of unpaid labour as a condition for the very existence
of labour power) that we can see how the expanded reproduction of
capital emerges as an eminent field of valorization and accumulation.
Even the issues of the so-called green transition and Green New Deal

---

93   See Günther Anders, *Die Antiquiertheit des Menschen*, München: C.H. Beck,
1956.

94   Moore, 'The Capitalocene, Part II', 247. See David Harvey, *The New Imperialism*, Oxford: Oxford University Press, 2003.

95   Sandro Mezzadra and Brett Neilson, *The Politics of Operations: Excavating
Contemporary Capitalism*, Durham, NC: 2019, 201–8.

96   Moore, 'The Capitalocene, Part II', 247.

can be analysed from a perspective that takes the expanded reproduction of capital as a site of investment and valorization for specific economic actors.

At least since Friedrich Engels's discussion of the 'ideal collective capitalist' in the *Anti-Dühring*, the analysis of capital's reproduction has implied in Marxist theory a reference to the key role played by the state.[97] Two of the most important aspects of reproduction – the frictions and clashes between fractions of capital on the one hand, and the coercive law imposed by aggregate capital on the other – can be grasped from the angle of the capitalist state's capacity to provide a representation of the national fraction of aggregate capital. Providing such a representation also means implementing in a specific way the coercive law of capital's accumulation with the establishment, well beyond the economic sphere, of what Pierre Bourdieu in his lectures on the state calls 'modes of reproduction', with their symbolic and social hierarchizing effects.[98] Seen in this context, the expanded reproduction of capital tends to shape society as a whole, with the state performing key roles that are foreshadowed and implemented by the institution of the family, education systems, and other social apparatuses. In the twentieth century, after the Soviet revolution, the reproduction of labour power became a crucial terrain of state's intervention, performed within multiple varieties of welfare and developmental structures.[99] While this led to the internalization of class struggle within the institutional structures of the state, in ways described in the 1970s by Nicos Poulantzas among others, the double role of the state (its representation of the unity of the national fraction of aggregate capital and its intervention to organize the reproduction of labour power) was important in entrenching the continuity of the accumulation of capital, as well as in assuring the stability of industrial capitalism.[100]

---

97   Friedrich Engels, *Herrn Eugen Dührings Umwälzung der Wissenschaft (Anti-Dühring)*, in *Marx Engels Werke*, vol. 20, Berlin: Dietz Verlag, 1975, 260.

98   Pierre Bourdieu, *On the State: Lectures at the Collège de France, 1989–1992*, Cambridge: Polity, 2015. See also Pierre Bourdieu and Jean-Claude Passeron, *Reproduction in Education, Society, and Culture*, London: Sage, 1977.

99   Michael Hardt and Antonio Negri, *Labor of Dionysus: A Critique of the State-Form*, Minneapolis: University of Minnesota Press, 1994, ch. 3.

100   See Nicos Poulantzas, 'The Problem of the Capitalist State', in James Marting (ed.), *The Poulantzas Reader*, London: Verso, 2008, 172–85; Mezzadra and Neilson, *Politics of Operations*, ch. 2.

Today, states continue to perform these roles in ways that are clearly different depending on their position in the world system and related power. Nonetheless, at least since the early 1970s, they have been challenged by a whole set of interrelated processes that have displaced the terrain both of the representation of the unity of aggregate capital (which also means of its expanded reproduction) and of the reproduction of labour power. New monetary and financial arrangements built the framework for the emergence of a new geography of production, materially enabled by new logistical techniques and by the stretching of supply chains. While no unified global capital is in sight, the world market became in new forms the necessary horizon for the representation of aggregate capital as well as for staging the frictions and tensions between its fractions. Financial markets assumed crucial roles in the expanded reproduction of capital, and the increasing relevance of new financial and monetary instruments (such as derivatives and so-called shadow money) ran parallel to the dismantling of the standard wage-labour relationship and to the proliferation of contractual forms for precarious labour.[101] At the same time, in the wake of the dispersed workers' and popular struggles of the 1960s and 1970s, the legal and political arrangements surrounding the reproduction of labour power became the target of multiple attacks. While many scholars drew on the notion of decommodification forged by Karl Polanyi to make sense of the operations of those arrangements, the overarching framework of the neoliberal hegemony that took shape in the 1970s introduced a set of processes that opened new spaces for capital's valorization and accumulation precisely in the field of the reproduction of labour power (which includes important sectors such as health and education).[102] Finance had prominent roles to play in this respect, and while subprime mortgages provide a good instance of financialization of social reproduction in the US, there is no shortage in Europe and elsewhere of examples of similar processes contributing to the financialization of the household.[103]

---

101 Melinda Cooper, 'Shadow Money and the Shadow Workforce: Rethinking Labor and Liquidity', *South Atlantic Quarterly* 114, no. 2 (2015), 395–423.

102 See Gøsta Esping-Andersen, *The Three Worlds of Welfare Capitalism*, Cambridge: Polity Press, 1990, 35–54.

103 Adrienne Roberts, 'Financing Social Reproduction: The Gendered Relations of Debt and Mortgage Finance in Twenty-First Century America', *New Political Economy* 18, no. 1 (2013), 21–42.

Neoliberal economists including Gary Becker have indeed explicitly posed the family as 'a comprehensive alternative to the welfare state', laying the basis for such processes.[104] More generally, the notion of a financialization of social rights effectively captures the violence and depth of a set of mutations that have radically reshaped the reproduction of labour power and the position of the state with respect to it.[105]

The politicization of reproduction was due to feminist interventions in Marxist debates, and above all to feminist and women's struggles across diverse geographical scales, and this continues to be true today.[106] Nonetheless, over recent decades several scholars have critically engaged in an analysis of the new position of reproduction in the workings of capitalism. Take, for instance, Romano Alquati, a leading figure in Italian workerism of the 1960s. In a book originally written in 2002, he reframes the problematic of the reproduction of labour power in terms of the reproduction of what he calls 'living human capacity', maintaining that it coincides today with the 'valorization and accumulation of capital'.[107] Speaking of living human capacity allows Alquati to stress the tensions and contradictions surrounding the process of the commodification of labour power, to expand the Marxian notion, and to identify a whole set of dimensions of its reproduction where the operations of capital intervene to open spaces for processes of valorization. This is not only true for education and healthcare, but also increasingly for the management of the household as well as for the new forms taken by the leisure industry, the media system, and related processes of digitalization. Indeed, for Alquati, the reproduction of living human capacity includes what he calls its *restoration*, a process active in generating a complex economic (but also social and cultural) system that figures today as an increasingly relevant terrain of capital's valorization and accumulation.[108] The process of restoration involves a dramatic expansion of reproductive labour writ large, performed mainly although not

104   Melinda Cooper, *Family Values: Between Neoliberalism and the New Social Conservatism*, New York: Zone Books, 2017, 9.

105   See Colin Crouch, 'Privatised Keynesianism: An Unacknowledged Policy Regime', *British Journal of Politics and International Relations* 11, no. 3 (2009), 382–99.

106   See Verónica Gago, 'Is Politics Possible Today?', *Crisis and Critique* 9, no. 2 (2022), 85–100.

107   Romano Alquati, *Sulla riproduzione della capacità umana vivente. L'industrializzazione della soggettività*, Rome: Derive Approdi, 2021, 17.

108   Ibid., 117.

exclusively by women. For Alquati, privatization, the spread of entrepreneurial rationality, and even the industrialization of the service sector are trends that correspond to the new position of reproduction in contemporary capitalism.

Alquati's peculiar interpretation of the Marxian notion of labour power allows him to speak of reproduction as a key dimension for the valorization of capital precisely because it leads him to expand the very understanding of value. In this respect, there is a continuity between his work and the interventions of Marxist feminists in the 1970s who, as we saw above in the case of Alisa Del Re, pointed to the crucial relevance of women in the production and reproduction of the 'special commodity' of labour power. We have already mentioned the Wages for Housework movement, which is a well-known instance of feminist politics articulated around such an understanding of reproduction, particularly active in Italy, in the UK, and the US.[109] Initiated in the early 1970s by activists and thinkers such as Mariarosa Dalla Costa, Silvia Federici, and Selma James, it was part of a wider conjuncture of struggles and theoretical interventions that, facing the incipient crisis of mass industrial production in the West, aimed to expand the notion of production, interrogating the boundaries between so-called productive and unproductive labour, as well as between production and reproduction. Nonetheless, as we implied earlier, the Wages for Housework campaign and its theoretical foundation did not go uncriticized in feminist debates. In the last chapter of her celebrated *Women, Race and Class*, for instance, Angela Davis took issue with an essay by Mariarosa Dalla Costa, arguing that she reduced women to their domestic functions 'regardless of their class and race'.[110] While this criticism sounds exaggerated, since Dalla Costa was explicitly referring to working-class women in her writings, which did not explicitly take up the subject of race, it is true that the female proletarian experience taken as standard by the Wages for Housework movement was indeed a specific experience forged in the age of the 'family wage'. That standard did not

---

109 See Louise Toupin, *Wages for Housework: A History of an International Feminist Movement*, London: Pluto Press, 2018. More generally, on reproductive labour in feminist debates, see Emmanuel Renault, *Abolir la exploitation. Expériences, theories, strategies*, Paris, La Découverte, 2023, 188–98.

110 Angela Davis, *Women, Race and Class*, New York: Vintage, 1983, 234. Davis refers to Dalla Costa and James, *The Power of Women*.

include in any way the other experiences discussed by Davis, like those of black cleaning women and waged domestic workers in the US and the 'intense assault' and destabilization of black women's family life in South Africa.[111]

Although this is an important point, we are unconvinced by Davis's central theoretical argument in her critical discussion of Dalla Costa's essay: that, since 'the industrial revolution resulted in the structural separation of the home economy from the public economy, then housework cannot be defined as integral component of capitalist production'. Related to production, she concludes, housework is rather a *precondition*.[112] It seems to us that such a statement reproduces the private–public divide that lies at the core of liberal political economy, and at the same time validates the subordination of reproduction to production (of reproductive struggles to struggles at the point of production) in orthodox Marxism. We think there is a need to move beyond such political and theoretical shortcomings, yet this should not entail falling back into the trap of considering a single female proletarian experience as standard. If one looks, for instance, from a feminist standpoint to the circulation of the peculiar commodity of labour power, which means to migration, there is a continuous reshuffling of the partition between spaces of production and reproduction, with migrant women occupying a wide array of heterogeneous positions in shifting geographies and arrangements of exploitation.[113] More generally, contemporary theories of social reproduction provide us with important tools to grasp the spread of processes of capitalist valorization across the domain of reproduction. Such theories, writes Tithi Bhattacharya, 'perceive the relation between labor dispensed to produce commodities and labor dispensed to produce people as part of the systemic totality of capitalism'.[114] This perspective has clear political implications for how we understand class struggle, which must include '*struggles over social reproduction*: for universal health care and free education, for environmental justice and access to clean energy, and for housing and public

111   Davis, *Women, Race and Class*, 236–7.

112   Ibid., 234.

113   See Enrica Rigo, *La straniera. Migrazioni, asilo, sfruttamento in una prospettiva di genere*, Rome: Carocci, 2022.

114   Tithi Bhattacharya (ed.), *Social Reproduction Theory: Remapping Class, Recentering Oppression*, London: Pluto Press, 2017, 2.

transportation'.[115] The struggles for women's liberation, against racism, colonialism, and war, are played out on this expanded field of class struggle.

Nancy Fraser, who has made important contributions to this debate, writes of a 'shift, theorized by Marxist- and socialist-feminists, from commodity production to social reproduction', of a new attention paid to care, affective labour, or subjectivation within the framework of an 'expanded conception of capitalism'.[116] We question the use of the word *shift*, as our concern lies in focusing the analysis on the nexus and articulation between production and reproduction, which requires a reframing of the meaning of both terms. Nonetheless, we consider it crucial to pay attention to the multifarious composition of labour and activities that crisscross the materiality of social reproduction, as well as to related processes of subjectivation. It is true that such composition works the boundaries between the economic sphere and a whole set of other domains (from cultural to social life, from moral economies to all kinds of emotional bonds) that are often imagined as free from the capital relation – but upon which capital structurally impinges. What Fraser calls 'boundary struggles' arise precisely from this aspect of social reproduction.[117] These struggles play important roles in social movements in many parts of the world, but they need to contribute to the formation of wider coalitions to confront effectively the processes of capital's valorization that permeate social reproduction today. Given the relevance of race and gender (as well as of a panoply of other attrubutes) in what we have just called the material composition of social reproduction, and their visibility in our preceding chapter's analysis of essential labour during the pandemic, intersectionality can be reframed here and become a method for a new class politics.[118]

---

115   Cinzia Arruzza, Tithi Bhattacharya, and Nancy Fraser, *Feminism for the 99%. A Manifesto*, London: Verso, 2019, 24–5.

116   Nancy Fraser and Rahel Jaeggi, *Capitalism: A Conversation in Critical Theory*, Cambridge: Polity Press, 2008, 31–5.

117   Ibid., 165–80.

118   Sandro Mezzadra, 'Intersectionality, Identity, and the Riddle of Class', *Papeles del CEIC*, 2021/2, 1–10.

Intersecting worlds

When it comes to struggles at the nexus of circulation and reproduction, intersectionality emerges not as the combined effect of separately constituted systems of oppression but as a matter of lived experience. One of the challenges of working with the concept of intersectionality is accounting for the mutual constitution of differently articulated relations of domination or oppression (including class, race, gender, sexuality, ability, coloniality), rather than approaching them as independent axes of power that, under certain circumstances, overlap each other. As David McNally observes, the origins of intersectionality in legal theory – 'with its foundational doctrine of discrete and autonomous legal subjects who possess property and rights' – are perhaps at the heart of this problem, which 'the most sophisticated proponents of intersectionality seek to escape.'[119] The preference of Patricia Hill Collins, for example, to describe a 'matrix of domination' as opposed to discretely constituted systems of oppression reflects the contours of this challenge.[120] The difficulty is pronounced when it comes to the conduct of political struggles, in which what Ashley Bohrer calls the *equiprimordality* of different forms of oppression and exploitation is often, and rightly, held as a principle of organization.[121] Squaring this commitment to equiprimordality with the tendency for a single axis of power to impose itself as a 'structure in dominance' under particular social and conjunctural conditions introduces a dilemma for political movements.[122] If, for instance, race emerges as a primary form of oppression and exploitation in the contemporary US, does it mean that all struggles for freedom and justice in this context need to emphasize racial politics above, say, questions of class or gender in their modes of organization and contestation? The issue is certainly an important one for political questions of strategy and tactics, especially as framed at the local or

---

119   David McNally, 'Intersections and Dialectics: Critical Reconstructions in Social Reproduction Theory', in Bhattacharya, *Social Reproduction Theory*, 99.

120   Patricia Hill Collins, *Black Feminist Thought: Knowledge, Consciousness, and the Politics of Empowerment*, London: Routledge, 1990, 276.

121   Bohrer, *Marxism and Intersectionality*, 198.

122   See Stuart Hall, 'Race, Articulation, and Societies Structured in Dominance', in *Sociological Theories: Race and Colonialism*, Paris: UNESCO, 1980, 305.

national levels. But it also has relevance for coalition building and the potential for struggles to scale and expand into mass movements capable of working across borders. What may prove strategic or tactical for political struggle in a particular space or time may also limit its possibilities to open itself to new forms of solidarity and opposition.

With these debates, the question of intersectionality, initially forged to contrast an exclusive focus on class struggle in leftist politics, flips around to become not an issue of identity but one of political organization. The opening made by intersectionality has certainly been crucial in displacing an understanding of class struggle, particularly prevalent in the Western world during the period of industrial and national capitalism, as the concern of white male workers in a standard employment relation. From this perspective, intersectionality correlates to the movement of political struggles beyond the point of production, which, for many critical thinkers, has expanded the range of struggles into the worlds of circulation and reproduction. In this regard, it is worth revisiting a work that articulates many of the issues that political movements and labour struggles were confronting in the 1990s when the introduction of the internet and rise in high technology industries substantially changed the world of production. In *Cyber-Marx: Cycles and Circuits in High Technology Capitalism*, Nick Dyer-Witheford argues that 'capital depends for its operations not just on exploitation in the immediate workplace, but on the continuous integration of a whole series of social sites and activities – sites and activities which, however, may also become scenes of subversion and insurgency'.[123] He focuses on struggles conducted by 'workers at the bottom of the hierarchy of labour power, whose networks of support are founded as much in gender and ethnicity as in the traditions of the labour movement'.[124] In analysing labour struggles in Silicon Valley, he turns not to high-skilled technology workers but to the Justice for Janitors movement, which, in the 1990s, was one of the initial instances of what Kim Moody labels 'social movement unionism'.[125] Furthermore, Dyer-Witheford's analysis extends to struggles in the realm of social reproduction, including

---

123   Nick Dyer-Witheford, *Cyber-Marx: Cycles and Circuits in High Technology Capitalism*, Champaign, IL: University of Illinois Press, 1999, 114.

124   Ibid., 96.

125   Kim Moody, *Workers in a Lean World: Unions in the International Economy*, London: Verso, 1997, 147.

health, education, and welfare, and to movements for environmental justice, especially those concerned with toxic waste dumping 'in communities of color, traditional working class neighborhoods, Native Indian Lands, and regions of the rural poor'.[126] Although his enthusiasm for computer-mediated communication opening the possibility for a 'circulation of struggles' needs rethinking in light of the subsequent corporatization of the internet and the rise of social media as a site of data extraction, Dyer-Witheford's analysis makes it evident that intersectionality enters into circulation struggles not as a moral imperative of representation or voice but as an effect of the stakes of the struggles themselves, especially as regards the bodies and minds that orchestrate them.[127]

Almost twenty years later, as we mentioned in the previous chapter, Joshua Clover's discussion of circulation struggles in *Riot. Strike. Riot: The New Era of Uprisings* makes a similar point. Drawing on the work of the Théorie Communiste group regarding the eclipse of production by circulation in contemporary capitalism, Clover argues that circulation struggles involve the unification of participants not by their 'possession of jobs' but rather by 'their more general dispossession'.[128] These struggles take the form of the riot (and related forms of blockade and occupation) rather than the strike. Above all, circulation struggles are not necessarily labour struggles because they revolve about the 'under- and unemployed', whom 'deindustrialization' has 'dramatically racialized' and 'left to informal economies'.[129] Again, the intersectional nature of the struggles at hand appears not as a question of strategy and tactics but as a matter of those surplus populations 'left to molder' in an era when 'the economy as such has receded into planetary logistics and the global division of labor into the ether of finance'.[130] We take these accounts of circulation struggles from Dyer-Witheford and Clover as preliminary attempts to discern the shape and contours of social antagonism and political insurrection at a time when relations among production, circulation, and reproduction are undergoing deep

---

126   Dyer-Witheford, *Cyber-Marx*, 114.
127   Ibid., 122.
128   Joshua Clover, *Riot. Strike. Riot: The New Era of Uprisings*, London: Verso, 2016, 151.
129   Ibid.
130   Ibid., 151 and 124.

change. It is necessary to supplement these perspectives, which are grounded in North American and Atlantic experiences, with an account of circulation and reproduction struggles in a wider global vista. It is also important to approach the question of struggles from an angle that encompasses more recent changes, including the plat-formization of economies and the shifting labour relations that became evident with the pandemic designation of the essential worker. We reserve this task for the final chapter of this book. For now, we want to emphasize that the changing relations among production, circula-tion, and reproduction do not unfold uniformly across the world, but rather proceed in uneven and entangled ways, meaning that it is always contentious to make general claims about the relative posi-tioning of these processes in the differentiated unity established by capital's operations.

The incomplete shift of industrial manufacturing from the North and West of the world to regions such as East Asia and Central America was a feature of the early stages of late-twentieth-century globalization, beginning in the 1970s and reaching a peak in the 1990s. As we have already discussed, this relocation was linked to the formation of global supply chains and special economic zones, the emergence of mass working classes in the global South (in quantity if not necessarily with regard to political subjectivity), the precarization of work in formerly industrialized regions, and the strong intertwining of productive and circulatory processes across global, regional, and local scales. Despite recent enthusiasms spurred by the current conjuncture of pandemic and war for reshoring and decoupling – which are phenomena that apply only to a few specialized sectors of the global economy, such as the high-technology industries – these movements have never really ceased. Although the pandemic and the Ukraine war have significantly lowered rates of industrial production around the world, as did the 2007–8 economic crisis, longer-term trends show steady growth since the 1990s, with emerging economies generally outpacing those in established manufacturing regions. To speak of circulation and repro-duction changing and moulding the world of production is thus neither to make a claim about the falling importance of the latter, nor to signal its diminution in quantitative terms. Rather, it is to point to momen-tous changes in the spatial organization of industrial production, which have been extensively studied by geographers such as David Harvey.[131] Indeed, the wide deployment of the concept of the 'production of space', introduced by Henri Lefebvre in the mid-1970s, to explain these transformations registers the extent to which industrial production shapes and reconfigures the spaces in which it unfolds rather than merely occurring within the boundaries of established territories or regional formations.[132] Lefebvre expands both the notion of production and that of space – the first by contending that economies not only produce goods and services but also spaces themselves, which, depending on the historical moment, play a crucial role in the turnover of capital and the distribution of wealth; the second by understanding space not as a neutral container within which events occur but as a product analogous to other economic goods, meaning not only that it can be bought and sold but that it is shaped by the interests of classes, capital, experts, racial dynamics, popular politics, and so on. In any case, this spatial perspective, although admittedly well-worked analytically, provides a first step in rethinking the workings of production, and one that proves crucial in confronting changes in the current global and planetary order, in which the increasingly violent intersection of geoeconomics and geopolitics is an inescapable feature.

The second point to emphasize regarding changes in the world of production is that the manufacture of material commodities no longer remains the most salient or economically important aspect of the global economy. That production pertains not only to the making of goods but also the provision of services is hardly a new revelation. The concept of 'immaterial labour' introduced in the early 1990s was a provisional attempt to register this fact, applying not only to the production of services but also of cultural products, knowledge, affects, or communicative practices.[133] Somewhat unfortunate in its naming and elaboration, the concept was criticized both by those who found it to obscure the continued economic and social importance of manufacturing and industrial

131   See, for instance, David Harvey, *Spaces of Capital: Towards a Critical Geography*, Milton Park: Taylor & Francis, 2001, and *Spaces of Global Capitalism: Towards a Theory of Uneven Geographical Development*, London: Verso, 2006.
132   Henri Lefebvre, *The Production of Space*, Hoboken, NJ: Wiley-Blackwell, 1992.
133   See for instance Maurizio Lazzarato and Antonio Negri, 'Travail immatériel et subjectivité', *Futur Antérieur* 6 (1991), 87–99.

production, and those fixed on pointing to the irrefutably material quality of the processes, infrastructures, and bodily exertion involved in this kind of productive activity. Undoubtedly, these were problems with which the progenitors of the concept were themselves grappling, and that they attempted to negotiate by noting that manufacturing was not eliminated but transformed by immaterial production, particularly in the informatic mode.[134] In the time since these debates, the basic tenets of the argument have received stronger empirical confirmation. Today, information and technology companies are the largest and most profitable in the world, with their activities having been amplified and deeply sunk into everyday lives, including those in the former peripheries, through the advent of social media and platform economies. The cultural and creative industries, themselves transformed by information technologies, have been promoted and governmentally supported as engines of economic renewal, particularly in urban environments. The production of affects and the conduct of labour in the bodily mode are central to economies and practices of care, which extend across the spheres of health, education, and domestic life, and whose crucial importance for social reproduction was made strongly evident in the pandemic. All these changes link to processes of financialization and logistification, which we have discussed earlier in this chapter. Together, they provide points of reference not so much for vindicating arguments about immaterial labour but for tracking wider transformations in the composition of living labour and in the world of production, including those linked to the production of space, which we have already mentioned, and those that revolve around the concept of productivity, which we now briefly discuss.

Productivity is a key concept for rethinking production insofar as it extends models of time management developed in the manufacturing sector into parts of the economy usually not considered productive, or primarily productive. Frederick Taylor pioneered the rise of scientific management in the late-nineteenth-century factory. His work was extended by figures such as Frank and Lillian Gilbreth, in the office and, significantly, the home. Along with Catherine Beecher and Christine Frederick, Lillian Gilbreth contributed to the founding of the field of

---

134   Michael Hardt and Antonio Negri, *Empire*, Cambridge, MA: Harvard University Press, 2000, 285–6.

home economics, teaching generations of women to be time-and-motion experts in the domestic space by applying productivity measures to reproductive work, generally considered until the time of the Wages for Housework movement to be unproductive labour.[135] There is thus a strong history for the migration of productivity measures beyond the factory walls and into economic sectors in which reproductive, circulatory, and extractive processes are primary. Today, productivity is not only the main metric used in national economic modelling and enterprise efficiency forecasting but also a measure regularly applied in sectors such as mining, banking, and logistics. Within the critical analysis of platform economies, there is a fierce debate about whether the resulting labour regimes can be characterized as practices of digital Taylorism.[136] There is even a debate about making finance productive, highlighting the role of national income statisticians in defining what counts as productive as what adds value to an economy.[137] These controversies insert themselves within a wider discussion about the possibility of measuring socially necessary labour time at a moment when the boundaries between life and work, productive and unproductive labour, seemingly collapse, and the gap between concrete practices of social cooperation and techniques of abstract labour measure increases.[138] It is important to maintain the conceptual distinction between production and productivity, but the extension of the latter across all sections of the economy is a factor in tracking the ways that production must be rethought today.

In summary, the world of production is changing in the pincers of circulation and reproduction. At the same time, key aspects that have historically characterized production expand into and reshape the domains of circulation and reproduction. The very notion of production undergoes profound transformations that result in a blurring of the boundaries that circumscribe it as the economic domain *par excellence*. This blurring has important implications for the spatial analysis of

---

135   Melissa Gregg, *Counterproductive: Time Management in the Knowledge Economy*, Durham, NC: Duke University Press, 2018, 48.

136   For a positive case, see Moritz Altenried, *The Digital Factory: The Human Labor of Automation*, Chicago: University of Chicago Press, 2022.

137   Brett Christophers, 'Making Finance Productive', *Economy and Society* 40, no. 1 (2011), 112–40.

138   Mezzadra and Neilson, *Politics of Operations*, 8.

contemporary capitalism. The intertwining of spaces of production, reproduction, and circulation deeply shifts the spatial configurations of processes of valorization and accumulation of capital. While the world market remains the horizon against which these processes are played out, its organization is becoming increasingly complex, marked by bottlenecks and chokepoints, and fractured across territorial arrangements that no longer fully abide the sovereign spatial imperatives that resulted from nineteenth-century colonialism and the rise of international law. As we argued in Chapter 1, these changes are particularly evident in the wake of the pandemic. The disruption of supply chains has led to the emergence of new maps of trade, which put pressure on geographies of production, while circuits of reproduction have been stressed and tested. Far from representing a temporary setback, the crisis of mobility brought by the pandemic has had deep economic and social effects, instantiated by the return of inflation, while also haunting the current remaking and persistent instability of global space.

As we will show in the next chapter, this instability has not been created solely by the pandemic. In the 1990s, visions of globalization were characterized by an emphasis on world order and peace, notwithstanding the many wars that were fought in this and successive decades, including those that followed the events of September 2001. The economic crisis of 2007–8 brought a deep fracture to this scenario, rearranging territorial assemblages and spaces of capital. That crisis was an important threshold in the emergence of a new geometry of power in which the global hegemony of the US was severely tested and the ascendence of the Rest reoriented the topologies of the world system. Within this changed landscape, there emerged new flashpoints and hotspots – from those surrounding the violent backlash against migration in many parts of the world to those linked to explicitly militarized scenarios, whether hot or cold, including the standoff in the South China Sea and the botched withdrawal of US and allied troops after twenty years of war in Afghanistan. It was only as the pandemic began to reach its long tail, however, that there exploded a conflict that would directly touch the sinews of the global system. We refer here to the war in Ukraine. With marked effects upon the economic, political, ecological, and imperial organization of the planet, this war poses the problem of how to assess shifts in the global organization of power outside of a zero-sum framework in which hegemony simply passes from one set of actors to another.

Although it is too early to know the extent to which Russia's reassertion of regional power will have lasting and global effects, it does not seem a stretch to argue, with Raúl Sánchez Cedillo, that this war will not end in Ukraine.[139] We begin the next chapter with a consideration of the unfolding trajectory of this war, always keeping in mind how its possible ends cross the endless accumulation of capital and the transformations of circulation and reproduction that span the vacillations of the planet and the globe.

---

139   Raúl Sanchez Cedillo, *Esta guerra no termina en Ucrania*, Pamplona: Katakrak, 2022.

3

Regimes of War

---

24 February 2022

There was no shortage of signs about the events that would unfold on the above date. Nevertheless, for many observers and even involved parties, it was a surprise. Russia's invasion of Ukraine confronted the world with a new set of challenges and existential dangers, while at the same time reframing some of the key questions raised by the pandemic. The global circulation of COVID-19 tested and disrupted supply chains. The war, on both sides, has stretched existing supply chains, often to the point of fracture, and necessitated the organization of new logistical routes and connections. In and around Ukraine, the military origins of logistics are once again evident, not to mention the violence, terror, and devastation that civilian populations have endured since the beginning of the assault. Writing on war, for us, means repudiating such violence, a defining feature of the many conflicts that continue to be fought in the world today. A peculiarity of the one in Ukraine is that, for the first time in several decades, the ghost of atomic warfare is starkly present, thanks to the technological developments that have led to the emergence of tactical nuclear weapons. If, as Jürgen Habermas argues, a war against a nuclear power cannot be won 'in any reasonable sense', a series of questions emerges about the ways in which this war can end.[1] Unlike many other recent conflicts, the Ukraine war is not fought on the fringes of the

---

1 Jürgen Habermas, 'Krieg und Empörung', *Süddeutsche Zeitung*, 29 April 2022.

world system. Moralizing rhetoric and invocations of 'just war' abound today on both sides, with a clear continuity in the West with discourses that justified the wars of the 1990s and 2000s (with significant changes in tone after 9/11). Those past discourses assumed the existence of a sole superpower that exercised police functions over a range of so-called rogue states, decentralized networks, and even hostile ethnic nationalisms. This is not an accurate picture of the situation today.

Over the past fifteen years, and particularly since the financial crisis of 2007–8, the world system has been disrupted and, in a way, shattered, to the point that Russia's invasion of Ukraine has radically challenged its stability and structure. The fact that President Putin himself often refers to the end of the unipolar world and even takes anticolonial tones in his speeches should not obscure the powerful shifts at hand. Putin's anticolonial rhetoric is disavowed by the long series of wars waged by Russia in recent decades – from Chechnya to Syria – and by the colonial design of a Russian imperial *Großraum* behind the invasion of Ukraine. To point to deep transformations in the world system, and to contend, as Adam Tooze puts it, that 'the new era of globalization is generating a centrifugal multipolarity' is not to support Putin's arguments.[2] Later in this chapter, we will discuss the notion of multipolarity in relation to the ongoing imperial ventures that wrack today's world. For now, we want only to note that the Ukraine war has accelerated and deepened the centrifugal tendencies in the world system. We are not speaking of a constituted multipolarity, of a renewed rules-based or liberal order, but rather of an unbalanced proliferation of poles across different scales that challenges the very idea of a centre. In this context, the Rest emerges not as a unitary category that opposes or balances the West, or that defines and delimits it. Clearly, the West appears decentred, and new axes of power are reconfiguring economic and political relations. Although the idea of an ascent of the Rest nicely captures these dynamics, it is important to say that we are not confronted here with a simple reversal of the vexed binary opposition between 'the West and the Rest'. As Naoki Sakai explains, we are, rather, experiencing a 'proliferating sense of worthlessness of such categories as the West, the Rest of the World, and so forth', which for us include metageographical oppositions such as global North

---

2 Adam Tooze, *Shutdown: How Covid Shook the World's Economy,* New York: Viking, 2021, 294.

and South, as well as the world systems theory categories of centre, periphery, and semiperiphery.[3]

We mentioned that the Ukraine war is not fought on the fringes of the world system. However, this war is certainly fought on Europe's fringes, in a border zone that historically connects Europe to the Asian landmasses. Ukraine's interstitial location is important for understanding the conflict's consequentiality for the world system as well as the nationalist rhetoric prevailing in the country today, which aims at removing any ambiguity regarding its full belonging to the West.[4] Indeed, Volodymyr Ishchenko writes, due to the war 'Ukrainians turn out to be not just the same as Westerners, but even better than them'.[5] Historically, and despite its vast geographical reach, Russia has held a liminal position with respect to Europe, having served, for several centuries, as a kind of mirror and asserted itself as both internal and external to the development of European modern identity, while often taking Europe as a model.[6] From this viewpoint, it is important to stress that the Ukraine war is a European war. This statement has multiple and contradictory implications because the war has shattered the very project of European integration. There has been a displacement to the east of Europe's central axis (particularly to Poland), and an overlapping of EU membership and fidelity to NATO. The question of gas, oil, and related pipelines is part of this picture. The US targeting of Germany's cooperation with and energy dependence on Russia surely played a role in triggering the war, as did internal developments in Ukraine, including economic turmoil, corruption, the Maidan movement in 2013–14, civil war–like clashes in the Donbas region, and Russia's annexation of Crimea. Although we do not go into the details of these processes, framing the Ukraine war as a European war offers a critical slant from which to probe these regional dynamics and fractures, without detracting from an analysis of the conflict's global implications.

---

3   Naoki Sakai, *The End of Pax Americana: The Loss of Empire and Hikikomori Nationalism*, Durham, NC: Duke University Press, 2022, 3; Sandro Mezzadra and Brett Neilson, *Border as Method, or, the Multiplication of Labor*. Durham, NC: Duke University Press, 2013, chapter 3.

4   See Francesco Strazzari, *Frontiera Ucraina. Guerra, Geopolitiche e ordine internazionale*, Bologna: il Mulino, 2022.

5   Volodymyr Ishchenko, 'Ukrainian Voices', *New Left Review* 138 (2022), 4.

6   See Dieter Groh, *Russland und das Selbstverständnis Europas*, Neuwied, Luchterhand, 1961.

Among the global ramifications of Russia's invasion of Ukraine was a series of abrupt changes in international relations. From the start, there were parallel worries about the situation in the Taiwan Strait, which, founded or unfounded, reached an apex after Nancy Pelosi's visit to Taipei in August 2022. In Asia, Latin America, and Africa support for the West was weak, and Russia's arguments found many willing ears. The US pressure to build a new aggressive West had consequences not only for the strong NATO support of Ukraine but also for changing power relations in the region that has been labelled the Indo-Pacific. The expansion of the security concept of NATO at the Madrid meeting in June 2022 to include the Indo-Pacific is an important aspect of this changing international and security landscape.[7] The position of India, an important pivot for US strategies in the region, has provided a kind of puzzle for international relations, because this subcontinental power refused to side with the West and maintained relations with Russia. Commentators scratched their heads when asking how the war affected India–China relations, which oscillated between new attempts at cooperation and escalating military tensions. And while the war put China in the difficult position of balancing its political support for Russia against its economic interest in widening networks of global exchange, the conflict provided new grounds for actors such as Turkey, which was able to use its position as a potential negotiator to blackmail Sweden and Finland, demanding the extradition of Kurdish militants as a condition to allow their NATO membership. Moreover, the architectures of the international world were unsettled and compromised, as bodies such as the United Nations Security Council were unable to act due to their structure and particularly Russia's right of veto.

The economic impact of the war is also momentous, and has been amplified by Western sanctions against Russia. Energy and food are the two main domains in which the war has led to supply chain blockages, shortages around the world, and price volatility with effects well beyond sectoral boundaries. These disruptions have reinforced in uneven ways the inflationary pressures that stemmed from the pandemic. While the war has prompted and reasserted the economic centrality of the fossil fuel industries to the detriment of any energy transition or Green New

---

7   NATO, *Strategic Concept 2022*, 11. Adopted by Heads of State and Government at the NATO Summit in Madrid, 29 June 2022.

Deal, waves of militarization have shifted public investments to pull against the welfare and stimulus initiatives that many governments and central banks launched in response to COVID-19. These changes are part of the regime of war that is spreading in the wake of Russia's invasion of Ukraine. With the term *regime of war*, we describe a militarization of political and economic life that exceeds the actual engagement of military forces on the ground and may even exist independently from such mobilizations.[8] Although it is important to recognize that the involvement of military forces in activities other than war often complements such militarization beyond war, these processes are also accompanied by a general tendency for civilian and economic life to reshape military affairs. Practices and paradigms of national security, which are a prominent expression of regimes of war, have a differentiated uptake across regions and state formations, assuming a steering role in countries such as the US and China but always mixing with other governmental imperatives. To write of the expansion of a regime of war in response to the events in Ukraine is to register the war's effects way beyond its territorial delimitation and purview as a European war.

The regime of war has a particularly strong grip in Russia, where the repression of dissent, the amplified circulation of the symbol Z, the explicit role of the Wagner company in the first year of war, martial masculinity, and the forced military conscription of civilian bodies, including convicted criminals otherwise languishing in prison cells, are among its most salient aspects.[9] Without mentioning similar tendencies in Ukraine and the world at large, which nevertheless need to be analysed to understand the uneven spread of regimes of war across diverse spaces and scales, we need to dwell for a moment on Russia to shed light on the dynamics underlying Putin's decision to invade Ukraine. Scholars including Georgi Derluguian and Immanuel Wallerstein stress the marginal role of Russia at the dawn of the capitalist world system, which resulted in the country taking what they call a semiperipheral position in this system as it evolved across the centuries. These thinkers point to the fact that modernization cycles in Russian history (including the Bolshevik

---

8   See also Raúl Sanchez Cedillo, *Esta guerra no termina en Ucrania*, Pamplona: Katakrak, 2022, 46–7.

9   Isabell Lorey, 'Martial Masculinity and Authoritarian Populism', trans. Kelly Mulvaney, transversal.at, April 2022.

revolution) run parallel to the 'hegemonic cycles of the capitalist center'.[10] While the USSR was characterized by repeated attempts to break the historical limits of Russia's semiperipheral position, the unwillingness of Brezhnev's *nomenklatura* to take up the challenge of 1968 (in Prague but also at home) laid the basis for the crisis that led to the eventual dissolution of actually existing socialism in 1991. Privatizations and nationalist separatism in the 1990s only reinforced the semiperipheral position of a weakened Russia, with the emergence of corruption and so-called oligarchs as distinctive features of a new capitalism.[11]

An approach to Russia from the perspective of world systems theory has been quite influential in recent critical debates, which have also registered an increasing concern with colonial and postcolonial issues and entanglements.[12] The peripheral or semiperipheral position of Russia is central to many attempts to characterize the country's political predicament, including an influential intervention by Rick Simon, and above all a book by the venerable figure of the Russian left Boris Kagarlitsky.[13] The latter describes Russia as an 'empire of the periphery', adapting the terminology of world systems theory in a seemingly paradoxical way. The imperial dimension of Russian history is evident not only in the country's vast territorial expanse but also because of the huge cultural, linguistic, and even ethnic diversity that its federal structure struggles to contain. In recent years it has become increasingly clear that Putin aims to relaunch an imperial politics, challenging what he calls the 'collective West' and claiming the establishment of a new security architecture in Europe, with global implications for Russia's position. In doing so, he has frequently used civilizational tones, emphasizing the patriarchal and orthodox traits of his reactionary political project, which is hostile not only to liberalism and democracy but also to any kind of social struggle. As Ilya Budraitskis writes, referring to Samuel P. Huntington's influential and perfidious manifesto *The Clash of*

---

10   Georgi Derluguian and Immanuel Wallerstein, 'De Iván el Terrible a Vladímir Putin: Russia en la perspectiva del Sistema-mundo', *Nueva Sociedad* 253 (2014), 53.

11   Ibid., 68.

12   See, for instance, Viatcheslav Morozov, *Russia's Postcolonial Identity: A Subaltern Empire in a Eurocentric World*, London: Palgrave Macmillan, 2015.

13   Rick Simon, '"Upper Volta with Gas?" Russia as a Semi-Peripheral State', in Owen Worth and Phoebe Moore (eds), *Globalization and the 'New' Semiperipheries*, London: Palgrave Macmillan, 2009, 120–37; Boris Kagarlitsky, *Empire of the Periphery: Russia and the World System*, London: Pluto Press, 2008.

Civilizations, Putin 'lives in the world that Huntington built'.[14] Influential ideologues, from Vladislav Surkov to Aleksandr Dugin, have worked for years to prepare the ground for Putin's political vision, harking back to the work of Ivan Ilyin (an extreme rightwing Russian thinker active during the first half of the twentieth century) and heralding the prospect of a so-called Eurasia, a concept with its own problematic historical roots. Interestingly, references to world systems theory are not absent from such debates, for instance in the work of Sergey Glazyev.[15]

Putin's imperial vision, which takes the USSR as an imaginary reference emptied of any socialist content, has economic as well as civilizational implications. Since the 1990s, Russian capitalism has undergone several transformations, including the trauma of Boris Yeltsin and Yegor Gaidar's 'shock therapy', and the subsequent alliance of political classes and oligarchs that facilitated Putin's provisional stabilization of the economy and political ascent. That such consolidation was achieved on the back of extractive processes, particularly in the oil and gas industries, is a salient feature that must be given due attention in any analysis of the dynamics that facilitated Russia's reach into the global economy. The country's position remained nonetheless subordinated to the limits of a specific form of political capitalism, established on the ruins of socialist welfare structures that became terrains of capital valorization against a background of widespread processes of dispossession. With the term *political capitalism*, we refer to a situation where the boundaries between politics and economy are not pre-established, due to the clearly political effects of capital operations. Recognizing that the porosity of these boundaries can work in very different ways opens the possibility of using the notion of political capitalism in ways that go beyond specific instances, which are usually limited to authoritarian states. As opposed to the category of state capitalism, which has its genealogy in Marxist debates on the nature of the USSR, political capitalism avows the extent to which capitalist activity drives state transformations, reconfigures various global divisions and lines (from the international division of labour to systems of political and military alliance), and shifts relations among states, firms, and other governance agents. It additionally enables

14   Ilya Budraitskis, *Dissidents among Dissidents: Ideology, Politics, and the Left in Post-Soviet Russia*, London: Verso, 2022, 7.

15   See Yurii Colombo, *La Russia dopo Putin*, Rome: Castelvecchi, 2022, 83.

an analysis of states' hierarchy based on trade, finance, and technological advance, and their rivalry for control over globalizing spaces and processes. In this sense, the notion of political capitalism has a conceptual and analytical ambit that extends beyond the instance of any one specific state or set of states, to provide an effective angle on contemporary capitalism writ large. As will become evident later in this chapter, the concept is one that sheds light on the global economic and political positioning of China and the US, as well as on their strategic competition.

To return to Russia, we can make sense of the country's positioning as an empire of the periphery in terms of political capitalism. While the size of the Russian economy dwarfs in comparison to China and the US, the sectoral concentration on the energy industries is pivotal to its functioning and global projection. It is no secret that the intertwining of power and wealth that has characterized Russia since the collapse of the USSR has extractive rent as its basis.[16] While the economy is not limited to the energy industries, the latter drive economic development and are at the root of the formation of the most powerful interest groups, which are always connected to the state. The resulting form of political capitalism has therefore a purely extractive foundation, which results in a lack of dynamism and innovation. To recall the analysis of the previous chapter, circulation plays a crucial role in this political capitalist formation, as becomes obvious from looking at the sanctions and infrastructures of energy distribution. By contrast, social reproduction appears to be narrowed and curtailed, as the state focuses on an attempt to channel its functions into heteronormativity and nationalism, and the role of migrants from post-Soviet states becomes an important factor in sustaining workforces, households, and military forces.[17] To offset the resulting social dispossession and allow sections of the population to negotiate continuing processes of neoliberalization, the state redeploys money drawn from energy rent in an array of projects that extend from urban housing to agricultural and fossil fuel subsidies.[18]

---

16   Tony Wood, *Russia without Putin: Power and Myths of the New Cold War*, London: Verso, 2018.

17   On the latter, see Caress Schenk, 'Post-Soviet Labor Migrants in Russia Face New Questions amid War in Ukraine', *Migration Information Source*, 7 February 2023, migrationpolicy.org.

18   See Sarah Wilson Sokhey, 'What Does Putin Promise Russians? Russia's Authoritarian Social Policy', *Orbis* 64, no. 3 (2020), 390–402; Andrea Chandler, 'Populism and Social Policy', *World Affairs* 183, no. 2 (2020), 125–54.

While we do not think that there is a linear or causal relation between the emergence of this specific form of political capitalism and the invasion of Ukraine, an analysis of the entanglement of political and economic powers provides an important background for understanding the conditions that contributed to the events of 24 February 2022. Russia's decision to challenge the international system confronts us with a set of pregnant questions. While many international relations commentators were focused on the competition between the US and China, Russia's actions reshuffled the cards and even altered the framework of that competition. The assumption that China's economic growth places it on a path of conflict with the US, often discussed in the framework of what Graham T. Allison calls the 'Thucydides trap', was overshadowed by an actor whose current economic power rests not on size but rather on the control of strategic resources and assets.[19] One can say that Russia's economic structure is somehow out of synch with the imperial dimension of its political project, which with the invasion of Ukraine took a turn that remains to be investigated and explained. Understanding this asynchronicity poses the challenge of rethinking imperialism in a multipolar world.

Hegemony unravelled

In Western international relations debates, there is no lack of awareness about the crisis and mutations in the world system. 'The global order', write Dani Rodrik and Stephen M. Walt in an article published in *Foreign Affairs*, 'is deteriorating before our eyes. The relative decline of US power and the concomitant rise of China have eroded the partially liberal, rules-based system once dominated by the United States and its allies.'[20] Interestingly, the focus here is on China, as is basically the case in the National Security Strategy released by the Biden administration in October 2022, which defines the PRC as the 'only competitor with both the intent to reshape the international order and, increasingly, the

---

19   See Graham T. Allison, *Destined for War: Can America and China Escape Thucydides' Trap?*, Boston, MA: Houghton Mifflin, 2017.

20   Dani Rodrik and Stephen M. Walt, 'How to Build a Better Order', *Foreign Affairs* 101, no. 5 (2022), 142.

economic, diplomatic, military, and technological power to advance that objective'.[21] This preoccupation with China does not mean that this strategy paper does not take into consideration Russia's invasion of Ukraine. The same document provides arguments to support the unprecedented military and economic aid offered to Ukraine by the US and the West. In the long run, however, the challenge posed by Russia appears subordinated to a more strategic and systemic challenge posed by China. Rodrik and Walt warn, in this respect, that the US reaction to the war might even have counterproductive effects. 'Russia's invasion of Ukraine', they write, 'may have revitalized NATO, but it has also deepened the divide between East and West and North and South.'[22] Such a statement registers the traps and pitfalls of the centrifugal multipolarity we discussed in the previous section of this chapter. While Russia's position within such multipolarity remains to be further investigated, this point needs due consideration in any analysis of China–US relations that avoids the traps of a bipolar approach.

Speaking of a relative decline of US power provides an important framework for the analysis of the war in Ukraine and of its global implications. From this point of view, it becomes important to discuss in more detail the work of world systems scholars such as Immanuel Wallerstein and Giovanni Arrighi, who were pointing to the relative decline of US power as early as the 1990s, amid prevailing rhetorical celebrations of the coming 'new American century' or what G. John Ikenberry would call the 'American unipolar age'.[23] Significantly, in his *The Long Twentieth Century*, Arrighi described the decentring of the West from an economic viewpoint, concluding his analysis of the shifts within the capitalist world system by asserting: 'For the first time since the earliest origins of the capitalist world-economy, the power of money seems to be slipping or to have slipped from Western hands.'[24] Although there are precedents for the adaption of the Gramscian notion of hegemony to the analysis of international relations and dynamics, Arrighi's work is particularly brilliant in this respect and deserves close

---

21   The White House, 'National Security Strategy', October 2022, 8.

22   Rodrik and Walt, 'How to Build a Better Order', 142.

23   G. John Ikenberry, 'Liberalism and Empire: Logics of Order in the American Unipolar Age', *Review of International Studies* 30, no. 4 (2004), 609–30.

24   Giovanni Arrighi, *The Long Twentieth Century: Money, Power, and the Origins of Our Times*, London: Verso, 1994, 367.

consideration.[25] He underscores that speaking of hegemony in an international or even global context does not simply imply a reference to
the power of the hegemon, but rather to an increase of 'collective
aspects of power', which means an augmentation of the 'collective
power of the entire system's dominant groups'.[26] This understanding of
hegemony guides Arrighi's discussion of hegemonic cycles in historical capitalism, as well as his approach to the hegemonic crises that
punctuate its transformations. It is within this conceptual framework
that the crisis of US global hegemony must be analysed. Entitling the
third part of *Adam Smith in Beijing* 'Hegemony unraveling', Arrighi
adopts from the subaltern studies historian Ranajit Guha the phrase
'domination without hegemony' to describe the position of the US as
a 'debtor country', increasingly 'dependent on a flow of money and
credit from the very countries that are most likely to become the
victims of that domination'. Although this implies a 'deterioration in
the competitive position of American business at home and abroad',
the 'collective aspects of power' that define hegemony appear severely
tested in the case of the US.[27]

Arrighi distinguishes what he calls 'signal' from 'terminal' crises of
hegemony, and proposes the US wars of the first decade of the twenty-
first century (in particular the Iraq war), as well as their impact on the
US's centrality in the global political economy, as a crucial moment of
acceleration in what he considers a terminal crisis of hegemony.[28]
Arrighi's analysis has become even more compelling fifteen years after
the publication of *Adam Smith in Beijing*, and it invites us to reflect upon
(in the language of world systems theory) *hegemonic transition*. There
are two aspects of this question that we want to discuss. First, as Arrighi
underscores, historical hegemonic transitions in historical capitalism –
from Dutch to British, and from British to US hegemony – 'eventually
resulted in a complete and seemingly irremediable break down in the
system's organization, which was not overcome until the system was

25 As an antecedent, see for instance Robert W. Cox, 'Gramsci, Hegemony, and
International Relations: An Essay in Method', *Millennium: Journal of International
Studies* 12, no. 2 (1983), 162–75.
26 Giovanni Arrighi, *Adam Smith in Beijing: Lineages of the Twenty-First Century*,
London: Verso, 2007, 150.
27 Ibid., 191 and 193.
28 Ibid., 150–1 and 189.

reconstituted under a new hegemony'.[29] It is crucial to stress that such an 'irremediable break down' passed through a concatenation of wars, including the two 'world wars' of the twentieth century. This perspective on hegemonic transition provides an unsettling lens through which to look at the Ukraine war, its global implications, and the spread of war regimes across diverse geographical scales and spaces. But there is a second question we would like to highlight. As Arrighi maintains in an essay written with Beverly Silver: 'In past hegemonic transitions, dominant groups successfully took on the task of fashioning a new world order only after coming under intense pressure from movements of protest and self-protection.' Arrighi and Silver add that this pressure from below 'has widened and deepened from transition to transition', and that therefore 'we can expect social contradictions to play a far more decisive role than ever before in shaping both the unfolding transition and whatever new world order eventually emerges out of the impending systemic chaos'.[30] This is, for us, a crucial point that foreshadows the investigation we undertake of the nexus of social struggles and geopolitical transformations in Chapter 5. Arrighi and Silver's argument points to the key relevance in world politics of actors and movements beyond those that usually take centre stage in analyses framed in terms of geopolitics and international relations – that is, states, great powers, and even landmasses.

Arrighi does not take Russia very seriously as a power doomed to play a decisive role in the hegemonic transition. Rather, he contrasts Russia with China to caricature the arguments of Western economists who in the 1990s celebrated the superiority of the former due to the 'shock therapy' that the latter did not adopt.[31] As is well known, it is precisely the option for gradual reforms that, according to Arrighi, enabled the spectacular ascent and dynamism of China's economy after the brutal crackdown on the Tiananmen movement in 1989.[32] Beginning with *The Long Twentieth Century*, Arrighi carefully mapped the powerful shifts of the dynamics underlying the capitalist world system

---

29   Ibid., 162–3.

30   Giovanni Arrighi and Beverly Silver, 'Capitalism and World (Dis)Order', *Review of International Studies* 27 (2001), 279.

31   See Arrighi, *Adam Smith*, 13–14.

32   See also Isabella M. Weber, *How China Escaped Shock Therapy: The Market Reform Debate*, London: Routledge, 2021.

towards East Asia. In *Adam Smith in Beijing*, he focuses on China, examining its ability to forge new, multi-scalar regional spaces, and positioning it as an emerging centre of economic power that is beginning to deploy a limited but no less effective hegemony. We agree with Arrighi that no account of the global condition can be pursued today without coming to grips with the position of China. Nevertheless, we are cautious regarding the tendency of world systems scholars to think of the current hegemonic transition in linear and straightforward terms, following the pattern of the historical hegemonic transitions we mentioned above. We note that such a tendency is less pronounced in Arrighi's last book, but Immanuel Wallerstein takes the missing prospect of an accomplished hegemonic transition as a sign that we are facing the end of the modern world system and of historical capitalism (adding, to be sure, that what comes next is perhaps going to be worse than capitalism).[33] In so doing, he confirms the relevance of the existence of a single hegemon – a territorial or national state – as a hallmark of the theoretical paradigm of world systems theory.

We do not believe that we are facing the end of historical capitalism. A couple of generations after Walter Benjamin lamented the signing of the Molotov–Ribbentrop Pact, we have lived the same experience he assigned to his generation: the realization 'that capitalism will not die a natural death'.[34] Although we take seriously the ascent of China, we consider that contemporary capitalism, while reproducing its fundamental logics of accumulation and exploitation, has taken a shape that is significantly different from those that have characterized its history. The very fact that today not only US hegemony is shaken, but that of the West as such, implies a difference with respect to previous historical hegemonic transitions. At stake is a kind of meta-hegemony, in the sense that since the origins of the capitalist world system hegemonic cycles were predicated upon an unquestioned European and Western dominance. Another point, to which we will return, is that the position of finance in the working of contemporary capitalism differs from how Arrighi portrays it, following

---

33   See Immanuel Wallerstein, *La Gauche global. Hier, aujourd'hui, demain*, Paris: Éditions de la Maison des Sciences de l'Homme, 2017.

34   See Walter Benjamin, *The Arcades Project*, Cambridge, MA: Harvard University Press, 2002, 912.

Fernand Braudel, in calling financial expansion 'a sign of autumn', or of hegemonic crisis.[35]

If we understand the transition under way to puncture a meta-hegemony, we are confronted with a global scenario that is often described using the concept of multipolarity. There is no need here to investigate historical instantiations of multipolarity, going back for instance to the time that preceded colonial modernity and the establishment of what Carl Schmitt calls the *jus publicum Europaeum*.[36] While the concept of multipolarity was used during the Cold War, for instance with reference to the Bandung moment and to the nonaligned movement, its more recent uses refer to the formation of new regional spaces where the relations among the economic and the political dimensions of power are always problematic and always at stake.[37] The invention of the acronym BRIC in 2001 is one mark of the emergence of such spaces, whose geographical coordinates were soon expanded by the inclusion of South Africa.[38] The changes in global power relations denominated by this concept are complex and multi-scalar and cannot be reduced to the ascendance of large continental states whose names provide the initials that compose the acronym BRICS. More important is the entanglement of each of those states within a fabric of networks and operations of capital that structurally exceed their boundaries and stretch across regional spaces through which global processes are articulated. It is important to mention that BRICS started to meet regularly at a forum in 2009, after the financial crisis of 2007–8, and that the fourteenth summit took place in June 2022 in Beijing. This summit meeting had obvious implications for the war in Ukraine because all the countries involved declined to support the imposition of sanctions at the UN general assembly.

The crisis of 2007–8 is an important threshold in the history of multipolarity, not only because its economic fallout extended beyond the US and its subprime market, but also due to its uneven impacts and

---

35   Arrighi, *Adam Smith*, 230.

36   Carl Schmitt, *The Nomos of the Earth in the International Law of the Jus Publicum Europaeum*, New York: Telos Press, 2006.

37   For uses during the Cold War see for instance Richard Rosecrance, 'Bipolarity, Multipolarity, and the Future', *Journal of Conflict Resolution* 10, no. 3 (1966), 314–27.

38   See Andrew F. Cooper, *BRICS: A Very Short Introduction*, Oxford: Oxford University Press, 2016.

circulation within the conduits of global capitalism.[39] While it is too simple to claim that the effects of the crisis were more severe in the global North, the ensuing turmoil allowed a reshuffling of geographical power relations. In Latin America, notably, some progressive governments saw the US financial crash as a historic opportunity.[40] Although this vision would prove illusory, the ways in which China reacted to the crisis and proved particularly effective in managing it is a salient feature of most histories of this period. In response to the outside shock posed by the market falls in the West, China was able to muster great resources and energies, which allowed it not only to overcome the impact of the collapse of global trade in 2008 but also to start a process of economic reorganization and renegotiate its interdependence with the US. Public investments in health, education, and infrastructure, especially on the part of the central government, were key to these efforts, which were also a response to powerful waves of workers' struggles (as became clear with the controversial reform of labour contract law in 2008, which bettered labour conditions, but was seen by many as a means of boosting domestic consumption). The recovery facilitated by such measures and investments in China was an important factor for the stabilization of the world economy. This had implications well beyond the economic sphere, reinforcing the sense of relative decline of US hegemony and transforming China's position in the world. These changes are crucial to understanding the rise of multipolarity in the contemporary world, but they are not the whole story.

We need to repeat that the critical analysis of China–US competition must reach beyond a bipolar scheme that eventually reinstates the structural logic of the Cold War. This kind of bipolar scheme ignores the relevance of such heterogeneous actors as India, South Africa, and Indonesia, which cannot be directly characterized as proxies or vassals for either China or the US. Even in vast stretches of Latin America or Africa, where the rivalry between these powers manifests in terms of influence and resources, it is impossible to understand the dynamics according to a logic of alliance or affiliation. Writing about multipolarity

---

39   See Adam Tooze, *Crashed: How a Decade of Financial Crises Changed the World*, New York: Viking, 2018.

40   As a telling example see the interview with Marco Aurélio Garcia, foreign affairs advisor to President Lula of Brazil in 2008: Martín Piqué, 'Hay que apostar al Mercado Regional: Entrevista con Marco Aurelio Garcia', *Página 12*, 5 October 2008.

means emphasizing the importance of regional and continental spaces, but we are wary of any definition of such spaces in territorial terms. Latin America and Africa, which we have just mentioned, are cases in point.[41] Historically constituted by different experiences of conquest, colonialism, extraction, and forced labour, these spaces have their own unique dynamics, including regional and national articulations such as those surrounding movements of migration, which are important for understanding how they fit into the world system. What is the meaning of a *pole* in the context of such complex dynamics and entanglements that challenge any stable definition of territory? To ask this question is not to disavow the conceptual, political, and even economic gravity of territorial arrangements and delimitations. Rather, it is to reframe the question of territory in ways that highlight its importance in the variable geometries that expose the fault lines of the contemporary world system.

The notion of multipolarity cannot be taken for granted today, due precisely to the difficulty of defining a pole. For this reason, Richard Haass, in an article written in 2008, introduces the challenging notion of *nonpolarity*. Central to his argument is the fact that in international relations poles are usually identified with nation-states, while in today's world we are confronted with 'dozens of actors possessing and exercising different kinds of power'.[42] Among such actors he mentions regional and global organizations, corporations, electronic networks, militias, and nongovernmental organizations (NGOs). The list could easily be extended. We take Haass's argument seriously because it stresses the heterogeneity of the global landscape of power. We also maintain, however, that the use of the concept of multipolarity does not imply the identification of poles with nation-states. For us, entities such as electronic networks, corporations, and regulating agencies all contribute to the composition of poles. This becomes particularly clear if we take stock of the changes that have taken place since 2008. If we consider the evolution of technology companies, financial markets, and even the regulation of NGOs in China, for instance, it is easy to see how the borders between state and non-state actors have been negotiated in ways

---

41 See, for instance, Walter D. Mignolo, *The Idea of Latin America*, Oxford: Blackwell, 2005; and Valentin Y. Mudimbe, *The Invention of Africa: Gnosis, Philosophy, and the Order of Knowledge*, Bloomington, IN: Indiana University Press, 1988.

42 Richard Haass, 'The Age of Nonpolarity: What Will Follow U.S. Dominance?', *Foreign Affairs* 87, no. 3 (2008), 44.

that respond to external pressure but also register shifts in internal governance. Such negotiation also shapes the global projection of China's economic power through the Belt and Road Initiative, the extension of digital platforms such as WeChat or TikTok far beyond mainland China, or transnational forums such as BRICS and the Shanghai Cooperation Organization (SCO). China is clearly emerging as a pole in the world system, and the state plays important roles in this respect. Nonetheless, this pole's operations cannot be reduced to statecraft, and its spatial constitution is not circumscribed by China's territorial boundaries.

To write of multipolarity is not only to signal that there are many poles in the world today; it is also to recognize that pole formation and maintenance are heterogeneous and contradictory processes that involve multiple means of assembling different entities and actors as well as articulating their operations. Looking, for instance, at the position of Brazil in Latin America, we can note that on the one hand its dependence on global markets has been entrenched over recent decades, while, on the other hand, its penetration into the economy of other countries in the region has happened through the giant oil company Petrobras and related logistical and infrastructural projects.[43] This is quite different from the case of China (despite the presence of Belt and Road projects in Latin America), and is different again from the case of India, whose regional projection takes place in a highly militarized environment. These are all instances of poles, characterized by different intensities and degrees of effectiveness, as well as by different practices of cooperation among state and non-state actors. Importantly, the spatial reach of poles can overlap, meaning their borders are never stable and do not take the familiar shape of a line. We want to repeat that although states have prominent and heterogeneous roles to play in the constitution of poles, this never coincides with geopolitical logics that assume relations between distinct territories. Such disjunction complicates the geographies of the world system today and opens an important perspective on the analysis of current conflicts, turbulence, and transition. A distinctive feature of contemporary capitalism (also due to the driving roles of circulation and reproduction) is that the relation among political spaces and spaces of capital has become more complex than in the past.

---

43   For a critique, see Raúl Zibechi, *The New Brazil: Regional Imperialism and the New Democracy*, Oakland, CA: AK Press, 2014.

The logistical production of space, for instance, follows logics that are quite different from the territorial ones of the nation-state. We will have more to say about this point in the next chapter. For now, we need to come back to the Ukraine war, and to Russia, whose initiatives seem rather to follow a territorial rationality and an imperial logic not fully rooted in economic gain.

The lowest point of capitalism?

We have already mentioned the concept of *Großraum* with respect to the political visions that have driven Russia's invasion of Ukraine. Without overemphasizing the origins of this concept in the writings of Carl Schmitt, it is important to note that, for him, the provenance of the notion of *Großraum* does not derive from the domain of the state but, rather, from the technical, economic, and organizational spheres.[44] Schmitt had in mind the profound transformations brought about by the 'total mobilization' of the First World War, which led to the stretching of supply chains well beyond national boundaries in Europe and emphasized the strategic relevance of infrastructures. To employ the notion of *Großraum* in the context of Russia's invasion of Ukraine is to take an approach to the economic dimension of the war that goes beyond the charting of immediate gains. If we consider the technical-organizational relations among economic processes and energy networks, for instance, we can see that the stakes of the war reach beyond a simple contravention by Russia of an international order based on the underlying principle of territoriality. There is, rather, a complex relation of infrastructures, space, and power at play, with economic and political implications at scales far wider than that of Ukrainian national territory, as has become obvious in the war's consequences for energy markets in Europe and beyond. We need to ask what kind of political power is projected through the control of energy and commodity flows, recognizing that such control has been a crucial issue in the Ukraine war.

---

44 See Carl Schmitt, *Stato, grande spazio, nomos*, Milano: Adelphi, 2015, 107 (the reference is taken from an essay on the concept of empire in international law, originally published in 1941).

The invasion of 24 February 2022 occurred only four hours after Ukraine's electricity grid had been unplugged from the Russian-operated network to which it had previously been connected. This step was necessary for its planned integration into the European grid – a task that was then accomplished at breakneck speed by 16 March.[45] Likewise, the continued payment by Russia to Ukraine of gas transit fees, plans to connect the nuclear power station at Zaporizhzhia to the Russian grid, and the systematic Russian targeting of vital electricity and water infrastructures in Ukraine show the intermingling of geographical scales, power relations, and economic arrangements that make the concept of *Großraum* relevant in the violent conjuncture of the war. If military and territorial logics strongly shape Russia's operations on the ground, its war aims include but do not appear to be limited to the conquest and annexation of specific territories. They rather encompass wider infrastructural and networked spaces that provide conduits to expand the operative dimension of Russian political capitalism. Even when considered from this angle, this peculiar formation of capitalism appears to be dominated by logics of power that curtail rather than spur dynamism and innovation, reproducing a prevailing extractivism that generates an authoritarianism crisscrossed by both economy and politics. In a multipolar world, Russia instantiates a particularly static and reactionary tendency to expand and guard its interests, which is clear not only from the viewpoint of social struggles and movements but also from the role of fractions of capital that are not directly linked to extractive industries. Kagarlitsky's characterization of Russia as an empire of the periphery is apposite here, and even the vexed notion of imperialism needs to be further tested if we are to understand the way in which Russia's position relates to other poles in the capitalist world system.

More than twenty years ago, in a book that continues to be relevant today, Michael Hardt and Toni Negri questioned the applicability of the notion of imperialism to the world conjuncture that existed at the end of the twentieth century. What they famously termed Empire was a decentred and multilayered system of rule in which the sovereignty of capital outweighed and overshadowed traditional logics of imperialism.

---

45   See Anna Blaustein, 'How Ukraine Unplugged from Russia and Joined Europe's Power Grid with Unprecedented Speed', *Scientific American*, 23 March 2022, scientific american.com.

Territorial conquest, the merging of industrial and financial capital to drive expansionist politics, and the scramble for colonies that characterized imperialism at the dawn of the twentieth century no longer figured as salient concerns in Hardt and Negri's theoretical project. In pointing to what they called the *limits* of imperialism, they emphasized that no nation-state (even the most powerful, the US) is able 'to form the center of an imperialist project'.[46] This situation exists because the operations of capital and the dense web of heterogeneous organizations and surrounding entities have radically altered the territorial logics constitutive of imperialism in its classical forms. Moreover, Hardt and Negri's argument is predicated on the idea that imperialism needs an outside to be colonized, while Empire internalizes all its outsides, including non-capitalist spaces, social arrangements, and pre-capitalist modes of production.[47] Importantly, the main reference for their discussion of imperialism is Vladimir Lenin's compelling description of the double process whereby the concentration of capital and power in the nation-state is the driver of imperialist expansion in the age of the Great War. While Hardt and Negri underscore that Lenin's political commitment led him to anticipate some aspects of the transition to Empire, they recognize that Lenin's description of the mechanisms of imperialism is difficult to adapt to an analysis of global capitalism after the end of the Cold War.[48] Indeed, for them, the nation-state is no longer the fulcrum around which relations of capital and power revolve.

This does not mean that Empire is an unstructured or anarchic totality. Hardt and Negri explicitly advance a model of mixed or hybrid constitution that articulates and layers – as in the classical theory of Polybius – different principles of political organization. They correlate the classical forms of monarchy, aristocracy, and democracy to different actors, including the US which occupies the pinnacle of the mixed constitution but 'prefers to act in collaboration with others under the umbrella of the United Nations'.[49] Among these other actors are the nation-states that form the aristocratic layer, while the democratic layer is occupied by heterogeneous 'organizations that construct and represent the People in

---

46 Michael Hardt and Antonio Negri, *Empire*, Cambridge, MA: Harvard University Press, 2000, xiv.
47 Ibid., 225–9.
48 Ibid., 231–2.
49 Ibid., 309.

the new global arrangement'. Across and in the interstices between these layers operate capitalist actors, including multinational corporations that 'directly structure and articulate territories and populations'.[50] The role played by institutions such as the World Bank and the International Monetary Fund is also a constitutive factor in the working of the mixed constitution of Empire, as are the activities of nongovernment organizations, which primarily fulfil a missionary function. This is a flexible and adaptable model, which continues to provide a useful framework through which to analyse the political constitution of the world. Nonetheless, the current global conjuncture is characterized by a series of tectonic shifts that have reorganized the relations among the actors mentioned by Hardt and Negri as well as the positioning of these actors within landscapes of capital and power. From the angle of the notion of multipolarity we have discussed, these shifts are particularly apparent. Not only do other states exercise the kind of network power once monopolized by the US, but we also observe a realignment of monetary and military might that fractures the mixed constitution and obstructs its workings. Furthermore, centrifugal tendencies in the multipolar world suggest that these processes will become even more pronounced. In this context, the challenge of rethinking imperialism is at once demanding and unavoidable.

Shifts in forms and shapes of imperialism precede conflagrations and conflicts in today's multipolar world. We need not go back to the classical debates of the late-nineteenth and early-twentieth centuries to trace these transformations. In the wake of the Second World War, dependency theories and discussions of uneven development and underdevelopment nurtured new strands of analysis of imperialism and 'neo-imperialism', the latter being understood as the specific form of US global projection of power.[51] More generally, the crisis of the 1970s spurred a rethinking of the notion of imperialism within Marxism. In an essay written in 1975, Luciano Ferrari Bravo points to the growing relevance of a 'process of internationalization of capital', discussing how the connected dynamics of capitalism at the level of the world market tend 'to eliminate the

---

50   Ibid., 311.

51   See Anthony Brewer, *Marxist Theories of Imperialism: A Critical Survey*, 2nd edn, London: Routledge, 1990, ch. 6; and Crystal Parikh, 'US Imperialism and Neo-Imperialism', in *Encyclopedia of Postcolonial Studies*, Hoboken, NJ: Wiley-Blackwell, 2016.

"economic" significance of the division of the world into nation-states'. Commenting on a text by Nicos Poulantzas, Ferrari Bravo adds that 'the traditional functions of the state' have been requalifying themselves under the pressure of multinational corporations as 'functions of the same international cycle of capital'.[52] We consider these points as notable anticipations of trends that have continued to unfold amid the turmoil and shocks that have characterized the mutations of capitalism at the global level since the 1970s. For the theory of imperialism, accounting for these tendencies means paying attention to the multiple borders and frictions that fracture and articulate the 'international cycle of capital', and prevent it from producing a smooth space of circulation. These borders and frictions provide us with a way to understand the persistent roles played in such a cycle by nation-states, which are displaced and transformed but not wiped out.

Imperialism is often linked to the most brutal forms of capitalist exploitation and even pillage. Hannah Arendt famously contends that imperialism 'forced the bourgeoisie to realize for the first time that the original sin of simple robbery', at the very heart of what Marx calls primitive accumulation, 'had eventually to be repeated lest the motor of accumulation suddenly die down'.[53] Arendt's remark highlights the prevalence of extraction that has characterized many imperialist practices in historical capitalism. Different theories of imperialism have emphasized extractive processes. These theories range from Rosa Luxemburg's argument about the necessary colonization of non-capitalist spaces by capital to Eduardo Galeano's and Walter Rodney's investigations of extractive endeavours in the imperial depletion of resources in Latin America and Africa respectively (the latter analysing the slave trade from this perspective).[54] Today the relations among imperialism and extraction appear more scattered and take incongruent forms across

---

52   Luciano Ferrari Bravo, 'Old and New Questions in the Theory of Imperialism (1975)', *Viewpoint Magazine*, 1 February 2018, viewpointmag.com. Ferrari Bravo refers to Nicos Poulantzas, 'L'internationalisation des rapports capitalists et l'Etat-nation', *Les Temps Modernes* 319 (1973), 1456–500.

53   Hannah Arendt, *The Origins of Totalitarianism*, New York: Harcourt, Brace, 1973, 148.

54   See Rosa Luxemburg, *The Accumulation of Capital*, New York: Routledge, 2013; Eduardo Galeano, *Open Veins of Latin America: Five Centuries of the Pillage of a Continent*, New York: Monthly Review Press, 2009; and Walter Rodney, *How Europe Underdeveloped Africa*, London: Bogle-L'Ouverture Publications, 1972.

the different poles of the world system. While violence continues to shape a huge variety of extractive activities, the operations of foreign capital and actors are often entangled in wider and more complex assemblages of power. From this viewpoint, Russia's project of a new *Großraum*, clearly connected to a further entrenchment of extraction particularly in the field of energy, displays a marked imperial quality, while it remains to be asked whether that quality is unique in comparison to other global players and poles.

Since the end of the Second World War, the global projection of power on the part of the US has prompted many debates on the nature of a form of imperialism that does not rely on territorial conquest and direct political control. The notions of US global hegemony and of a new empire that we discussed above are part of those debates, which have encompassed for instance the forceful arguments of Paul Baran and Paul Sweezy for the applicability of the notion of imperialism to the US.[55] There is no need for us to go into the details of these contentions, which were shifted by developments in the wake of the fall of the Soviet Union. A further fillip to these discussions came after the events of September 2001 and the ensuing so-called global war on terror. The arguments presented by David Harvey in his book *The New Imperialism* were prominent in this new conjuncture. With a focus on oil, Harvey joined Luxemburg and Arendt by connecting his analysis of imperialism to the question of primitive accumulation, leading him to introduce the notion of accumulation by dispossession. For Harvey, the undisputed role of the US as a sole superpower (the neoconservative project pursued by the Bush Jr administration after 9/11) was not destined to bring stability to the global capitalist system, which faced various elements of disorder and crisis. From a theoretical point of view, Harvey understood imperialism as 'a contradictory fusion' of a political moment related to state and empire and of the 'molecular processes of capital accumulation in space and time'.[56] In describing this problematic amalgam, he drew directly on Arrighi's analysis of the combined but also contradictory logics of 'territorialism' and capitalism.[57] In this way,

55   See Paul A. Baran and Paul M. Sweezy, *Monopoly Capital: An Essay on the American Economic and Social Order*, New York: Monthly Review Press, 1966.
56   David Harvey, *The New Imperialism*, Oxford: Oxford University Press, 2003, 26.
57   Ibid., 27.

Harvey's reading of contemporary capitalist imperialism cannot be separated from an understanding of political relations within the interstate system.[58]

'Only the unlimited accumulation of power', writes Hannah Arendt, 'could bring about the unlimited accumulation of capital.' Foreign investments and capital export, she adds, 'became a permanent feature of all economic systems as soon as it was protected by export of power'.[59] This interpretation of imperialism as a political concept is important for both Harvey and for Arrighi, the latter already arguing in a book published in 1978 that 'there is a substantial unity between the tendency to the formation of the world market and the ascent of the nation-state as dominant entity within the international system'.[60] Nonetheless, while Arendt's analysis focuses on the intertwining of accumulation of power and capital *within states*, Arrighi stresses the need to study such dynamics 'in an *evolving system of states*'.[61] He takes this approach to territorialism ('the territorial logic of historical capitalism') as well as imperialism, focusing on the vexed question of the overaccumulation of capital and related processes of financialization. For Arrighi it is important to understand the implications of these processes for the spatial arrangements needed, to use the term popularized by Harvey, to 'fix' the ensuing problems of stagnation. He attempts to explain the peculiarity of the US project of world rule in the twentieth century, underscoring the aspects that distinguish it from 'the fusion of capitalism and imperialism' that was the constitutive feature of British hegemony within the world system.

Interestingly, Arrighi emphasizes that the US 'had "internalized" imperialism from the very beginning of its history'. He contends that its reluctance to pursue territorial gains abroad until the end of the nineteenth century (it did not follow the European powers by engaging in colonial expansion) was predicated on what Gareth Stedman Jones calls 'an unprecedented territorialism "at home"'.[62] Internal processes of territorialization shape the formation of 'the continent-sized US "island"' and anticipate its position within the 'new historical geography of

58 Ibid., 33.
59 Arendt, *Totalitarianism*, 137.
60 Giovanni Arrighi, *Geometria dell'imperialismo*, Milano: Feltrinelli, 1978, 93.
61 Arrighi, *Adam Smith*, 229.
62 Ibid., 247.

capitalism', which emerged from the hegemonic transition in the early twentieth century. 'Mastery of the balance of power in the interstate system' was essential to the rise of the US as the new hegemon, but the combination of 'protection, state-making, war-making, and extraction' characteristic of US global hegemony depended on shifting configurations of capitalism and territorialism, where direct rule abroad was a last resort.[63] We can add to this observation that mutations of capitalism during the Cold War, and even more clearly after its end, have altered the very notion of territory, both with respect to the operations of capital and to political configurations of power, including nation-states.

We have written extensively on such mutations of territory elsewhere and we will come back to this issue in the next chapter.[64] For now, we want to register the persistent importance of territorial assemblages and logics as well as of the notion of territorialism, although there is a need to adapt this approach to the new emerging configurations of capitalism if they are to continue to provide an effective analytical approach to the question of imperialism. As we earlier contended, the relation between spaces of capital and political spaces has become complex and at times illegible. The image proposed by Hardt and Negri of 'two nested spheres – the planetary networks of social production and reproduction, and the constitution of global governance – that are increasingly out of synch' captures this predicament nicely.[65] The 'system of states' can no longer offer a stable point of reference for the analysis of capitalism and territorialism, since it appears fractured and obstructed by the emergence of powers that constitutively challenge the principle of the 'sovereign equality of all its members' that figures in Article 2 of the UN Charter. This is not simply to make the banal point that some states are more powerful than others. The fact is that the powers that matter in the contemporary world have a territorial expanse and material constitution that are completely different from those of the European nation-states upon which the UN charter is tailored. They have rather evolved as *imperial* or *continental states*. This is true for Russia no less than for the US and China. But a few other states can be mentioned here, whose

63 Ibid., 249.
64 Mezzadra and Neilson, *Politics of Operations*, 24–32.
65 Michael Hardt and Antonio Negri, 'Empire, Twenty Years On', *New Left Review* 120, 2019, 68.

nature can be deemed imperial or continental not only due to their territorial reach but also because of their colonial and postcolonial histories, from Brazil to India and Turkey. One could also say that, during the Cold War, the US and the Soviet Union were states of this kind. But the bipolar logic of the international architecture in those decades cannot be easily replicated and adapted to the presence of multiple imperial or continental states.[66]

It would be wrong to identify such states with the poles composing the emergent multipolar world. But any attempt to come to grips with imperialism in today's world must take these imperial or continental states into due consideration. The disjunction of capitalism and territorialism is an important factor to account for in any analysis of the tensions and conflicts surrounding the constitution of a multipolar world. Giving appropriate analytical attention to these conditions means admitting the possibility of the existence of multiple forms of imperialism, each with different proportions of capitalist and territorial components contributing to their political manifestations and imprints. Returning to the case of Russia, we can observe an excess of territorial logics at work in the invasion of Ukraine. The pursuit of a *Großraum* that we mentioned earlier was theoretically possible by other means, including agreements, political and economic pressure, and infrastructural investments. This is not to claim that capital is not at stake in Putin's war. Specific fractions of capital, particularly in the energy and arms sectors, benefit from these military actions, and provide impetus to the war effort. The territorial stakes of the war also have implications for the distribution of capital interests across the borders of Ukraine and Russia, with the industrial and mining sectors in the Donbas playing important roles in this regard. The question of Russian imperialism in history and in the present has been contentious in recent years, as has the role played by Western imperialism in the dynamics that led to the war.[67] Russia projects its power not only in Ukraine but also in the Middle East and sub-Saharan Africa, engaging in bold and reckless

---

66 See Carlo Galli, 'Il "grande Stato" nella politica internazionale', in Paolo Colombo, Damiano Palano, and Vittorio Emanuele (eds), *La forma dell'interesse. Studi in onore di Lorenzo Ornaghi*, Milano: Vita e Pensiero, 2018, 181–95.

67 Volodymyr Ishchenko and Yuliya Yurchenko, 'Ukrainian Capitalism and Inter-Imperialist Rivalry', in Immanuel Ness and Zak Cope (eds), *The Palgrave Encyclopedia of Imperialism and Anti-Imperialism*, London: Palgrave Macmillan, 2019, 9–15

military adventures but also expanding the tentacles of its specific form of political capitalism.

If one can note a prevalence of territorial logics in Russian imperialism, other varieties of imperialism are present in the multipolar world. The US, an imperial state that uses the sovereign position of its currency to manage its huge external debt, seems to instantiate an opposing type of imperialism, reliant more on capital operations than on expressions of territorialism. What Daniela Gabor describes as the updating of the Washington Consensus to form a Wall Street consensus, based on the reorganization of development initiatives through partnerships with global finance, paints a telling portrait of the evolving imperial dynamics of capital in the US.[68] The use of sanctions as an economic weapon that was taken to a new level against Russia during the Ukraine war is also emblematic of the role played by capital in this specific form of imperialism, which constellates around US global influence and alliance building.[69] This is not to say that this form of imperialism is fully deterritorialized. Suffice it to recall the unprecedented military might of the US and the hundreds of bases it maintains around the world. The many wars fought by the US in recent decades, from Korea and Vietnam to Iraq and Afghanistan, demonstrate that territorial logics were never absent in this capitalist imperialism. Under conditions of centrifugal multipolarity, territorial conflicts can flare up in highly unpredictable ways and even become more pronounced as a feature of the capitalist world system. The rapid, although uneven spread of regimes of war in the wake of Russia's invasion of Ukraine is an alarming symptom of this volatile and increasingly unstable situation.

Imperialism today is not confined to powers such as the US and Russia. Without going into a discussion of the position of China as well as of other imperial or continental states, we note that the disjunction we have been describing between territorial and capitalist logics is at the root of a potential proliferation of multiple and even overlapping imperialisms. It is an irony of history that the definition of imperialism provided at the end of the Great War by Joseph Schumpeter as 'atavistic

---

68 See Daniela Gabor, 'The Wall Street Consensus', *Development and Change* 52, no. 3 (2021), 429–59.

69 See Nicholas Mulder, *The Economic Weapon: The Rise of Sanctions as a Tool of Modern War*, New Haven, CT: Yale University Press, 2022.

in character' may resonate today, at least in some cases.⁷⁰ This is not
to say that Schumpeter was right in his refusal to link imperialism to
capitalism. The opposite is the case, since it is precisely the long history
of that link as well as of anti-imperialist struggles that led to a situation
in which imperialism can appear as what we might call 'the lowest
point of capitalism'. We use this description of imperialism only
semi-ironically, since the circumstances we describe in the previous
chapter, by which production and circulation cannot guarantee the
reproduction of capital at the aggregate scale of the state, do indeed
suggest a low point in capital's ability to sustain and perpetuate social
and biological life. Under these conditions, in which states cannot fully
orient, shape, or regulate the operations of capital, the scramble to
control spaces of globalization leads to a situation in which imperialist
tendencies and conflicts bubble up and dissipate, either quickly or
protractedly. There is no doubt that imperialism today can facilitate
processes of valorization and accumulation of capital, even as it dis-
seminates wars and devastation across territories. In many cases,
however, imperial wars and manoeuvres signal a limit to these processes, and importantly this limit is one that imperial ventures are often
unable to overcome. As Russia's war in Ukraine shows, nation-states
continue to play a role under these conflagratory and variable circumstances. But we take seriously what Naoki Sakai writes, when he claims
that with 'the demise of Pax Americana, a new iteration of imperialism
may well be emerging, but it will no longer be sustained by the territorial national sovereignty of a nation-state'.⁷¹ Such a process of iteration
is doubtless uneven in its spatial logics, stochastic and sometimes
backward-looking in its temporal elaborations; but in a multipolar
world, imperialism is impelled and sustained by a potent mix of driving
factors that cannot be reduced to territorial logics alone. We agree with
Volodymir Ishchenko and Yuliya Yurchenko that we are confronting
today a 'combination of competing geopolitical and economic imperialisms (which are more than one), yet ideologically they remain
capitalist to the core'.⁷²

---

70   Joseph Schumpeter, *Imperialism and Social Classes*, Cleveland: Meridian Books,
1966, 65.
71   Sakai, *End of Pax Americana*, 183.
72   Ishchenko and Yurchenko, 'Ukrainian Capitalism', 1.

China beyond China

We earlier characterized the Ukraine war as having rocked the centre of the world system. One register of this conflict's seismic effect is how it has displaced and complicated narratives about global power dynamics that had become slowly but surely entrenched in the time since the 2007–8 financial crisis. We refer to the growing tensions between China and the US – two imperial or continental states, which despite their strong economic entwining, found themselves engaged in 'strategic competition' by the last part of the second decade of the twenty-first century. We do not need to rehearse here the reasons for this mounting situation; suffice it to say, we do not take seriously the many screeds that attribute the downward spiral of China–US relations to the proclivities and excesses of their respective leaders. Just as Tony Wood uses the phrase 'Russia without Putin' to suggest that an obsessive focus on a country's leader obscures an analysis of the wider political and economic forces at hand, we see a need to talk about China without Xi, the US without Trump, or for that matter, the US without Biden.[73] Undoubtedly, a leader's decisions and foibles can influence geopolitical dynamics or even prove emblematic of them, but the tendency to link international political developments to leadership style or personality traits, pronounced in the case of Putin, reveals little of the undercurrents at stake. As is often remarked, the milder disposition of Biden compared to Trump has not resulted in a winding back of Beltway hostilities towards China; these have continued strongly, although in a more multilateral and predictable frame. Despite the ongoing enmity between China and the US, we do not place much credence in linear accounts of hegemonic transition that assume the inevitability of military conflict between these powers. Without discounting the possibility of such a confrontation, we ask if the antagonism between China and the US already constitutes a war, given the tendency among many commentators to define war as encompassing such situations as trade war, information war, and financial war.

These inclusions are by no means novel in discussions about transformations in warfare. As long ago as 1999, Chinese Airforce colonels

---

73 Wood, *Russia Without Putin.*

Qiao Liang and Wang Xiangsui described in their tract *Unrestricted Warfare* the propensity for war to become more generalized – that is, for war to be conducted not only through military but also through non-military means. Qiao and Wang's list non-military warfare forms, which proliferate alongside military actions other than war, is extensive and includes, beyond the categories already mentioned, ecological warfare, resource warfare, intelligence warfare, foreign aid warfare, sanctions warfare, drug warfare, media warfare, and regulatory warfare.[74] Without suggesting that Qiao and Wang provide a master plan for China's US strategy, which has certainly evolved in the past twenty years, we can note that their expansion of warfare beyond military conflict provides a kind of checklist against which to measure the escalation of China–US antipathy. The picture has included: tariffs; computer hacking; the quest for soft power influence; 'wolf warrior' diplomacy; export controls on GPU chips and other high-technology items; heightened media rhetoric in venues such as Fox News and the *Global Times*; extraditions; the West's banning of Huawei from 5G and other digital networks; denunciations of the treatment of Uighurs and other Muslims in Xinjiang; Beijing's blocking of the Ant Group's initial public offering on the Hong Kong exchange; the suspension of scientific collaboration on climate change; control of undersea data infrastructures; foreign interference legislation; vaccine nationalism; and allocation of blame for the COVID-19 pandemic. To take stock of these factors is not to discount parallel military developments, including on the Chinese side the growth and modernization of the People's Liberation Army, the building of military installations in the South China Sea, skirmishes on the China–India border, the opening of the Djibouti naval base, and the arrival of doctrines and technologies of intelligent warfare. Overall, however, China has been a largely peaceful nation, internal skirmishes and violence against minority populations aside, and has not sent forces into major combat operations since the invasion of Vietnam more than four decades ago. It is thus difficult to know the detail of China's military capabilities and operational concepts. By contrast, given its many invasions and interventions in recent decades, the military strength of the US is a known and potent quantity. Additional security arrangements

---

74   Qiao Liang and Wang Xiangsui, *Unrestricted Warfare*, Beijing: PLA Literature and Arts Publishing House, February 1999, 146.

such as the Quadrilateral Security Dialogue with Australia, India, and Japan, and the AUKUS technology-sharing agreement, which aside from increasing interoperability among military forces aims to deliver nuclear-powered submarines to Australia, are explicitly directed towards containing China.

The extension of China–US hostilities into civilian and technological spaces beyond military build-ups and alliance making reinforces our argument that the formation of poles and the spread of war regimes are not limited to the arts of statecraft, international relations, or military preparation. As we contended in Chapter 1, building on the argument of Lee Jones and Shahar Hameiri, even the most militarized zones of the China–US standoff are crossed by multiple state and non-state interests.[75] In the case of the South China Sea, for instance, heterogeneous actors are at work on the Chinese side, including the China Coast Guard, national oil companies, provincial governments, environmental agencies, and entities charged with the regulation of fishing, vessel inspection, and port management. It is worth remembering that the neologism Chimerica, used to describe the symbiotic economic relationship between China and the US, was in vogue less than a decade ago. Nowadays, talk of decoupling has become predominant, even as the separation of world's two largest economies has proceeded primarily in the technology sector, with uneven and mixed results in terms of foreign direct investment and currency exchange, and muted effects on capital markets. Nonetheless, US exercises in reshoring and friendshoring, and China's dual circulation economic model, which aims to bolster domestic demand and reduce dependence on imports, are likely to have significant effects. Ho-fung Hung attributes the fracture in China–US economic relations to 'intercapitalist competition in the Chinese market', which 'eventually aligned US corporate dispositions toward China with that of the foreign policy elite on the side of enmity'.[76] This analysis seems, to us, too committed to a formal divide between economic and political powers even as it finds them to work in concert. Our interest lies more in understanding the political effects of capital operations

75   Lee Jones and Shahar Hameiri, *Fractured China: How State Transformation Is Shaping China's Rise*, Cambridge: Cambridge University Press, 2021.
76   See Ho-fung Hung, *Clash of Empires: From 'Chimerica' to the 'New Cold War'*, Cambridge: Cambridge University Press, 2022.

themselves, and this gives us a particular analytical perspective on the different forms of political capitalism that have become entrenched in both China and the US, and their implications for the strategic competition between these powers.

It is no secret that Hong Kong and Taiwan have become hotspots in the China–US rivalry. To say this is not to ignore the political will of populations in these territories, where civil tensions have been heightened and geopolitical considerations mix with social and historical factors to create highly fractious situations. There is some merit in grouping together the Hong Kong and Taiwan scenarios, given affinities in political dynamics and expressive practices among the Umbrella and Sunflower movements, which struggled for democratic recognition in the mid-2010s. The positioning of Hong Kong and Taiwan in a 'liminal island chain', which extends to Okinawa, adds a geopolitical dimension to this likeness.[77] From the PRC perspective, however, the political and territorial arrangements surrounding Hong Kong and Taiwan are vastly different, given the status of the former since 1997 as a Special Autonomous Region ruled under the 'one country, two systems' principle and the view of the latter as an inalienable part of China's territory that should be reunified with the mainland under the internationally recognized One China policy. In Chapter 5, we will have more to say about the remarkable social struggles that unfolded in Hong Kong in 2019–20, and the relevance of these movements for the mounting social contradictions that accompany geopolitical transitions. In the case of Taiwan, the presence of a fully formed democratic nationalism, vouchsafed by US military support and economic interests, and the fragility of the 1992 consensus, by which Taiwan and the PRC agreed on the One China approach but agreed to disagree on their understandings of what China meant, have led to a parlous situation in which expectations of and paranoia about military intervention are rife. We cannot go into detail here about the debates in the Taiwanese left regarding the prospects of independence, reunification, or the tightrope walk of maintaining the status quo, however that might be defined or understood. Suffice it to say that there have been calls to dissociate the current

---

77   Chih-Ming Wang, 'Post/Colonial Geography, Post/Cold War Complication: Okinawa, Taiwan, and Hong Kong as a Liminal Island Chain', *Geopolitics* 29, no. 2 (2024), 398–422.

predicament from a nationalist perspective or that of China–US relations, and to read it instead in terms of the fractures created by global capitalism.[78] There have also been suggestions that the recognition of Taiwan as part of a Sino-world (Zhonghua) might ease cross-strait tensions.[79] Such propositions have regularly met with charges of ignoring Chinese imperialism.[80] As should be clear from the previous section of this chapter, we think the question of imperialism is unavoidable in accounting for contemporary geopolitical and capitalist transitions, but we hold that rising world multipolarity works against an analysis that links imperialism to states and territories in straightforward ways. A wider analytical ambit – which links political capitalism to challenges of social reproduction on the one hand and attempts to exert control over spaces of globalization on the other – is required.

Alain Brossat's analysis of the Taiwan situation as involving a China–US competition for *Großraum* is compelling insofar as it understands the face-off not only in terms of strategic interests in maritime and land space but also in terms of struggle over markets, logistical routes, zones of influence, and models of governance.[81] That military conflict over Taiwan could involve a naval blockade, like that enacted by the PRC in the wake of Nancy Pelosi's August 2022 visit to Taipei, and a retaliatory blockade of the Malacca Strait by the US and its allies, which would clog trade routes critical for China, highlights the importance of technical, economic, and organizational matters for the unfolding geopolitical scenario. The parallels with our analysis of the Ukraine war cannot go unnoticed, with all necessary methodological cautions as regards the differing forms of political capitalism that have taken root in Russia,

---

78 See, for instance, Joyce C. H. Liu, 'Yu zhaogang shangque: Women xuyao shenme yangde "zhongguo" linian', in *Women xuyao shenme yangde 'zhongguo' linian*, 1st edn, Taipei: Renjian, 2015, 117–28.

79 See Mark McConaghy, 'Can Taiwanese Nationalists Think *Zhonghua* Once Again?', *Positions Politics*, 7 August 2022, positionspolitics.org.

80 See, for instance, Brian Hioe, 'The Debate about the Sunflower Movement in the Pro-Unification Left', *New Bloom: Radical Perspectives on Taiwan and the Asia Pacific*, 4 July 2015; and Brian Hioe, 'Can Chinese Nationalists (or Their Apologists) Please Shut Up about *Zhonghua*', *New Bloom: Radical Perspectives on Taiwan and the Asia Pacific*, 18 August 2022.

81 Alain Brossat, '"Large Space" and the (New) Cold War', in Alain Brossat and Juan Alberto Ruiz Cascado, *Culture of Enmity: The Discursive Struggle for Taiwan in the Making of the New Cold War*, Singapore: Springer Nature, 2023, 109–18,

China, and the US. The drawing of comparisons between Ukraine and
Taiwan has certainly been a preoccupation of commentators since the
beginning of the war on Europe's fringes. PRC pundits have been quick
to point out that they consider the Taiwan question a domestic matter
and thus separate from any situation involving the invasion of a sovereign state. US observers have tended to speculate over whether Russia's
actions make a Chinese move on Taiwan more or less likely. In our view,
the relevance of the Ukraine war for China–US relations is different
from both these concerns. At stake is a stark and violent reminder that
multipolar dynamics overshadow and problematize any attempt to
understand the world's future as balancing in a China–US bipolar frame.
Not only has the reductiveness of reading global political and economic
developments in terms of a great power rivalry between an established
and emerging hegemon been exposed, but the narrative of a linear
transition from the American to the Chinese century, or from Pax Americana to Pax Sinica, has been thoroughly displaced and questioned.

To note these effects of the Ukraine war is not to deny that China–US
tensions will continue to have marked effects on the capitalist world
system. As we mentioned earlier, though, Russia's actions have put China
in an unenviable position, where it must carefully balance its enmity
towards the US and political friendship with Russia against its trade,
resource, and infrastructure interests as a participant in the global economy.
Although it is unclear whether China was apprised of Russia's intentions
before the outbreak of war, Beijing has been careful not to breach
Western imposed sanctions, even as it criticizes them as disruptive and
illegal. In the meantime, China supports Russia as far as it can – for
instance, by becoming the premier buyer of Russian oil and gas, supplying Moscow with high-tech items such as silicon chips, or even indirectly
providing ammunition and other military needs, although the latter is a
contested claim pushed by Western media. Significantly, much China–
Russia trade since the beginning of the war has been denominated in
Chinese currency, making it part of a more general Chinese drive for
RMB internationalization that pushes back against the dollar domination of global trade and financial systems, as well as seeking pre-emptively
to insulate China from any future sanctions it may face.[82] While US

---

82   Diana Choyleva and Dinny McMahon, *China's Quest for Financial Self-Reliance*,
London: Enodo Economics, 2022.

commentators warn that China seeks to make the world safe for autocracy, voices from within China have risked taking the Ukraine invasion as an opportunity to advocate for a break with Russia.[83] For its part, the Chinese party-state professes its interest to continue participating in a rules-based international order, but its ambition to contribute to setting the rules is increasingly evident. In general, China prefers a Westphalian order in which principles of state sovereignty and non-interference are paramount, and liberal efforts to persuade or compel other states to alter their own domestic arrangements are muted. Clearly, China's positions on Taiwan and Xinjiang are relevant in this regard, but this does not lessen its advocacy for an open international trade order. The spirit of Xi Jinping's 2017 and 2021 Davos interventions, paeans to economic globalization and free trade, lives on. China's commitment to a liberal economic order remains extant, even if, as the US National Security Strategy claims, it 'frequently uses its economic power to coerce countries' – an ironic observation, indeed, if one considers the role of US economic strength and dollar imperialism in the post-1945 world.[84]

When it comes to China's engagement with the global South, the question of whether colonial relations of economic coercion are in place is hotly debated. That many of the countries in question hold experiences of Western colonialism in living memory muddies the issue, and even affords China a point of negotiation and solidarity, given its own history of opium wars, concessions, and nationalist struggle. Likewise, uncertainties about what constitutes the global South and the sheer diversity of countries that might claim to be part of it poses problems, raising the matter of whether China has a consistent approach to its activities across nations and localities in regions as internally heterogeneous and as different from each other as sub-Saharan Africa, Central America, South-East Asia, the Pacific islands, and Central Asia. One thing is for sure, however: the idea of China as a rising or emerging power makes little sense in many of these contexts, where China is already the main trading partner, aid provider, technology supplier, or source of direct foreign investment. In her landmark

---

83   See Jessica Chen Weiss, 'A World Safe for Autocracy?', *Foreign Affairs*, July–August 2019, 92–102; and Hu Wei, 'Possible Outcomes of the Russo-Ukrainian War and China's Choice', trans. Jiaqi Liu, US–China Perception Monitor, 12 March 2022, uscnpm.org.

84   White House, 'National Security Strategy', 23.

study *The Specter of Global China: Politics, Labor, and Foreign Invest-ment in Africa*, Ching Kwan Lee finds 'the frame of colonialism (or neocolonialism) not intellectually productive' to explain China's inter-actions with the global South. She observes that there 'is no military occupation by China in Africa, no chartered companies with exclusive or sovereign trading rights, no religious proselytizing'.[85] On this basis, she rebuffs claims that the 'phenomenon of global China' is about 'imperial influence' and argues, rather, that China seeks 'spatial and political fixes to its resource and profit bottleneck, in the context of a national and global overaccumulation crisis, with no preordained or guaranteed outcome'.[86] Furthermore, taking what she calls a 'varieties of capital' approach, Lee contends that 'Chinese state capital's encompass-ing imperatives – for which it is often assailed as "colonialist" – in reality compel it to be more open to political negotiation and concession than profit-maximizing private global capital'.[87] These are poignant argu-ments based in close ethnographic observation, and they confirm what other researchers, including those who question the meme of 'debt trap diplomacy', conclude about China's globalizing economic activities or, as Lee puts it, 'China beyond China'.[88]

Although we broadly agree with Lee's conclusions, our approach to questions of imperialism, multipolarity, statehood, and territory through the lens of political capitalism gives us a slightly different perspective. We need to make two points in this regard. First, our use of the term *imperialism* to describe both the facilitation of different patterns of capital valorization and accumulation across the poles of world power and the often-unsuccessful attempts of states, firms, and other entities to overcome the limits of these processes means that it cannot be easily separated from 'political and spatial fixes' that seek to reorganize capital operations across national and global scales. In this light, the analytical deployment of the term imperialism need not measure itself against the

---

85   Ching Kwan Lee, *The Specter of Global China: Politics, Labor, and Foreign Investment in Africa*, Chicago: University of Chicago Press, 2017, vi.

86   Ibid., vi–vii.

87   Ibid., xiii.

88   Ibid., xiv. On 'debt trap diplomacy', see Deborah Brautigam, 'A Critical Look at Chinese "Debt Trap Diplomacy": The Rise of a Meme', *Area Development and Policy* 5, no. 1 (2020), 1–14; and Pádraig Carmody, 'Dependence Not Debt-Trap Diplomacy', *Area Development and Policy* 5, no. 1 (2020), 23–31.

presence of features that typically accompanied Western imperialism in the period of its modern territorial expansion: military occupation, chartered companies, missionary zeal, and so on. Rather than becoming a term of moral judgement or symbolic condemnation before which the representatives and ideologues of today's continental states are doomed to baulk, imperialism becomes a more flexible analytical category whose deployment needs not imply violent political and economic subjugation, although this can certainly still be the case, as the example of the Ukraine war shows. The term works for us in more elastic ways that enable description and analysis of how power operates in conjunction with state entities, private actors, and technical systems, expanding and contracting in ways immanent to the vagaries of capital. To speak of Chinese imperialism, then, is not necessarily to vouchsafe the arguments of Taiwanese independence activists or to affirm the claim that China's so-called century of humiliation drives its current reassertion on the world stage. Instead, it is to observe a predominantly non-territorial expansion of economic interests that can take promissory as well as concrete forms, and that exists in necessary tension with US and Russian imperialism, among others, although it takes more infrastructural shapes than the former and involves less militarized undertakings than the latter. These observations contribute to a clarification of how a view of China as an imperial power can coexist with the recognition that, as Minqi Li explains, it continues to transfer more surplus value to the historical imperialist states in the capitalist core than it draws from countries in Africa, South-East Asia, or Latin America.[89] It also helps explain why China's Belt and Road Initiative, which we will discuss in Chapter 4, has been subjected to so many competing and contradictory interpretations, being understood, for instance, as a form of 'offensive mercantilism' in some quarters, and as an exercise in South–South solidarity, an attempt to build a 'new Bandung', in others.[90]

Our second point concerns the status of the *Chinese* in Chinese imperialism, or for that matter, in Chinese capitalism or the Chinese state

---

89   Minqi Li, 'China: Imperialism or Semi-Periphery?', *Monthly Review* 73 (2021), 31–46.

90   See Jonathan Holslag, 'How China's New Silk Road Threatens European Trade', *International Spectator* 52, no. 1 (2017), 46–60; and Wondam Paik, 'The 60th Anniversary of the Bandung Conference and Asia', *Inter-Asia Cultural Studies* 17, no. 1 (2016), 148–57.

capital that Lee finds to offer more scope for political negotiation in Africa than private global capital. For us, the term *Chinese* offers a convenient descriptive tag, but not a comprehensive analytical category that accurately captures the forms of power, social organization, and capital at hand in China's economic expansion and globalizing strategy. The same applies to our use of the terms *US* and *Russian*, as well as to our references to other national denominations. To make this claim is not to deny the ongoing effects of political power as manifest at national or continental scales or the relation of aggregate economic forces to state budgets, policies, and international agendas. Rather, it is to question the capacity of states to represent fully the aggregate operations of capital as they unfold across the multipolar arrangements of today's world. Lee specifies that 'the *Chinese* in *Chinese state capital* . . . refers to Chinese state interests, not to Chinese culture or ethnicity'. She contrasts her argument with on 'the one hand, studies of Chinese state capitalism' that 'emphasize centralized party-state control over political and economic institutions', and on the other with discussions of 'capitalism in China', which point to 'decentralized, dispersed, bottom-up initiatives, even anarchic competition by local state and corporate actors'. Both approaches, she suggests, 'conceptualize capital as abstract and aggregate' and thus miss its 'concreteness and contestedness'.[91] In particular, Lee contends, these perspectives are unable to give adequate analytical attention to the role of host states in China's globalizing initiatives and how the operations of Chinese state capital enable these actors to exert a 'counteragency' that is 'more easily short-circuited by finance-driven, globally mobile, private capital'.[92]

For us, there is an analytical and political necessity to attend both to the concrete ways in which capital hits the ground and to the wider, more aggregate ways in which operations of capital mesh with each other to produce distinct forms of capitalism. On this basis, it is possible to heed Lee's arguments about the operations of Chinese state capital while also considering how these operations interact with others to forge particular kinds of capitalism with variegated effects across China and the world. To speak of Chinese capitalism in this context is not necessarily to submit to the methodological nationalism implicit in

---

91   Lee, *Specter of Global China*, 4.
92   Ibid., 11.

the concept of state capitalism. Nor is it to affirm the anarchic interaction of different types or fractions of capital without guiding
principles or national containment. We can observe that China's globalizing activities are carried out by a variety of entities and agents,
including state-owned enterprises, private firms, and provincial governments, without contending that these actors' interactions are void of
a shape or logic given by a range of governance factors, among them
central state regulation. Equally, we can discern that state-guided initiatives, such as the RMB internationalization drive mentioned earlier,
have effects that extend way beyond the territorial boundaries in which
the renminbi functions as legal currency. In this case, the combined
actions of banks, payment systems, foreign exchanges, and other institutional and market actors compel the use of the RMB as a currency of
finance and trade, a change that if accomplished widely will have
important political and monetary implications for relations among the
poles of world power. We describe the forms of capitalism that result
from these kinds of arrangements as *political capitalism*, but before
continuing our analysis we need to give greater analytical and historical
substance to this term.

Global capitalism in a multipolar world

Is Chinese capitalism an instance of political capitalism? Our answer to
this question is affirmative, provided we further qualify the concept we
introduced and started to discuss earlier in this chapter. Max Weber,
who is often credited as having forged it, uses the term political capitalism mainly with respect to the ancient, and particularly to the Roman
world.[93] From this perspective, the concept is clearly opposed to the
rational market capitalism that prevails in European modernity. Weber
associates what he calls 'politically oriented capitalism' with modes of
profit making, such as 'opportunities for predatory profits from political
organizations' and from 'unusual transactions with political bodies',
which are undoubtedly also present in modern capitalism. But it is easy
to see that such profiteering borders on clientelism or corruption and

---

93   See John R. Love, *Antiquity and Capitalism: Max Weber and the Sociological
Foundations of Roman Civilization*, London: Routledge, 1991, 36–7.

is therefore deemed 'irrational from an economic point of view'.[94] This situation may have changed in the age of imperialism, since it is a general rule for Weber that 'imperialist capitalism, especially colonial booty capitalism based on direct force and compulsory labor, has offered by far the greatest opportunities for profit'.[95] Nonetheless, the notion of political capitalism in Weber's work was just a remnant of his laborious elaboration of the concept of 'rational capitalism', and we can say that it signals deviations from the standards and working logics of this 'ideal type'.

This original imprint of political capitalism remains apparent in more recent uses where it is usually connected to authoritarian countries, political control over the economy, kleptocracies, distortions of market dynamics, and the like. Even a more nuanced definition, such as the one provided by Randall G. Holcombe who characterizes political capitalism as 'an economic and political system in which the economic and political elite cooperate for their mutual benefit', immediately points to 'the fascist and corporatist economies of Germany and Italy' between the World Wars as explicit implementations of that system.[96] The fact that Holcombe adds Eisenhower's warning about the dangers of the 'military-industrial complex' as an instance of political capitalism is important since it refers to the issue of national security and its relevance in contemporary uses of the concept. Even more interesting for us is the discussion of bailouts in the wake of the financial crisis of 2007–8 and of the 'too big to fail doctrine', where 'government allows private firms to retain their profits but underwrites their losses', as 'the most obvious manifestation of political capitalism'.[97] Nonetheless, it is also clear that the initiative here comes from the state, and that this is the privileged angle from which the concept of political capitalism operates. This is also evident in the recent use of the term political capitalism by Dylan Riley and Robert Brenner to describe 'a new regime of accumulation' in which 'raw political power, rather than productive investment, is the key determinant of

---

94 Max Weber, *Economy and Society*, Berkeley, CA: University of California Press, 1978, 164–6.

95 Ibid., 918.

96 Randall G. Holcombe, 'Political Capitalism', *Cato Journal* 35, no. 1 (2015), 41.

97 Ibid., 45.

the rate of return'.[98] Riley and Brenner have in mind a series of interventions in the domestic economy on the part of governments and other
organs of the US state, such as tax breaks, privatization of public assets,
quantitative easing and low interest rates, and massive state spending
directed at private industry. With regard to the latter, they mention
Bush's Prescription Drug legislation, Obama's Affordable Care Act,
Trump's CARES Act, Biden's American Rescue Plan, the Infrastructure
and CHIPS Acts, and the Inflation Reduction Act. Although Riley and
Brenner offer some poignant observations about class politics, the scope
of their discussion is strictly limited to the US, itself an interesting cir-
cumscription given the usual association of political capitalism with
authoritarian regimes. To give a different example, one of the most
astute analysts of Russia's war, Volodymyr Ishchenko, uses the phrase
'political capitalists' to denote not only a specific faction of the Russian
political class but also Ukrainian oligarchs who 'emerged during the
post-Soviet collapse'. And judging by his assertion that 'transnational
capital will likely benefit from the reconstruction of Ukraine', he seems
to think that the age of political capitalism may be over for his country
after the war.[99] Again, what defines the notion of political capitalism
here is the primacy of the state and its power to enable specific capitalist
actors to dominate the economy.

We do not want to deny the salience of such processes, which we have
already analysed with respect to Russia. Nevertheless, we are convinced
that the concept of political capitalism can be also framed in a different
way to become a razor that we can adopt as a general framework for
the analysis of contemporary capitalism. To do that, a conceptual reversal is needed. Instead of taking the state as the main analytical thread,
we contend that the intrinsic political nature characterizing operations
of capital has acquired an unprecedented intensity in the present. Therefore, political capitalism first refers, for us, to the fact that capitalism
today necessarily impinges on politics, deploying its own logics of

---

98   Dylan Riley and Robert Brenner, 'Seven Theses on American Capitalism', *New
Left Review* 138 (2022), 6. For a critical discussion, see Tim Barker, 'Political Capital-
ism?', *New Left Review* 140/141 (2023), 35–51; and Lola Seaton, 'Reflection on "Political
Capitalism"', *New Left Review* 142 (2023), 5–27.

99   Volodymir Ishchenko, interviewed by Małgorzata Kulbaczewska-Figat, 'Why
Russia's Political Capitalists Went to War – And How the War Could End Their Rule',
International Viewpoint, 4 September 2022, internationalviewpoint.org.

political subjectivation and power that cannot be completely disentangled from those vested in the state. This has, of course, significantly different manifestations in different countries and world regions. Nevertheless, it provides an effective angle from which to analyse a second dimension of political capitalism: the extent to and forms by which a panoply of political actors, from states to international organizations, frame, shape, and even drive the valorization and accumulation of capital across diverse geographical scales. Understood in this way, political capitalism becomes a flexible and adaptable concept, which allows us to grasp the peculiarity of the distinct capitalist formations that populate the global landscape today while at the same time shedding light on common elements that would otherwise remain hidden.

Chinese capitalism is then political not only due to the position of the state within its operations, which has been significant since Deng's economic policy, which allowed the country to avoid shock therapy, and has taken on new characteristics in recent years.[100] Equally important is what Wang Hui describes as the 'corporatization of government during market reform', which means the penetration of capital and its rationality within state and party, as well as the increasing shaping of social relations through processes of financialization and logistification.[101] Harking back to our analysis of the strategic competition between China and the US, there are clearly differences between their respective capitalist formations. But there are also common grounds that the concept of political capitalism allows us to flesh out. In a recent book, Alessandro Aresu uses a specific definition of the notion to pursue a parallel analysis of capitalism in the US and China. Mobilizing a wide array of theoretical references, from Adam Smith to Werner Sombart (to mention just two), Aresu focuses his attention on 'the problematic relation between capitalism and security'.[102] What we find interesting in this approach is the fact that security does not

---

100   See Weber, *How China Escaped*.

101   See Wang Hui, *China's Twentieth Century*, London: Verso, 2016, 155; Giulia Dal Maso, *Risky Expertise in Chinese Financialization: Returned Labour and State-Finance Nexus*, Singapore: Palgrave Macmillan, 2020; and Xiang Biao, 'The Gyroscope-Like Economy: Hypermobility, Structural Imbalance, and Pandemic Governance in China', *Inter-Asia Cultural Studies* 21, no. 4 (2020), 524.

102   Alessandro Aresu, *Le potenze del capitalismo politico. Stati Uniti e Cina*, Milano: La Nave di Teseo, 2020, 14.

emerge as a logic (geopolitical, military, or otherwise) that impinges on capitalism from its outside but is rather cast as internal to its development. Nevertheless, Aresu's description of political capitalism in China and the US is dominated by the issue and prevailing roles of 'national security'. His emphasis on 'innovation' in both instances of capitalist development enables him to provide analyses that are sometimes brilliant; but in China that emphasis points to 'an extension of the domain of security, led by the party and under the principle of the fusion of military and civilian issues', while in the US innovation appears subordinated to the 'scientific-military apparatus and its endless frontier'.[103] This is part of an understanding of political capitalism that once again privileges the state, to the point that Aresu, echoing Carl Schmitt, writes that 'sovereignty decides on the economic state of exception'.[104]

The relevance of national security cannot be overlooked, particularly in a conjuncture in which war regimes proliferate across regions and continents. But, while we are committed to struggle against such regimes, which also means against the imperative and logics of national security, it is perhaps even more important, from a theoretical point of view, to stress that our notion of political capitalism continues to be predicated on the Marxian understanding of capital as a social relation, open to class struggle. In contrast to a *geopolitical* theory of capitalism, we analyse the political implications and impact of capital's operations, but, methodologically as well as politically, we give primacy to the antagonistic fabric within which they are encapsulated – to put it briefly, to class struggle writ large. From this angle, differences and common traits between capitalist formations in the US and China, which should be analysed in the wider perspective of our analysis of multipolarity, present themselves in an alternative manner. As we wrote earlier, the dynamics of labour struggles in China – often led by internal migrants – were one of the factors spurring and altering the pace and quality of development in that country.[105] Similarly, in the US, a 'new terrain' of struggle has emerged in recent years, part and parcel of what Kim

---

103   Ibid., 261 and 302.

104   Ibid., 370.

105   See Pun Ngai, *Migrant Labor in China: Post-socialist Transformations*, Cambridge: Polity Press, 2016.

Moody calls 'the remaking of the US working class'.[106] No analysis of political capitalism in China and in the US is valid for us if it does not take such struggles prominently into account. Moreover, other movements should be added to the picture, from the struggles in Hong Kong in 2019–20 to the powerful Movement for Black Lives in the US after the outbreak of the pandemic and to the manifold forms of negotiation and contestation of the 'zero COVID' policy of the Communist Party of China. We will have more to say on this in the final chapter of the book, but it is important to stress, at this point, the relevance we attribute to the understanding of capital as a *social relation*.

With this point in mind, rehearsing the vexed questions regarding capitalism and its contemporary manifestations is crucial to advancing our investigation of centrifugal multipolarity. First, we must ask again whether we are confronted with multiple *varieties* of capitalism today, even beyond the ones registered by theories that go under that label.[107] In the West, critical scholars have continued to add new definitions to the proliferating nomenclature originating in recent decades by the attempt to come to grips with the peculiarity of contemporary capitalism. For example, to such notions as financial, absolute, communicative, or cognitive capitalism, has been added 'Amazon capitalism'.[108] Looking beyond the West, geographical definitions of specific instantiations of capitalism, such as for instance the 'Andean-Amazonian capitalism' theorized by Bolivia's former vice-president Álvaro García Linera, are matched by other sector-specific forms, including petrocapitalism.[109] The latter is close to the common understanding of political capitalism, given the relevance of concessions, often tied to clienteles, and to a so-called rentier state, where corruption is structural. Nevertheless, as Matthew T. Huber writes, the widespread tendency to pathologize governments obscures the fact that 'in the context of increasing neo-liberalization of oil policy the vast majority of the wealth generated is

106   See Kim Moody, *On New Terrain: How Capital is Reshaping the Battleground of Class War*, Chicago: Haymarket Books, 2017.

107   See, for instance, Peter A. Hall and David W. Soskice, *Varieties of Capitalism*, Oxford: Oxford University Press, 2001.

108   See Jake Alimahomed Wilson and Ellen Reese (eds), *The Cost of Free Shopping: Amazon in the Global Economy*, London: Pluto Press, 2020; and Into the Black Box, *Futuro presente. I piani di Amazon*, Rome: Manifestolibri, 2024.

109   See Álvaro García Linera, *Geopolítica de la Amazonía. Poder hacendal-patrimonial y acumulación capitalista*, La Paz: Vicepresidencia de la Nación, 2012.

captured by private transnational corporations'.[110] Processes of neoliberalization and the related precarization of labour have indeed transformed
since the 1990s even a country like Iran, which nurtures a peculiar
instance of petrocapitalism hit hard by US sanctions in the past four
decades.[111] This combination of US sanctions and neoliberal reforms is
uncanny, since it points to unexpected commonalities and complicities
of capitalism even among sworn enemies.

It is interesting, in this respect, to note Huber's comment that the
term petrocapitalism, originally forged to define '*specific* forms of accumulation tied up with the extraction of oil', is today employed in a much
wider sense. Ecological concerns have led to the combination of a focus
on extraction and a concern with 'consumptive petrocapitalism' and its
geographically dispersed manifestations, so that petrocapitalism 'virtu-
ally includes the entirety of capitalism itself'.[112] While this expansion of
the meaning of petrocapitalism is predicated on the pervasiveness of oil
in the conduits of global capitalism, it may also have symptomatic value.
We do not want to deny the relevance of differences between capitalist
formations, which have, for instance, long been analysed by postcolonial
scholars as well as by diverse critical schools.[113] But to grasp and understand those differences theoretically, we find it more productive to
employ, with Jamie Peck and Nick Theodore, the umbrella term 'variegated capitalism', rather than mapping and bordering distinct types of
capitalism, defined in geographical, political, or sectoral terms.[114] What
we find compelling in this concept is its capacity to make sense of the
vast heterogeneity that characterizes contemporary capitalism without
obscuring the common features and driving forces that compose its

110   Matthew T. Huber, 'Petrocapitalism', in David A. Snow (ed.), *International
Encyclopedia of Geography: People, the Earth, Environment, and Society*, Hoboken, NJ:
Wiley-Blackwell, 2016, 3.
111   See Kayhan Valadbaygi, 'Hybrid Neoliberalism: Capitalist Development in
Contemporary Iran', *New Political Economy* 26, no. 3 (2021), 313–27; and Kayhan Valadbaygi, 'Neoliberalism and State Formation in Iran', *Globalizations*, 17 January 2022,
published online. On US sanctions, see Narges Bajoghli, Vali Nasr, Djavad Salehi-
Isfahani, and Ali Vaez, *How Sanctions Work: Iran and the Impact of Economic Warfare*,
Stanford, CA: Stanford University Press, 2024.
112   Huber, 'Petrocapitalism', 1.
113   See for instance John T. Chalcraft, 'Pluralizing Capital, Challenging Eurocentrism: Toward Post-Marxist Historiography', *Radical History Review* 91 (2005), 13–39.
114   Jamie Peck and Nick Theodore, 'Variegated Capitalism', *Progress in Human
Geography* 31, no. 6 (2007), 731–72.

unitary framework. It calls attention to a proliferation of differences (for instance, in the organization of labour, in the circulation of commodities, in the role of money) produced by those very driving forces when they 'hit the ground' – when they are translated onto distinct material settings.[115] Perhaps even more importantly, the use of *variegated capitalism* challenges any understanding of nationally denominated capitalisms as homogeneous and invites us to analyse in detail the processes of variegation that disrupt the territorial unity and institutional coherence of those formations. Just to give an example that is pertinent to our current discussion, in their investigation of Chinese variegated capitalism, Jamie Peck and Jun Zhang emphasize the relevance of 'the internal geographical, social, and regulatory differentiation of the Chinese economy', giving way to 'regional styles of development', which remain distinct from each other while being deeply networked into a panoply of global production networks and offshore economies.[116]

Such processes of internal variegation characterize capitalism, with uneven intensity and different results, across regions and continents despite the presence of vectors of homogenization that can be strengthened by shocks such as a war and the related spread of war regimes. Even theories and politics of development, which in the wake of the Second World War were driven by projects of national homogenization of economy and society, appear much more fractured and elusive today. We already mentioned Daniela Gabor's description of what she calls the Wall Street Consensus, which aptly describes financial globalization as the main axis along which Western countries pursue 'international development' in the twenty-first century. Importantly, Gabor stresses the link between finance and infrastructural projects; she describes an attempt 'to extend the infrastructural dependence of the state on private finance – and thus the infrastructural power of the latter – from its two traditional domains of monetary and fiscal policy to other arenas of the government', including 'water, housing, energy, health, education, transport, and even nature'.[117] In the next chapter, we will analyse in more detail the Chinese global projection of economic power, in which

---

115 See Mezzadra and Neilson, *Politics of Operations*.

116 Jamie Peck and Jun Zhang, 'Variegated Capitalism, Chinese Style: Regional Models, Regional Models, Multiscalar Constructions', *Regional Studies* 50, no. 1 (2016), 65.

117 Gabor, 'Wall Street Consensus', 436.

infrastructures play prominent roles. And we will see that the intertwining of finance and infrastructures takes different but no less compelling forms in that case, which also addresses issues of development. For now, suffice it to say that finance and infrastructures, working as the main related axes of development intervention, compose a framework that facilitates processes of diversification in so-called developing countries. And, while this framework can become a serious limit to the policies of such countries, current conditions of centrifugal multipolarity can also open unexpected margins for them. Take, for instance, Nepal, which was able to negotiate a favourable agreement with China in 2017, in the framework of the Belt and Road Initiative, by playing the card of its 'geostrategic position' with respect to India.[118] While the implementation of the agreement and issues of Chinese investment in Nepal remain to be tested, we take this as a symptomatic instance of the possibility of breaking the straitjacket and constraints of international development.

Such a possibility is part of multipolarity, although the current conjuncture of war may restrict margins of autonomy and exasperate the imperialist tendencies that are also inherent to multipolarity, and may inflect it in a territorialist direction, as is happening in the case of Russia. Due to the dynamics of contemporary capitalism, however, poles remain much more than territorial formations. And it should be clear by now that, although there are huge differences between capitalism in different parts of the world (in China and in the US, but also in India, Brazil, and Turkey), the poles that we are discussing cannot each be defined by a distinct type of capitalism. Within each pole we are confronted, rather, with processes of interlacing and exchange that are as important as differences in facilitating the valorization and accumulation of capital. The extractive dimension of contemporary operations of capital (which, as we explained in Chapter 1, extends well beyond the realm of literal extraction to include the workings of logistics, digital platforms, and finance) cuts across regions and poles to define capitalism at the global scale, despite issues of interoperability that can obstruct the mobility of data and commodities. Likewise, the growing relevance of circulation and reproduction that we discussed in the previous

---

118   See Samir Sharma and Preksha Shree Chhetri, 'Nepal, China, and "Belt and Road Initiative": Prospects and Challenges', *India Quarterly: A Journal of International Affairs* 78, no. 3 (2022), 458–75.

chapter describes a global tendency that takes uneven forms but is equally compelling in its manifestations. While the pandemic has increased the visibility of that tendency, the war has given it frightening characteristics, bringing into view the relevance of military logistics, with its lethal effects for energy and food supply chains, as well as for the social reproduction of societies under siege and attack, as can be seen in Ukraine.

For these reasons, we need to stick with the notion of global capitalism in an age of pandemic and war, supply chain disruptions, export and import controls, and disputes over technology and strategic minerals. It goes without saying that, by global capitalism, we do not mean a tendency towards economic homogenization and marketization of the world, brought about by unimpeded flows of capital and commodities (while the mobility of labour has always been hampered in more or less violent ways). Critical debates long moved beyond such an unrealistic vision, which worked as a kind of ideological mantel for the US globalization project of the 1990s. The role of international politics and of the system of states in the constitution and working of global capitalism has been stressed from different angles since the beginning of the century, while Katharina Pistor has recently pointed to the fact that the 'legal infrastructure' that builds the 'backbone for global capitalism' is 'ultimately backed by states'.[119] We duly register such important observations, but our concept of political capitalism is also relevant here. Our analysis focuses primarily on the global processes that cut through heterogeneous capitalist formations and work the boundaries of their territorial denomination due to the political effects they generate. As we emphasized earlier, such processes are far from being homogeneous in the ways in which they translate into different geographical settings. They are, rather, characterized by a high degree of variegation, which makes global capitalism a variegated capitalism.

A detailed analysis becomes necessary, exploring both the nature of the global capitalist processes (apparent, for instance, in finance, infrastructures, digitalization, and logistics) and the ways in which they are contained, managed, and even territorialized in a conjuncture of

---

119   See, for instance, Robert Gilpin, *The Challenge of Global Capitalism: The World Economy in the 21st Century*, Princeton, NJ: Princeton University Press, 2000, 13; and Ellen Meiksins Wood, *Empire of Capital*, London: Verso, 2003, 24. Katharina Pistor, *The Code of Capital: How the Law Creates Wealth and Inequality*, Princeton, NJ: Princeton University Press, 18.

pandemic and war. To give just one example of this, the notion of 'the Stack', introduced in 2015 by media theorist Benjamin H. Bratton to describe a planetary-scale infrastructure of computation and govern-ance profoundly altering the working of sovereignty, has since been rethought by Bratton to allow for the emergence of 'hemispherical Stacks', among which a 'Chinese Stack' figures prominently.[120] While the nature of the Stack was presented as opposed to territorialism, a point nicely encapsulated by such phrases as 'the Nomos of the Cloud' and 'a Google *Großraum*', qualifying the term through the adjective 'hemi-spherical' (to which we could add regional or continental) or even more explicitly 'Chinese' introduces an opposing territorial logic which deserves close investigation and theoretical elaboration. It is to ques-tions such as this that we turn in the next chapter.[121]

---

120   See Benjamin H. Bratton, *The Stack: On Software and Sovereignty*, Cambridge, MA: MIT Press, 2015, and 'On Hemispherical Stacks: Notes on Multipolar Geopolitics and Planetary-Scale Computation', in Shaoqiang Wang (ed.), *As We May Think: Feedfor-ward: The 6th Guangzhou Triennale*, Guangzhou: Guangdong Museum of Art, 2018, 77–85. See also Gabriele de Seta, 'Gateways, Sieves, and Domes: On the Infrastructural Topology of the Chinese Stack', *International Journal of Communication* 15 (2021), 2669–92.

121   Bratton, *The Stack*, 31–40.

4

Working the Poles

Operative spaces

In an age of pandemic and war, global space appears as fractured and even disrupted. This is true both from the point of view of new political and civilizational divides intensified by the wars in Ukraine and then in Gaza and with respect to the supply chain disruptions as well as to the crisis of mobility engendered by the pandemic. The West seems to be aware of being just a part of the world, as the prevailing rhetoric of friendshoring signals in a quite effective way. The logistical reorganization of the conduits of global circulation of commodities and people is under way, carving out new regional and continental spaces. Trade and technology wars are challenging established geographies of capitalism, while territorial disputes in Ukraine, along the Taiwan Strait, and elsewhere in the world spur a proliferation of war regimes. How are we to make sense of the tensions and trends crisscrossing such a landscape? As we explain in the previous chapters, we do not think that the rhetoric of a new Cold War, as well as the related opposition between *democracy* and *autocracy*, is adequate to grasp the stakes of the present. We consider that rhetoric as a kind of political weapon, which is being used by specific actors within international politics (not merely from the West, to be sure), and that might lead to an intensification and crystallization of the competition between China and the US. There is a need to articulate a different analytical framework, such as the one we have attempted to build around the notion of centrifugal multipolarity, and broadening the understanding of the term *poles* beyond a unilateral territorial context. It is from this point of view that we undertake in this chapter an investigation of the emerging spaces of capital, paying attention to the tensions that characterize their relations with existing political spaces.

We are convinced that today, more than in other ages of its historical development, the relation of capitalism with what Arrighi calls territorialism is deeply problematic, marked by gaps, frictions, and asynchronicity. This is not to say that political control over, and territorialization of, capitalist accumulation is no longer possible. Our notion of political capitalism enables an understanding of such processes, which are particularly apparent in a country like Russia, for instance, but also – although differently – in cases such as the US CHIPS Act of 2022 or Xi Jinping's recent move to tighten control on Alibaba, Tencent, and other tech companies in China. Despite Western attitudes that single out China's supposed authoritarianism to explain this clampdown, it is clear that 'the US and China share concerns over monopolies in the tech industry'.[1] Nonetheless, the intensified political character of contemporary operations of capital can be tamed but not eliminated by such forms of control. And one of the most apparent manifestations of that political character lies precisely in a production of space that does not abide by the territorial logic of the state. Again, we do not contend that operations of capital today are completely deterritorialized, as a naïve view of digital platforms or financial markets would suggest. The opposite is the case. Both the working of financial markets and the operations of digital platforms are predicated on complex spatial arrangements and impinge, in a more or less violent way, on multiple territories. But the territorial demarcations circumscribing even imperial states are not always the most relevant for them. The aim of this chapter is to provide at least a first map of contemporary spaces of capital, shedding light on their political dimensions and meanings as well as on the ways in which they contribute to foreshadow and constitute the elusive space of poles.

In so doing, we take three privileged and combined analytical angles, provided by infrastructures, finance, and technology. One of the reasons behind this choice is that these three domains play crucial roles in the

---

1 Lin Zhang and Julie Yujie Chen, 'A Regional and Historical Approach to Platform Capitalism: The Cases of Alibaba and Tencent', *Media, Culture and Society* 44, no. 8 (2022), 1455.

articulation of circulation and reproduction, that we identify as driving capitalist processes of valorization and accumulation today. In Chapter 1 we have already examined the expansion of the notion of infrastructures, to include digital infrastructures and infrastructures of care. We will keep in mind this wide spectrum of meanings, which is particularly relevant for our discussion of circulation and reproduction. However, even when considered simply as 'built networks that facilitate the flow of goods, people, or ideas and allow for their exchange over space', infrastructures enable an analysis of the spatial implications of the ways in which operations of capital literally hit the ground.[2] Infrastructural geographies reflect, at the same time, the spread and scope of a specific form of power, defined by Michael Mann as 'infrastructural power'.[3] While Mann links this form of power to the state and even more narrowly to 'political power relations', we want to explore the possibility of its relative autonomy, connecting it to the operations of specific capitalist actors and to the emergence of an 'extrastatecraft' manifest in specific governmental codes and protocols.[4] If one considers the role of infrastructural and logistical projects in the global projection of China's economic power in the framework of the Belt and Road Initiative (now countered by a US global infrastructure programme announced in June 2022), the relevance of such questions for any investigation of global spaces becomes apparent. Recent work on infrastructures, including the so-called 'infrastructural turn' in anthropology, has made important contributions on the issue but has focused quite heavily on exchange, commerce, and interconnection.[5] Our emphasis on infrastructural power is meant to draw attention to the moments of conflict, antagonism, and struggle surrounding infrastructures, a point that has been often stressed with respect to urban infrastructures.[6] Equally important

---

2 Brian Larkin, 'The Politics and Poetics of Infrastructure', *Annual Review of Anthropology* 42 (2013), 328.

3 Michael Mann, 'The Autonomous Power of the State: Its Origins, Mechanisms, and Results', *European Journal of Sociology* 25, no. 2 (1984), 189.

4 Michael Mann, 'Infrastructural Power Revisited', *Studies in Comparative International Development* 43 (2008), 358; Keller Easterling, *Extrastatecraft: The Power of Infrastructure Space*, London: Verso, 2014.

5 Geoffrey Aung, 'A "Becoming Logistical" of Anthropology?', *Focaal – Journal of Global and Historical Anthropology* 91 (2021), 115–24.

6 AbdouMaliq Simone, 'People as Infrastructure: Intersecting Fragments in Johannesburg', *Public Culture* 16, no. 3 (2004), 407–29; Claudio Sopranzetti, *Owners of the*

for us are what Neil Brenner and Nikos Katsikis call 'operational land-scapes', as a way to register capital's drive to reorganize hinterland zones and increase 'labor productivity' and 'interspatial connectivity' through 'the construction of large-scale infrastructural configuration'.[7]

A second entry point for our analysis of the reorganization of spaces of capital is provided by finance. Even beyond the emerging Wall Street Consensus described by Daniela Gabor and discussed in the previous chapter, finance has always played key roles in the opening of new markets and in expanding the frontiers of capital. That was no less true for the operations of European chartered companies in early modernity than at the height of the age of imperialism, as Lenin famously demon-strated. More recently, the role of finance, and financial institutions including the World Bank and the International Monetary Fund, has been prominent in spurring global processes as well as the disruption of social and political arrangements in many parts of the world. One has only to think of the long list of debt crises in the wake of the Mexican default of 1982 and of the ensuing structural adjustment programmes. We do not need to rehearse here the discussion of the violence of finance, although we remain acutely aware of the persistent relevance of the issue. What we first need to stress, for the purpose of our investigation, is that the analysis of finance cannot proceed separately from the analysis of infrastructures, since not only the funding of big infrastructural projects but also their implementation requires financial interventions and the adoption of a financial rationality. Second, if one looks at the global projection of China's economic power, it is easy to see that the link between infrastructures and finance is again apparent in terms of lending and restructuring of debt. Third, in an age of emerging multi-polarity, we are confronted with a diversification of financial markets, while new financial institutions – the Asian Development Bank, for instance – emerge and complicate the landscape of capitalist develop-ment. More generally, there is a need to take stock of the mutations of finance in an age of pandemic and war, which must be analysed as part of wider monetary and fiscal dynamics and tensions, including

---

Map: Motorcycle Taxi Drivers, Mobility, and Politics in Bangkok, Berkeley: University of California Press, 2018.

7   Neil Brenner and Nikos Katsikis, 'Operational Landscapes: Hinterlands of the Capitalocene', *Architectural Design* 60, no. 1 (2020), 22–31.

processes of incipient de-dollarization that may have been accelerated by US financial sanctions on Russia after the invasion of Ukraine.[8] We will return to this issue later on.

The field of technology is the third angle from which we analyse emerging spaces of capital in a multipolar world. Again, there is no need to rehearse here a discussion of the vexed question of the relation between capitalism and technology, although we will have something to say on the new technological paradigm associated with the digital world and the expanding frontiers of artificial intelligence. More relevant for the analysis we pursue in this chapter is, first, the shifting geography of supply chains that enable the circulation and distribution of strategic resources, including energy, pharmaceutical ingredients, and critical minerals, as well as the production of semiconductors and large-capacity batteries, which are supposed to spur the digital and ecological transition of capital (technological innovations are unthinkable without the working of such supply chains). Second, focusing on technology implies, for us, a further extension of our interest in infrastructures, as the infrastructural skeleton that sustains supply chains makes clear. While we analyse the multiple ways in which technological innovations transform capitalism and have an impact on the social relation that constitutes it, both intensifying exploitation and providing a new terrain of struggle, we also remain attentive to how such innovations are produced and circulate across spaces. The analysis of the governance of 'large technical systems', defined by Maximilian Mayer and Michele Acuto as 'large infrastructural entities' – for instance, national rail systems, maritime shipping networks, or supranational innovation systems – provides further evidence of a hybridization of territorial and capitalist logics that shapes contemporary spaces of capital accumulation.[9]

The spaces we chart in this chapter are *operative spaces*. We draw this definition from the language of logistics, which beginning in the 1960s brought about what Deborah Cowen calls 'a revolution in the calculation and organization of economic space', enabling new maps for the spatial distribution of key operations of capital and providing a new

8   Daniel McDowell, *Bucking the Buck: US Financial Sanctions and the International Backlash Against the Dollar*, New York: Oxford University Press, 2023.
9   Maximilian Mayer and Michele Acuto, 'The Global Governance of Large Technical Systems', *Millennium: Journal of International Studies* 43, no. 2 (2015), 660–83.

logic 'for how, and so *where*, to do business'.[10] Importantly, Cowen stresses that the operative spaces of logistics cut through the political geography centred upon the bounded spaces of states, and nevertheless compose a 'network geography' of corridors and hubs, zones, and maritime routes that is in itself political since it reworks issues such as the management of mobility and security that are usually considered to lie within the purview of the state.[11] The political dimension of the operations of capital looms large in the operative spaces of logistics, although – or precisely because – they cannot be easily superimposed on a traditional geopolitical map. While logistics is important for our investigation of the emerging spatial configurations of capital, we look at a wider nomenclature of operative spaces, including for instance financial, infrastructural, and digital spaces that stretch across territories and work both in tension and concord to build the non-territorial architecture of poles in the contemporary world. This is not to say that territorial logics play no role in the establishment of these operative spaces. It is, rather, to call attention to the frictions between the principle of territoriality characterizing the state and a different, capitalist logic of production of space and territory. Such a logic intersects not only the working of imperial or continental states – such as, say, China and the US – but also processes of regional integration, including the ones epitomized by formal organizations such as ASEAN and NAFTA, the Organization of American States, and the Shanghai Cooperation Organisation.

Operative spaces therefore provide an effective analytical slant on the processes that constitute poles beyond state and territory. Again, this is not to say that state and territory do not matter; it is, rather, to call attention to the formation of spaces of capital that cannot be reduced to the nation, and at the same time intersect and rework its composition. Poles are constituted by processes of exchange and infrastructural investments, financial arrangements, scientific, and technological cooperation that foreshadow the building of a *Großraum*, although the territorial inflection of such a space, as in the case of Russia, is not the only or even the more effective available variant. In different ways,

---

10 Deborah Cowen, *The Deadly Life of Logistics: Mapping Violence in Global Trade*, Minneapolis: University of Minnesota Press, 2014, 24–5.
11 Ibid., 64.

China and the US already have a capacity to produce a space – what we can call an operative *Großraum* – that exceeds the Russian search for territorial expansion. The discussion we offer in the previous chapter allows us to discern different forms and degrees of imperialism in these cases, ranging from war and conquest to imperial practices of trade and financial subjugation as well as to military presence abroad. Crucial here is an analysis of the ways in which operative spaces intersect and, at the same time, enable the formation and working of poles, shedding light on mutations of capitalism underlying the current conjuncture of pandemic and war. Take for instance China's Digital Silk Road project, part of the wider Belt and Road Initiative. In Central Asia, Kazakhstan has signed a comprehensive agreement to support the modernization and digitalization of the economy through access to inexpensive Chinese software and hardware, including cutting-edge surveillance systems.[12] While this agreement nurtures concerns regarding Kazakhstan's dependence on China, it also creates an operative space within which capitalist corporations are doomed to be prominent actors.

A key aspect of operative spaces regards how they are governed. What John Agnew calls 'low' or 'hidden geopolitics', to evoke the way in which 'the geography of power works both globally and nationally to structure and govern the workings of the world's political economy', finds privileged sites of manifestation in these spaces.[13] Hidden geopolitics is characterized by the proliferation of forms of governance, where states figure as actors among other actors, part of assemblages of power that they usually concur to establish but that often develop a separate authority and governmental rationality. The public–private partnerships and governmental bodies established to manage large, transnational logistical projects are a good example of such forms of governance in which non-state and capitalist actors have prominent roles to play.[14] Moreover, a range of regulative agencies such as the International Organization for Standardization set protocols and rules that create 'a "soft law" of global exchanges' and concur to regulate 'infrastructure space' as well as the dense web of existing productive

---

12   Sergey Sukhankin, 'Tracking the Digital Component of the BRI in Central Asia, Part Two: Developments in Kazakhstan', *China Brief* 21 (2021), 9.

13   John Agnew, *Hidden Geopolitics: Governance in a Global World*, London: Roman & Littlefield, 2022, 3.

14   See Giorgio Grappi, *Logistica*, Rome: Ediesse, 2016.

and logistical chains, financial flows, and interconnected communication networks.[15] To give another example, US-based credit-rating agencies such as Moody, Fitch, and Standard & Poor 'have cropped up historically to serve purposes for private actors underserved through the channels provided by territorialized entities such as states' and have ended up monopolizing sovereign competences, even over states, in the operative spaces of finance.[16] The rise of a Chinese credit-rating industry over recent years, with the state playing a different role, signals a diversification of the world of finance but at the same time a further proliferation of a governmental logic which attributes key functions in the management and regulation of what we call operative logics to non-state actors.[17] A similar point can be made about the activities of consulting firms such as McKinsey or PricewaterhouseCoopers, although the Chinese crackdown on companies including Capvision, Bain & Company, and Mintz registers the unstable and always negotiable relations among these private actors and states amid the shifting sands of political capitalism.[18]

Expert knowledge and legal practice across borders continue to characterize the working of governance in operative spaces, while it is important to note that the involvement of a wide array of private and capitalist actors is at the root of the resulting assemblages of power, and that this mixed constitution obscures 'the opposition between states and markets that has prevailed in much thinking about geopolitical order'.[19] While this contributes to explain our distance from a mainstream geopolitical approach, it is important to stress that the mixed constitution of governance is open to shifts and disruptions, and this deserves careful investigation. In an age of war and rising international tensions, states could take drastic initiatives to simplify the working of governance, even in the operative spaces of capital, asserting their leading role and invoking national security as an overwhelming political

---

15   Easterling, *Extrastatecraft*, 18.

16   Agnew, *Hidden Geopolitics*, 139.

17   Scott Kennedy, 'China's Emerging Credit Ratings Industry: The Official Foundations of Private Authority', *China Quarterly* 193 (2008), 65–83.

18   Laleh Khalili, 'In Clover', *London Review of Books* 44 (15 December 2022), 25; David Pierson and Daisuke Wakabayashi, 'China's Crackdown Widens as Police Raid Another Firm with Foreign Ties', *New York Times*, 8 May 2023.

19   Agnew, *Hidden Geopolitics*, 17–18.

criterion. The multipolar world would then retreat into an archipelago of territorialized, militarized, and fenced enclaves. We do not deny that such trends exist today and may be further entrenched by the spread of aggressive nationalisms, which are apparent in several countries and world regions. But we also know that such scenarios would radically curtail the life and social reproduction of huge masses of people across the world, whose movements, behaviours, and desires push in a different direction. And while there are powerful fractions of capital that take the regime of war as an extraordinary opportunity for valorization and accumulation, contemporary capitalism also comprises actors, processes, and trends that aim at further valorizing operative spaces that cannot be fully reduced to the logic of territoriality.

The notion of a multipolar world in which poles are not defined in merely territorial terms points to an emerging tendency whose further development depends on many factors, among which, for us, class and social struggles figure prominently. But it also requires a careful analysis of the processes on the ground that foreshadow the actualization of such a multipolar world, taking account of the materiality of operations of capital and at their heterogeneous articulation in relation to the shifting assemblages of political power. Moreover, understanding poles beyond territoriality calls attention to the moment of intersection and nesting between the multiple spaces that constitute them, be it in terms of trade, technology, or communication. The realization of a multipolar world requires the establishment of global junctures, a capability contingent upon an informatic and logistical model of interoperability (the ability of different systems to cooperate despite differences in language, interface, and platform). Take, for instance, the issue of network-based technological infrastructures for worldwide interbank exchange, which has become highly politicized in the wake of Russia's invasion of Ukraine. The key Western sanction of the immediate expulsion of Russia from the SWIFT circuit drew attention to the Chinese CIPS banking system as a potential alternative. The relevant point for us is that, in a multipolar world, the existence of multiple circuits of interbank exchange is possible, but the interoperability (the global juncture) among them remains crucial. This is also the case with the working of financial markets and with the monetary regulation of global exchanges. While in recent years, as we mentioned earlier, we have been witnessing a diversification of reserve currencies and an erosion of dollar dominance, the latter is a lasting trace of US global hegemony and the material basis of a specific form of US imperialism.[20] For the future of globalization, the mutations of the global monetary landscape, the possible emergence of a monetary pluralism, and the way in which it will be managed are far from being secondary issues.

The distributed world

We have already mentioned the concept of decoupling, especially with reference to the trade and technology wars between China and the US. It is difficult to know the extent to which the ends and effects of so-called decoupling are driven by global economic and political trans-formations, and the degree to which they are the result of policy commitments that cater predominantly to domestic constituencies and act as self-fulfilling prophecies. In any case, the use of the notion of decoupling to refer to China–US trade dynamics assumes a scenario in which increasing pressures towards protectionism or self-reliance in the world's two largest economies splits the globe in two, forcing other countries to join a camp, if not in terms of political alliance then at least for credit arrangements, technological standards, infrastructural devel-opment, and so on. The concept of friendshoring, which we have also mentioned, is the corollary of such a split, insofar as it refers to practices of redesigning supply chains according to geoeconomic and geopolitical imperatives that reinforce or reorganize this division. In both decou-pling and friendshoring, there are two important tendencies to observe. The first is the deployment of economic relations for political ends. We understand this use of economic measures in terms of political capital-ism, which means not the reduction of economic to state logics but an effect of the political operativity of capital itself, beyond any easy dis-tinction between economic rationalities and the institutional power of states, international organizations, or other bodies usually identified as political in the narrow sense. The second point to make regarding decoupling and friendshoring is that they are often conceived in relation to trade, and particularly in terms of declining trade relations among

---

20   Raffaele Sciortino, *Stati Uniti e Cina allo scontro globale*, Trieste: Asterios Editore, 2022.

powerful continental states. Debates about decoupling usually take the form of citing and comparing trade statistics, quantifying the effects of tariffs on trade in specific sectors, and assessing shifts in overall trade deficits.[21] We have an interest in these accounting exercises, but our vision of global processes extends far beyond trade or even the economic sphere as narrowly conceived. Far from being unprecedented, this approach to trade and decoupling aligns with longstanding arguments that broadened the investigation of globalization way beyond its economic dimensions.[22] However, even within discussions restricted to economic globalization, there is a need to attend to financial operations above and beyond matters of trade. This is not merely because, since the late 1990s, financial flows have vastly superseded trade in goods and services, accounting for approximately 90 per cent of cross-border capital movements.[23] It is also because finance has assumed a coordinating role over other aspects of economic life, providing an 'abstract point of synchronization' for capital operations in general.[24]

Many commentators observe that decoupling dynamics apply mainly to strategic commodities. The policy momentum in the US around initiatives such as Biden's 2021 Executive Order on Critical Supply Chains, aiming to safeguard interests in the supply of critical minerals, large capacity batteries, semiconductors, and pharmaceutical ingredients, certainly points in this direction. The CHIPS Act of 2022 also suggests the linking of US industrial policy to the control and reshoring of supply chains for high-end technological products, framed in a context that simultaneously promotes environmental sustainability and seeks to deprive China of goods vital for civilian and military innovation. Nonetheless, China–US trade proceeds apace, hitting an all-time high for goods in 2022.[25] Similar dynamics can be observed regarding finance.

---

21   See, for instance, Chad P. Bown, 'Four Years into the Trade War, Are the US and China Decoupling?', Peterson Institute for International Economics, 20 October 2022, pile.com.

22   See, for instance, Roland Robertson, *Globalization: Social Theory and Global Culture*, London: Sage, 1992; or Arjun Appadurai, *Modernity at Large: Cultural Dimensions of Globalization*, Minneapolis: University of Minnesota Press, 1996.

23   Benn Steil and Robert E. Litan, *Financial Statecraft: The Role of Financial Markets in American Foreign Policy*, New Haven, CT: Yale University Press, 2006, 2–3.

24   Sandro Mezzadra and Brett Neilson, 'On the Multiple Frontiers of Extraction: Excavating Contemporary Capitalism', *Cultural Studies* 31, nos 2–3 (2017), 200.

25   US Bureau of Economic Analysis, 'US international Trade in Goods and Services, December and Annual 2022', 7 February 2023, bea.gov.

The integration of Chinese and US capital markets remains pivotal in the global economy, despite the delisting of some high-profile Chinese companies from US financial markets, slowdowns in direct foreign investment that have been in train since the 2007–8 crisis, and the Chinese push to denominate international transactions in renminbi. Such observations are important when it comes to understanding the intensity and selectivity of decoupling processes. However, the insights they generate come at the price of treating trade and finance as separate sectors, each with its own account balances and dynamics. As such, this approach fails to provide an analytical framework attentive to the role of finance in orchestrating capital operations, or to processes of financialization by which financial rationalities become increasingly crucial to the functioning and outcomes of other economic activities, such as industrial investment, energy prospecting, or supply chain coordination. Analyses of decoupling that set trade and finance apart tend to replicate arguments that separate finance from the *real* or productive economy, as if there were something merely fictitious or self-referential about financial operations. We emphasize, conversely, how finance interpenetrates the economy writ large, including the world of trade, whether that involves the cross-border movement of goods or, through processes of platformization, trade in services. Seen in this perspective, finance becomes central to geopolitical arguments about decoupling, and not simply a single domain in which the effects of decoupling might be observed or disavowed. Consequently, it becomes important to analyse financial operations closely in the context of global processes and the operative spaces in which they unfold.

The Shanghai and Shenzhen stock markets were established in 1990 and 1991 respectively with a design feature that endures to this day: shares were divided into two classes, A and B. Both classes list PRC-incorporated companies. A shares are traded in renminbi and were available only to Chinese investors until 2002, when the recognition of qualified foreign institutional investors allowed overseas transactions according to a quota. B shares are denominated in foreign currency, usually dollars, and were available only to foreign investors until 2001, when the China Securities Regulatory Commission (CSRC) allowed their sale to Chinese investors with foreign-currency holdings. Since 2000, the total value of B shares has remained under 3 per cent of China's total stock market capitalization. By contrast, the A market has been characterized by a large number of small investors, the so-called *sanhu*. Many of these investors turned to financial markets in an attempt to compensate for the social and economic displacement resulting from the dismantling of the *danwei* or work unit, which, in Maoist China, had provided a series of 'traditional social safety nets – such as state work allotment, fixed salaries, medical assistance, retirement funds, council houses, social security and funeral fees'.[26] Nonetheless, the staggered opening of the A market to foreign investors has been a consistent feature of finance in China, with the Hong Kong market often playing a mediating role between the mainland and global financial environments. Far from decoupling, China's integration into the world financial system has accelerated since its domestic stock market crisis in 2015, with an emphasis on attracting capital into the country and restricting its outflow. Entry of capital into China's financial markets has been facilitated by the introduction of cross-border investment channels such as Shanghai–Hong Kong Stock Connect in 2014, Shenzhen–Hong Kong Stock Connect in 2016, Bond Connect in 2017, Shanghai–London Stock Connect in 2019, and, in 2022, the expansion of the latter scheme to include the stock markets in Zurich and Frankfurt. Although the percentage of foreign investment on Chinese financial markets lags behind that in countries such as South Korea and Japan, the sheer size of the market continues to make it attractive to investors, among them some of the US's most serious financial players. In 2018, A shares were incorporated in the MSCI Emerging Markets Index, a move followed in 2019 by the Bloomberg Barclay Global Aggregate Index. Goldman Sachs and Morgan Stanley stepped up their ownership in Chinese venture capital firms in 2020, while JP Morgan received CSRC approval to operate a wholly foreign-owned futures firm in China. In 2021, BlackRock recommended that diversified global portfolios should increase their allocation of Chinese assets two or three times, 'ahead of Japan but still well below the US'.[27] Even US credit ratings agencies such as S&P Global and Fitch now operate in China's domestic market. These developments contrast declines in Chinese direct investment in the US

---

26 Giulia Dal Maso, *Risky Expertise in Chinese Financialisaton: Returned Labour and the State-Finance Nexus*, Singapore: Palgrave Macmillan, 2020, 150.
27 Steve Johnson, 'Lift Allocations to China's Markets, BlackRock Tells Investors', *Financial Times*, 17 August 2021.

resulting from the country's controls on capital exports as well as the Trump administration's 2018 Foreign Investment Risk Review Modernization Act. They also need to be understood in the context of Biden administration initiatives to introduce greater scrutiny on outbound US investment in China, particularly into conglomerates with military or national security connections.

The limited opening of China's financial market relates to rising processes of financialization within China itself, especially since 2012. Many analyses of financial dynamics in China tend to confirm the thesis of state capitalism, by arguing that the country's currency practices, trade-distorting subsidies, and state control of the central bank and commercial banking system inhibit cross-border monetary flows and result in the misallocation of capital.[28] Absent from these arguments is an appreciation of how the Chinese state has itself been an object of financialization and how this process has contributed to state transformation. Certainly, China is not the only state in which such transformation has occurred, but, as Yingyao Wang argues, in China 'the state and finance are even more endogenously connected to each other than is usually understood, in that the exercise of state power has been constitutive of the rise of finance'.[29] Reaching beyond the financialization of public debt, the Chinese state has harnessed financial reasoning and techniques to reinvent its role in managing its assets as well as in governing financial markets in general. Wang examines the case of state-owned enterprises (SOEs), which were corporatized according to the financial conception of firms and the model of shareholder value. While many strategic SOE assets remained off-limits to financial markets, other segments were traded actively. This arrangement enabled the Chinese political class to deal with the problem of averting privatization, a priority under Xi Jinping, while raising the value of state assets. Wang notes that the resulting state transformation had both epistemic and organizational dimensions. A reclassification of state assets in terms of marketability 'transformed the government from

28   See, for instance, James A. Fok, *Financial Cold War: A View of Sino-US Relations from the Financial Markets*, Chichester: Wiley, 2021.

29   Yingyao Wang, 'Financialization and State Transformations', in Philip Mader, Daniel Mertens, and Natasha van der Zwan (eds), *The Routledge International Handbook of Financialization*, London: Routledge, 2019, 197.

a passive to an active institutional investor'.[30] This reclassification accompanied new forms of organization building in the Chinese state, specifically in the form of the emergence of state asset-management organizations or so-called financing platforms, often established by local governments. Under these auspices, entities such as management companies, trusts, investment groups, and holding companies created chained and nested sets of subsidiaries and spinoffs, which, combined with the rise of China's shadow banking sector, became part of an institutional infrastructure for securitizing government debt.[31] Local governments, for instance, used these financing platforms to generate new revenue streams, most often through the mortgaging of public lands, allowing them to provide collateral against bank loans previously inaccessible to them. While an implicit assumption of sovereign support from the central government allowed the system to expand, there was an increase in experimentation and risk taking. A spiral effect led at once to the augmentation of state power and to financial innovation that seemed to outpace that occurring in more liberalized economies.

Although the 2021–22 debt crisis involving property developers such as Evergrande and Country Garden marks the limits and contradictions of this financial experimentation, many commentators argue that state control of China's financial system has contributed to decoupling dynamics. Writing in the journal *International Security*, Margaret M. Pearson, Meg Rithmire, and Kellee S. Tsai attribute the backlash against China in the world's major developed economies to state-led financialization, the assertion of party-state authority within firms, and the enforcement of fealty among economic actors. For these authors, 'escalating tensions over economic interdependence with China are best explained in terms of security dilemma dynamics triggered by changes in China's domestic political economy since the beginning of the 2010s'.[32] Part of an effort to introduce geoeconomic considerations into international relations, this analysis extends the concept of state capitalism by positing a 'party-state capitalism' that prioritizes political and

30   Ibid., 194.
31   Andrew Collier, *Shadow Banking and the Rise of Capitalism in China*, Singapore: Palgrave Macmillan, 2017.
32   Margaret M. Pearson, Meg Rithmire, and Kellee S. Tsai, 'China's Party-State Capitalism and International Backlash: From Interdependence to Insecurity', *International Security* 47, no. 2 (2022), 140.

security imperatives over developmental goals. Although it is undeniable that the blending of state power and capital operations in China has raised suspicion and hostility from the US and other Western powers, this approach tends to attribute increased geopolitical tension to the distinctiveness of China's political economy alone. By contrast, Lin Zhang and Tu Lan seek to understand state transformation in China by challenging 'the epistemologically Euro-American-centric literature of state capitalism'.[33] Their analysis foregrounds 'interactions between locally situated problems of the post-reform subcontracting system and specific challenges faced by emerging economies like China in consequence of the protracted global economic crisis'. Engaging with technological innovation initiatives pursued by Tsinghua University, Zhang and Lan situate state-led financialization and public–private fusions not only as ways to confront domestic economic problems but also as responses to conjunctural challenges and geopolitical pressures. In this regard, they observe that many policy tools that have contributed to the financialization of the Chinese state – including university spinoffs, local government-funded high-tech zones, and state-led venture capital – have correlates across industrialized countries and developing states. Moreover, they suggest that, because China's economic strategies are, in part, driven by security concerns, 'its innovation strategy resembles more that of the United States than the strategies of East Asian developmental states such as South Korea'.[34] This sense of confluence between Chinese and US state strategies, as opposed to arguments that claim the exceptionality of one or the other, lends credence to our concept of political capitalism.

As argued in the previous chapter, the observation of such confluence need not obscure the differences and discrepancies that invest varieties and variegations of capitalism as they manifest within and across the borders of territorial states. The thesis of state capitalism, as Jamie Peck writes, emerges in the 'cracked mirror' of neoliberalism, positing 'an ostensibly normal, purer, less corrupted' model of capitalism operative primarily in the West.[35] By contrast, the concept of political capitalism

---

33   Lin Zhang and Tu Lan, 'The Whole New State System: Reinventing the Chinese State to Promote Innovation', *Environment and Planning A: Economy and Space* 55, no. 1 (2023), 216.

34   Ibid., 217.

35   Jamie Peck, 'Wrestling with "the New" State Capitalism', *Environment and Planning A: Economy and Space*, 55, no. 3 (2023), 760.

describes the impingement of capital operations upon political decisions, processes, and forms of organization while also registering how
political actors shape and drive the valorization and accumulation of
capital. As such, this approach offers a means to explain why economic
interdependencies can coexist with harsh political rivalries and even
war regimes. When it comes to China–US dynamics, there is no starker
evidence of this than China's vast holdings of dollar reserves, which,
combined with the pegging of the renminbi below the dollar, have kept
the country's export prices low, furthering the integration of its manufacturing industries into global supply chains, not least those directed
towards the US. Nonetheless, the willingness of the US to use dollar
domination as an economic weapon, made particularly evident with the
sanctions imposed upon Russia following the invasion of Ukraine, has
catalysed China's efforts towards renminbi internationalization. Usually
understood as an instance of financial decoupling by which China seeks
to establish its own economic sphere of influence, renminbi internationalization requires establishing a large pool of the currency outside of
China. Doing so means not only getting foreign entities to accept
payment from Chinese firms in renminbi, as for instance in purchases
of Russian energy products, but also getting foreigners to invest in
Chinese financial assets. China's push to internationalize its currency
has thus hastened the opening of the A share market through investment channels such as the aforementioned Connect programmes, which
require investors to source renminbi outside China before using their
funds to buy stock from the mainland. Paradoxically then, de-dollarization
opens China's financial system to greater foreign investment, including
from the US. What counts as decoupling in one arena drives integration
in another, illustrating the difficulty of positing any inevitable or one-
way process in this regard.

The Belt and Road Initiative (BRI) is undoubtedly an important element
in China's capital export efforts, mixing infrastructural development
with financial expansion. We will not enter here into the debate about
debt-trap diplomacy, which has been so roundly refuted in the case of
countries such as Angola, Sri Lanka, and Venezuela by Deborah Brautigam.[36] What interests us is the nexus of Belt and Road and renminbi

---

36   Deborah Brautigam, 'A Critical Look at Chinese "Debt-Trap Diplomacy": The
Rise of a Meme', *Area Development and Policy* 5, no. 1 (2020), 1–14.

internationalization, because the combination of the two constitutes a powerful step towards financial multipolarity. Although the People's Bank of China allows trade settlement along the Belt and Road in renminbi, and investment in the BRI countries can also be invoiced and settled in the Chinese currency, the dollar has remained the dominant currency in BRI projects.[37] One problem is that BRI countries tend to have a higher renminbi outflow than inflow, contributing to the currency's illiquidity in their markets. A host of financial instruments have been introduced to address this situation, including currency-swap mechanisms, clearing houses, the issuance of yuan-denominated bonds in BRI countries such as Kazakhstan, and the use of so-called dim sum bonds, which are denominated in renminbi and traded in financial centres such as Hong Kong and London to finance infrastructure projects. More recently, moves by China's central bank to create a digital currency have fed visions of improved efficiency and reduced costs in cross-border renminbi transactions in BRI and beyond. These measures combine with the changing focus of BRI, which is arguably slowing in momentum after ten years and transformed by new Chinese policy schemes such as the Global Data Security Initiative of 2020, the Global Development Initiative (GDI) of 2021, and the Global Security Initiative of 2022. In particular, the focus of GDI on education, clean energy, and poverty suggests a potential recasting of BRI towards smaller targeted projects, conceived in a South–South frame. It is also necessary to consider the relevance of China's dual-circulation economic strategy, which was part of the Fourteenth Five Year Plan released in 2021 and aims to bolster domestic consumption in the face of a changed international trade and financial environment. In this context, China's currency internationalization efforts could mutate towards the provision of renminbi financing for industrial projects in BRI countries, producing goods for the Chinese domestic market, which would, in turn, be paid for in renminbi. Such a development would position the Chinese household as a consumer of last resort, at least within a certain economic pole, and the BRI, whatever its current limitations, would have been pivotal in bringing this about.

As discussed in Chapter 3, sanctions are an important manifestation of political capitalism. Notably, China itself practices sanctions, both

---

37   Yan Liang, 'RMB Internationalization and Financing Belt-Road Initiative: An MMT Perspective', *China Economy* 52, no. 4 (2020), 317–28.

formally through instruments such as its Unreliable Entities List, and practically, for instance, through the raising of tariffs. Dollar hegemony and financial globalization, however, have made sanctions a preferred policy tool in Washington, and use of this economic weapon by the US has rapidly expanded since the 1990s. Nicholas Mulder notes the contradictory tendency of sanctions to encourage both self-sufficiency and adaptation among targeted nations, feeding nationalism and militarism, and thus often exacerbating the phenomena they were supposed to penalize.[38] Such adaptation is clearly visible in Russia's reaction to the unprecedented sanctions imposed upon it after the Ukraine invasion. There have been, for instance, stabilizing moves from the Russian central bank, the promotion of national manufacturing and import substitution, the denomination of natural gas payments in roubles, and the rise of a vast shadow shipping and finance infrastructure. In the export of Russian crude oil, finance and insurance have shifted from Geneva to Hong Kong and Dubai, and a vast grey fleet of Aframax and Suezmax tankers has emerged, primarily to supply India and China, where oil is refined and even shipped on to Europe.[39] More mundane goods such as car parts, industrial materials, and chemicals have found new ways into Russia through third countries, involving for instance trucking routes starting in Turkey and passing through Georgia.[40] These changes may be coordinated, improvised, or selectively blocked but they contribute further to the making of multipolarity in the economic and financial world. The same is true of India's and South Africa's efforts to achieve waivers to intellectual property rules surrounding the manufacture of vaccines to fight the pandemic. Likewise, these tendencies are visible in the way some Chinese firms have reacted to US technology clampdowns by accessing high-end US chips through cloud services and in China's redoubling of its own semiconductor innovation efforts.[41] While one line of liberal thought criticizes sanctions for

---

38   Nicholas Mulder, *The Economic Weapon: The Rise of Sanctions as a Tool of Modern War*, New Haven, CT: Yale University Press, 2022.

39   'Ships in the Night: How Russia Dodges Oil Sanctions on an Industrial Scale', *The Economist*, 29 January 2023.

40   Ivan Nuchepurenko, 'How Western Goods Reach Russia: A Long Line of Trucks through Georgia', *New York Times*, 13 January 2023.

41   Eleanor Olcott, Qianer Liu, and Demetri Sevastopulo, 'Chinese AI Groups Use Cloud Services to Evade US Chip Export Controls', *Financial Times*, 9 March 2023.

distorting capital allocations, it is by now clear that the world market is becoming increasingly fragmented. Such fragmentation does not mean that capital operations cease to play themselves out against a global horizon. It points rather to the emergence of multiple poles of political capitalism.

The 2022 Annual Report of the Valdai Discussion Club, the Moscow think tank close to the Putin regime and dubbed the Russian Davos, closes with a section entitled 'The Distributed World'. Central to this document is the search for a 'system of self-regulation' in which 'hierarchy' among powerful states 'gives way to distributed interaction'.[42] The report posits a world in which the US is no longer a dominant superpower but the global infrastructure that serves it remains in place, with the result that China is unable to emerge as a hegemon. For the authors of the Valdai report, countries must unite to limit the effectiveness of the infrastructure that was built to sustain superpower hegemony, and 'the most urgent issue – the world's dependence on the dollar-based financial system – will also be resolved more easily by a group of stakeholder countries that can agree among themselves on alternative forms of settlement and trade that bypass the US sphere of influence'.[43] There is plenty to disagree with in this document, which quite accurately pinpoints emerging struggles over global processes and infrastructures, the operative spaces that 'contain' them, and the control of junctures that articulate different arenas and technologies of economic, financial, and geopolitical interest. The absence of any mention of empire, imperialism, and capital from the report's geopolitical analysis underlies its proposal to build new formats of interaction in the international sphere. Likewise, its call for 'respecting a pluralism of opinions and assessments' masks an implicit support for Putin's imperial venture and the extractive forms of political capitalism that have taken root in Russia.[44] One might also contest its identification of de-dollarization as the world's most urgent issue, given the Anthropocenic dimensions of the fossil fuel bonanza unleashed by the Ukraine war. As we shall see in the next section of this chapter, the nexus of

---

42   Oleg Barabanov et al., *A World Without Superpowers*, Annual Report of the Valdai Discussion Club, October, 2022, 20.

43   Ibid., 20.

44   Ibid., 20.

energy and infrastructure remains a key factor articulating geo-economics and geopolitics under conditions of centrifugal multipolarity and planetary catastrophe.

Energy interconnections

Who blew up the Nord Stream pipelines? The US? Russia? Ukraine? Norway? Britain? Some unspecified pro-Ukrainian group? The actors populating conspiracy theories, news reportage, and formal investigations surrounding this incident attest the grip of traditional geopolitics on our understandings of war and global processes. Although we know that, on 26 September 2022, four explosions damaged these crucial undersea energy infrastructures transporting cheap natural gas from Russia to Germany, our imaginations cannot drift beyond attributing the blasts to a state or some party acting in state interests. Releasing a devastating amount of methane into the earth's atmosphere, the detonations register not only the geopolitical significance of energy flows and infrastructures to the Ukraine war but also the planetary and environmental dimensions of the conflict. It is often noted that Russia's invasion commenced two days after German chancellor Olaf Scholz announced that the Nord Stream 2 pipeline, completed in 2021, would remain inoperative. In June 2022, Gazprom, the majority Russian state-owned multinational corporation that operates the pipelines, reduced supply through Nord Stream 1 by 40 per cent, leading to a massive increase in the European benchmark gas price. Following a pause in July for repairs, supply was halted; it resumed, and then stopped again, supposedly for maintenance, leaving the pipelines pressured at the time of the explosions. These adjustments and restrictions were part of the ongoing gas dispute between Russia and the European Union that has raged since the war's beginning. The friction has involved Russia limiting supply and requiring payment in roubles, European countries substituting gas with coal and imported fossil fuels, and, in a startling demonstration of the importance of global junctures in a time of conflict, the almost uninterrupted flow of gas from Russia to Europe through Ukraine, although after the closure of the Sokhranvika gas valve on the Donbas border in May 2022 only via the Sudzha metring point. Not only has energy been used as a weapon, but the war has exacerbated the world's addiction to fossil fuels, despite claims that their decreased availability and inflated cost will hasten the transition to renewables. Ironically, one group that has not been accused of causing the Nord Stream explosions is a usual suspect when it comes to sabotage of fossil fuel infrastructures: climate activists of the type that inspired Andreas Malm's revolutionary manifesto against carbon capitalism, *How to Blow Up a Pipeline*.[45]

That the pipelines were pressured at the time of the explosions is an important detail, which not only explains why the blasts released so much methane into the atmosphere but also highlights the materiality of natural gas as a physical substance. Because it is lighter than air, natural gas dissipates quickly and needs to be kept under pressure to move through a pipeline. Although it can be liquefied to facilitate more flexible transportation, the costs of doing so are high and the conversion processes at either end are energy intensive. Pipelines remain the most efficient means of transportation. As Margarita M. Balmaceda explains in *Russian Energy Chains*, this means natural gas is a far less adaptable commodity than the two other fossil fuels most intensively exported by Russia, oil and coal, both of which are more easily stockpiled, moved, and substituted. Reliance on pipelines has 'increased the importance of midstream actors, especially those able to provide the shortest route between producer and export markets and set the basis for Ukraine's key role as transit state for exporting Russian natural gas to Western Europe'.[46] Importantly, Ukraine's natural gas transmission system, including the pipelines that link to Europe, was built in the Soviet era, a fact conditioning the field of geopolitical practice in which the war has unfolded. The construction of the Nord Stream pipelines was undoubtedly part of Russia's attempt to diminish its reliance on the Ukraine corridor for gas exports. Yet, regardless of who was responsible for the explosions, the war has forced Europe to wean itself off Russian gas. The process of adaptation has been rapid, multifaceted, and incomplete. Europe has become a boom market for liquefied natural gas (LNG), especially that made from so-called shale gas extracted by fracking in the US. LNG contracts and infrastructures have proliferated, locking

---

45   Andreas Malm, *How to Blow Up a Pipeline*, London: Verso, 2021.
46   Margarita M. Balmaceda, *Russian Energy Chains: The Remaking of Technopolitics from Siberia to Ukraine to the European Union*, New York: Columbia University Press, 2021, 118.

in decades of future extractions and emissions. Elaborate governmental and market mechanisms such as Germany's *Gaspreisbremse* (gas price break) have been part of the picture. Italy and Spain have competed over access to natural gas supplies from Algeria, which, like Egypt and Israel, has boosted production. Nuclear power plants slated for closure have had their tenure extended and coal inputs to electricity grids have been ramped up, often through the revival of mothballed infrastructures. Germany has invested in a green hydrogen project with Namibia, marking the intersection of renewable energy projects and old imperial fealties. Amid these myriad changes, the importance of energy markets and interconnections to the Ukraine war is manifest. These transformations suggest the presence of another geopolitical dimension to the war, less shaped by statecraft and formal territorial boundaries than by the infrastructures, operative spaces, and junctures that enable contemporary global processes.

We have already mobilized the concept of *Großraum* to analyse the production of space implicit in the articulation of global processes. It is important to emphasize that we adopt this concept for the logistical, infrastructural, and economic aspects present in its initial formulation, and not for its legal, political, or, indeed, civilizational elaborations. To understand *Großraum* as a kind of operative space is not to deny that its making can acquire territorial or imperial dimensions, as is clear from Russia's invasion of Ukraine. But it is to acknowledge that these attributes can be variable and variegated, leading to the production of networked and/or non-contiguous spaces, as is the case with China's BRI, which has uneven financial and infrastructural reach across continents and even within the bounded territories of states that have signed up to the scheme. The multiple poles of today's political capitalism cross and require such operative spaces, but they cannot be equated with them directly, not least because these poles are registers of power whose spatial elaborations are mutable, shifting with capital operations and not necessarily pinned to territorial fixtures or contestations. While it is necessary to analyse the geopolitical dimensions of operative spaces and how they intersect state-based principles of territoriality, this task cannot be undertaken without attending to the specific details of the infrastructures involved. When it comes to transregional energy infrastructures, such as the Nord Stream gas pipelines or those passing through Ukraine, these rationalities are mediated through specific control points or junctures, and the geographical and territorial location of these is significant. The physical qualities of the energy being transported are also crucial. Oil pipelines function differently to gas pipelines, which again work differently to electricity grids. In this section of the chapter, we focus primarily on electricity grids, not only because the energy platforms feeding into them encompass the fossil fuels whose extraction has haunted the Ukraine war, but also because they embody the continuity between these commodities and the renewables that will supposedly enable the energy transition for which the war has amplified calls.

Talk of energy transition clearly predates the Ukraine war and has been strongly driven by climate politics, regardless of debates about whether the tipping points in global warming have already been passed. We cannot hope here to detail the geophysical aspects of climate change or their implications for the conjoined histories of the planet, the human species, and industrial and finance capital.[47] Nor can we describe the global challenges of governing the human response to climate change, whether mediated through international organizations, national governments, private firms, market mechanisms, or social movements. Our concerns centre on the geopolitical dimensions of the infrastructures vital to the energy transition and their relevance for arrangements of power and capital that make the multipolar world. Electricity grids are not the only salient objects in this regard, as a consideration of China's sway over critical mineral and large-capacity-battery supply chains demonstrates.[48] However, electricity grids foreground the geopolitical aspects of the energy transition due to their wide spatial extension, which as we shall see increasingly spans national borders. Grids also need to change their topologies to accommodate inputs from renewable energy sources such as solar and wind. Because electricity is uneasily stored, and travels almost at the speed of light, the logistical challenge of matching supply to demand has been a constant of grid management. In many ways, electricity grids have been the ideal type of just-in-time production systems, with peak consumption periods matched by

---

47   See Dipesh Chakrabarty, *The Climate of History in a Planetary Age*, Chicago: University of Chicago Press, 2021.

48   See Henry Sanderson, *Volt Rush: The Winners and Losers in the Race to Go Green*, New York: Simon & Schuster, 2022.

increased generation, made easy by stockpiled fossil fuels that could simply be loaded up and burnt to meet demand. By contrast, renewable energy inputs are variable, depending on meteorological conditions. An obvious remedy is to extend grids across greater spatial expanses, joining sites amenable to renewable power generation to centres of population and industry that are sufficiently energy-hungry to use the electricity as it is produced. Addressing the planetary catastrophe of climate change requires its own *Großraum*, but it is not produced according to territorial logics of state expansion.

The integrated national grids that evolved from scattered local infrastructures across the twentieth century were artefacts of industrialism and mass consumption. It is hard to forget the famous quote from Vladimir Ilyich Lenin: 'Communism is Soviet power plus the electrification of the whole country.'[49] However, even in capitalist countries, electricity was eventually considered a public utility, shielded from competition. In the US, where grids were initially constructed and regulated at the state level, governments set rates to reimburse electricity companies for providing a service while also allowing them to turn a profit and attract investors. Katharine Southard describes these arrangements as the first public–private partnerships.[50] It was not until the late-twentieth century that synchronized alternating current grids began to span continents. Lenin's dream of an integrated Soviet grid was not realized until the 1970s. The North American power system evolved into four giant networks, imperfectly linked together, as recent outages in Texas attest. These grid vulnerabilities derive partly from the deregulation of electricity markets, which, beginning in the 1990s, introduced wholesaling and price wars that benefited consumers at the cost of maintaining and upgrading grids, for instance, for purposes of decarbonization. Connecting grids with high-voltage direct-current (HVDC) cables is a means of addressing these problems – for instance, the Texas grid, which has remained largely separate from other North American networks for political reasons, is currently being joined to grids in the US

---

49   Vladimir Ilyich Lenin, 'Our Foreign and Domestic Position and Party Tasks: Speech Delivered to the Moscow Gubernia Conference of the R.C.P. (B.)', 21 November 1920, available at marxists.org.

50   Katharine Southard, 'US Electric Utilities: The First Public-Private Partnerships', *Public Contract Law Journal* 39, no. 2 (2010), 395–410.

South-East.[51] In China, such interconnections are more advanced. Since 2009, the country has built multiple grid interconnectors to link its coal and hydro-generation capacities in the west to its major eastern cities.[52] Grid interconnection technologies were pioneered in Europe, where cross-border interconnections began in the 1950s. Today Europe boasts the world's largest electricity-transmission network, spreading from Portugal and Scandinavia to Italy and Greece, and including East European countries such as Poland, Hungary, Slovakia, the Czech Republic, and most recently Ukraine, which, as we discussed in Chapter 3, was connected only twenty days after the war's start. As this latter instance illustrates, grid interconnections have geopolitical relevance. On the one hand, they stitch countries into a common energy destiny. On the other, they can leave countries open to energy dependence and political blackmail, given the need for electricity to support critical systems such as the internet, logistics, telecommunications, water supply, and healthcare. Apart from having environmental and technical benefits, then, grid interconnections project political power and reorder greater economic spaces.

Tracing the global proliferation of grid interconnectors in recent times reveals 'a fluid interplay of infrastructure, space and power that has the effect of undermining territoriality as a principle of international order'.[53] China's prodigious construction of HVDC lines, for example, provides a backbone for extending control of electricity flows beyond its territorial borders. In 2015, Xi Jinping announced the Global Energy Interconnection, an ambitious plan to connect the world's electricity networks using smart grid technologies to achieve cleaner energy futures. Entwined with BRI efforts to reorient global infrastructures and commercial flows, the results of this programme have been modest.[54] However, China is involved in extending grid ownership, for instance through investments in Greece, Portugal, Brazil, Cambodia, and the

51   Edward Klump and Peter Behr, 'What a $2B Texas Project says about US Quest for CO2-free Grid', *EnergyWire*, 28 October 2021.

52   Molly Lempriere, 'China's Mega Transmission Lines', *Future Power Technology*, 19 March 2019.

53   Kirsten Westphal, Maria Pastukhova, and Jacopo Maria Pepe, *Geopolitics of Electricity: Grids, Space and (Political) Power*, Berlin: German Institute for International and Security Affairs, 2022, 6.

54   Edmund Downie, 'China's Vision for a Global Grid', *Reconnecting Asia*, Washington, DC: Center for Strategic and International Studies, 2019.

Philippines, propagating technical norms and standards, and gaining control over equipment supply chains, including both hardware and software. In terms of interconnectivity, the country is not only developing transmission links with neighbours such as Mongolia, Myanmar, and Laos, but also negotiating the construction of three HVDC lines with Kazakhstan and Kyrgyzstan. In 2016, the State Grid Corporation of China signed agreements with stakeholders in Japan, South Korea, and Russia for the development of a North Asian Super Grid. In 2021, the same entity agreed with the International Renewable Energy Agency to assist with the transition of Central American and African grids to sustainable energy. Moreover, China has been strengthening grid interconnectors within BRI countries, including Pakistan, Cambodia, Nepal, and Kyrgyzstan, and has committed to upgrading the link between Uzbekistan and Tajikistan. These developments create complex, multivectoral operative spaces, which, while functioning through connectivity more than territoriality, also establish geopolitical tensions – for instance, with India, which has interconnectors with all South Asian countries excepting Pakistan and aims to synchronize its grid with Nepal and Bangladesh. Similar patterns repeat themselves in other world regions, where the actual and projected construction of interconnectors turns peripheral zones into spaces of infrastructural development and geopolitical contest. A report published by Germany's Institute for Security and Public Affairs details these spatial and technopolitical changes, focusing on the Eastern Mediterranean, the Black and Caspian Sea regions, and Central Asia. In these zones, the EU, Russia, and China compete to reconfigure electricity grids, and across the Black Sea, especially in the South Caucasus, Turkey and Iran are also active.[55]

The point we are making by examining these grid dynamics is not merely about geopolitics being played out through infrastructural connections rather than territorial logics. The operative spaces made by these electricity networks and the junctures that necessarily exist between them offer a basis for thinking about geopolitics differently, outside the frame of statecraft and international relations. Doubtless, the operative dimensions of critical infrastructures such as electricity grids cross back into state spaces and systems of power, generating novel interactions of geoeconomics and geopolitics that give rise to the multiple poles that inhabit and provisionally structure today's world of shifting hegemonies and war regimes. As Alke Jenss and Benjamin Scheutze argue, these infrastructures 'prefigure politics', locking publics out of their design, and 'fixing specific energy futures in place, while preventing others', often in the name of sustainability claims.[56] Jenss and Scheutze examine two transregional electricity grid projects: SIEPAC, built in the 2010s to connect the North and Central American grids; and MedRing, envisaged to link North African energy production to the EU. In both cases, they highlight how the vested states facilitate 'capital accumulation between related sites with different social struggles'.[57] In the case of SIEPAC, connections between resource sites and industrial hubs were privileged while blind spots were created around affected populations. In the instance of MedRing, the creation of a transcontinental energy flow bolsters colonial dispossession, the Moroccan occupation of the Western Sahara, and the exploitation of racialized labour in the European agricultural sector. Jenss and Scheutze contend that an overlooked 'element of electricity grids is the increasing intertwinement with migration containment infrastructures'.[58] At stake is not simply the claim that the cooperation required for building transregional energy grids reinforces the international cooperative efforts spurred by the fight against migration. Energy infrastructures, they argue, are 'an integral part of coercive, militarized landscapes of migration deterrence'.[59]

This observation adds credence to arguments about how the complex networked topologies that support global processes cross the world of borders and migration control in a time when the former mutates at the intersection of states, technology, and infrastructures, while the latter takes on an increasingly logistical rationality.[60] It is not a matter of grids, networks, and junctures facilitating the movement of people,

56   Alke Jenss and Benjamin Schuetze, 'Prefiguring Politics: Transregional Energy Infrastructures as a Lens for the Study of Authoritarian Practices', *Globalizations*, arnold-bergstraesser.de, 28 February 2023, 1.

57   Ibid., 12.

58   Ibid., 9.

59   Ibid., 5.

60   Huub Dijstelbloem, *Borders as Infrastructure: The Technopolitics of Border Control*, Cambridge, MA: MIT Press, 2021; Moritz Altenried et al., 'Logistical Borderscapes: Politics and Mediation of Mobile Labor in Germany after the "Summer of Migration"', *South Atlantic Quarterly* 117, no. 2 (2018), 291–312.

things, and energy while borders exclude and block such mobility. As we wrote in an article published over a decade ago, borders are 'not devices that block or obstruct global flows' but 'parameters that enable the channeling of flows and provide coordinates within which flows can be joined or segmented, connected or disconnected'.[61] It is important to remember this point when articulating arguments about the role of operative spaces in a time of pandemic and war to concerns about social struggles, global inequalities, and migration infrastructures. Whether one follows Xiang Biao and Johan Lindquist in understanding migration infrastructure as a nexus of commercial, regulatory, technological, humanitarian, and social systems or heeds activist researchers who emphasize the concept's relevance for organizing resistance strategies (among migrant domestic workers, for instance), there is a need to return the analysis of greater economic and infrastructural spaces to grounded situations of exploitation, extraction, and class struggle.[62] This is a task we take up in the book's final chapter. Before doing so, we need to add further detail around the technopolitical and institutional factors that contribute to expanding logics of political capitalism and multipolarity, particularly with regard to data politics, artificial intelligence, and processes of platformization.

The highest stage of decoupling?

Since the mid-2010s, technology has been at the forefront of China–US strategic competition. This conflict has impacted 5G telecommunications, undersea communication cables, semiconductors, chip-manufacturing equipment, artificial intelligence, digital currencies, large-capacity batteries, and solar panels. Given the ongoing entanglement of Chinese and US capital markets, as well as the junctures that join infrastructural initiatives supported by these large continental states, we might say, employing the

---

61   Sandro Mezzadra and Brett Neilson, 'Between Inclusion and Exclusion: On the Topology of Global Space and Borders', *Theory, Culture and Society* 29, nos 4–5 (2012), 58–75, 59.

62   Xiang Biao and Johan Lindquist, 'Migration Infrastructure', *International Migration Review* 48, no. S1 (2014), S122–48; Mouna Maaroufi and Neva Löw, 'Challenging Infrastructures of Domestic Labor: Implications for Labor Organizing in Lebanon and Belgium', *Journal of Labor and Society* 22, no. 4 (2019), 853–73.

same half-irony we exercised in describing today's imperialism as the lowest stage of capitalism, that technological competition represents the highest stage of decoupling. Media headlines and political rhetoric confirm this thesis, with US export controls on silicon chips and associated Dutch restrictions on semiconductor printing technologies occupying pride of place. Maximilian Mayer and Yen-Chi Lu, who made the effort to construct a Digital Dependence Index to measure countries' reliance on digital technologies from abroad, report that the US is the least digitally dependent country while in the last ten years China has done the most to catch up.[63] Nonetheless, China and the US remain the world's leading collaborators on artificial intelligence research.[64] Even reading Lulu Chen's *Influence Empire*, the story of Chinese tech giant Tencent, one is struck by how China–US ties mark the biographies of some of the company's most senior players, including President and Executive Director Martin Lau and Chief Exploration Officer David Wallerstein, who started as a US expat kicking around Shenzhen.[65] It is naïve to underestimate the impact on China's technology development of US measures such as the CHIPS Act or the far more comprehensive RESTRICT Act, of which social media platform TikTok promises to be the first victim. Likewise, it would be imprudent to underestimate the ability of Chinese researchers and industry to catch up in silicon chip production, or even to outstrip the West in the development of other key technologies, as a recent report from the Australian Strategic Policy Institute claims has already happened.[66] However, our interest is not to assess or predict changing state or commercial capacities for technological innovation. Rather, we ask how large technological systems recast geopolitics and produce emerging spaces of capital in a multipolar world.

How does technology cross the discourse and practice of multipolarity? The question has become important for thinkers who struggle

63   Maximilian Meyer and Yen-Chi Lu, 'Digital Autonomy? Measuring the Global Digital Dependence Structure', ssrn.com, 30 March 2023.

64   Edmund L. Andrews, 'China and the United States: Unlikely Partners in AI', Stanford University Human-Centered Intelligence, 16 March 2022.

65   Lulu Chen, *Influence Empire: The Story of Tencent and China's Ambition*, London: Hodder & Stoughton, 2022.

66   Jamie Gaida, Jennifer Wong Leung, Stephen Robin, and Danielle Cave, *ASPI's Critical Technology Tracker: The Global Race for Future Power*, Report No. 69, Canberra: Australian Strategic Policy Institute, 2023.

with the Eurocentrism implicit in the concept of technology, for instance in the philosophy of Martin Heidegger. At stake in these discussions is the relation of technology to tradition. For some, such as conservative political analyst Aleksandr Dugin, who posits the existence of a Russian episteme, thinking through this relation results in civilizational visions and a geopolitical perspective rooted in a state-centred and ultimately mystical notion of *Großraum*. By contrast, Yuk Hui, in his book *The Question Concerning Technology in China*, proposes to rethink technology beyond the Chinese philosophical frame of *Qi* (tool) and *Dao* (wholeness), which, in the late-nineteenth and twentieth centuries, was used to argue that China could adopt Western technologies for utilitarian purposes while maintaining a substantive and authentically Chinese tradition – a view that also characterizes the 'departure moment' of Indian nationalism.[67] For Hui, the challenge is 'to desubstantialise tradition in order to set it free from nationalism and consumerism'; this means rejecting a theory of multiple modernities in which technology nonetheless synchronizes the 'global time axis' and negotiating 'a new relation between tradition and technological development'. Working from this angle, Hui envisions a different kind of globalization in which what is changed is not only the 'geographical configuration of power' but also arrangements of data, sovereignty, and computation that are currently captured by war regimes.[68] Although it grapples with Heideggerian precepts that we think can be sidestepped in discussions of technology, Hui's outlook resonates with our understanding of multipolarity. What counts is not merely the spatial extension of states or empires that ground their claims to legitimacy in national or civilizational longings. Rather, the articulation of power through infrastructural and technological systems becomes a relevant concern in a world in which cloud platforms and computational networks take on roles traditionally performed by states. For us, the condition of multipolarity cannot be understood in isolation from related operations of capital. Examining the role of large technical systems means not only contesting traditional views of geopolitics but also rethinking notions of capital circulation and reproduction.

---

67   Yuk Hui, *The Question Concerning Technology in China*, Cambridge, MA: MIT Press, 2016; Partha Chatterjee, *Nationalist Thought and the Colonial World*, London: Zed Books, 1986, 73.

68   Hui, *The Question Concerning Technology*, 59, 56, 55, and 61.

In Chapter 2, we argued that the growing incapacity of states to guarantee the reproduction and turnover of capital within their borders has led them to seek advantage by strengthening their control over transnational circulatory processes. Now we need to add a point about how processes of recursion affect the circulation of capital, keeping in mind that these processes are central to the cybernetic models that have shaped today's digital technologies. Although its genealogy lies outside political economy, cybernetics offers a radically different theory of circulation than that which emphasizes reproduction. Rather than understanding circulation as the temporal shape of the structure of reproduction, it understands circulation according to principles of feedback, control, and communication. As Philip Mirowski explains, cybernetics started as 'a set of technologies to restrain entropy and chaos through feedback and later was transmuted into theories of self-organization, where entropy would itself under certain circumstances give rise to "higher" levels of order'.[69] What began, for Norbert Wiener, as a gun control problem evolved to provide the basis for a general theory of human–machine interaction, a philosophy of technology, the engineering of control systems, and, in the hands of Niklas Luhmann, a theory of society as a set of functionally differentiated autopoietic systems.[70] Yet if cybernetics is characterized by a tendency to universalize the notion of feedback, it was not the first knowledge system to emphasize this feature of circuits. In *Capital*, volume 3, Marx uses the concept of reflux (*Rückfluss*) to describe the capacity of circuits to turn back upon themselves, specifically through processes of financial reinvestment or the return of payments on loaned capital. 'The *manner* of the reflux', Marx writes, is 'determined in each case by the actual cyclical movement of capital as it reproduces itself and its specific varieties.'[71] There is a relation between reproduction and reflux (or feedback), and its shape derives from the qualities and specific forms of capital's circulation.

As discussed in Chapter 2, the reproduction of capital obeys a logic of self-expansion, driven by the coercive law of accumulation that crosses

---

69   Philip Mirowski, *Machine Dreams: Economics Becomes a Cyborg Science*, New York: Cambridge University Press, 2002, 54.

70   Niklas Luhmann, *Theory of Society*, vol. 1, Stanford: Stanford University Press, 2012.

71   Karl Marx, *Capital*, vol. 3, trans. David Fernbach, London: Penguin, 1981, 458.

its operations. The seeming metamorphoses accomplished by this process involve the return of circuits to their starting point, where capital's enrichment can be quantitatively measured, either as profit or loss. Yet the temporality of capital accumulation also has a linear aspect, which proceeds endlessly, or entropically, until subjected to the reflux of circulation, otherwise known as reinvestment. At stake in this dynamic are complex interactions of flow, equivalence, and circulation that unfold in potentially contradictory ways, resulting in blockages (underconsumption) or floods (overproduction) that threaten the continuation of the circulation process itself. This is why, for Marx, the theory of circulation is, at the same time, a theory of crisis.[72] This perspective on circulation has implications for the understanding of multipolarity.

Theories that explain China's Going Out and BRI activities as a spatial and infrastructural fix resulting from a crisis of overaccumulation offer a radically different explanation for these developments than geopolitical notions of grand strategy.[73] Seen from the angle of reproduction, China's unstable lurch into the world economy has another series of implications, both in sites where these activities hit the ground and within China itself. A recent report finds that, since 2016, China's international lending patterns have pivoted away from infrastructure financing to emergency rescue lending, primarily to middle-income countries along the Belt and Road.[74] These bailout measures reflect debtor countries' troubles in reproducing capital. Yet in extending such loans, China is ultimately trying to protect its own banks while it also aims at internationalizing its currency, the renminbi. The fact that China is a position to export capital does not mean that capital reproduction within its own borders is robust. This is partly why the country has turned to the dual-circulation model, seeking to augment its export-oriented growth by strengthening domestic consumption. In terms of social reproduction, this shift has consequences that extend beyond changes to population management. For instance, 2016 saw the abandonment of the One Child policy and the formal abolition of the

---

72   Peter Osborne, *Crisis as Form*, London: Verso, 2022, 65.

73   See, for instance, David Harvey, *Seventeen Contradictions and the End of Capitalism*, New York: Oxford University Press, 2014.

74   Sebastian Horn, Bradley C. Parks, Carmen M. Reinhart, and Christoph Trebesch, *China as an International Lender of Last Resort*, Working Paper 31105, Cambridge, MA: National Bureau of Economic Research, 2023.

urban–rural distinction from the *hukou* household registration system, while alerts regarding an impending demographic crisis multiplied in the following years. Pronatalism, party-state backing of patriarchal family values, and a focus on educational outcomes for left-behind children have forced many female rural–urban migrants of the 2000s back into provincial villages, where they not only bear the temporal, monetary, and labour costs of childrearing but also often moonlight in workshops that subcontract light manufacturing tasks from coastal factories at low cost. As a result, 'gender is playing a more significant role in informal work than in previous eras'.[75]

In seeking to boost the education and consumption levels of Chinese households, the dual-circulation model meshes with China's ambitions to achieve self-reliance by strengthening its domestic market. This is where technology and resources come back in, fuelled by trade wars, export controls, and delistings, combined with efforts to shore up external demand along the BRI, and importantly in Russia, in the context of Western containment. Although the scope of Chinese technological development is wide, we focus here on data-intensive technologies, including data storage, e-commerce, and artificial intelligence. This choice is driven by the realization that data has become a sovereign substance, something over which and from which sovereignty is claimed. Although localization laws requiring the storage of certain data (such as citizens' health data) in state territories are by now a feature of many jurisdictions, China occupies a special place in the global nexus of data and sovereignty, given the role of the Great Firewall not only in shielding Chinese internet users from foreign content but also in creating and protecting data markets at the national scale. Bolstered by the Cybersecurity Law of 2017 and the Data Security Law of 2021, the fire-walling of the data generated by China's vast population has inspired the description of the country as 'the Saudi Arabia of data'.[76] Yet, while this state-centric vision of data sovereignty may seem attractive to many governments around the world, not least for its potential in training artificial intelligence, China also pursues programmes such as the

---

75   Yiran Zhang, 'The Social Reproduction of the Informal Migrant Workforce in China', *Critical Legal Thinking*, 20 October 2021.

76   Kai-Fu Lee, *AI Superpowers: China, Silicon Valley, and the New World Order*, New York: Houghton Mifflin Harcourt, 2018, 54.

Digital Silk Road Initiative and China Standards 35, which aim to enhance its international data connectivity. Chinese companies are involved in the construction of undersea communication cables, satellite connections, and software platforms to improve local, interregional, and planetary information exchange – and, in 2020, China proposed a Global Data Security Initiative to promote, in the words of Xi Jinping, 'peaceful, secure, open, cooperative, and orderly' cross-border data flows.[77] Clearly, an account of Chinese data politics that emphasizes closure, territoriality, and subordination of data to state sovereignty is as inadequate as one that preaches openness, connectivity, and the capacity of data to create its own territorial and sovereign formations.

To understand and analyse these tensions, we need to probe the infrastructural layer of Chinese data power. Institutional framings of technology such as laws and policy are significant, but without technical capacity and physical infrastructure, systems remain inoperative. States have the capacity to set legislation and can turn regimes of intellectual property to their advantage, as has occurred with patent registrations in China. In the past decade, the latter have boomed for technologies such as semiconductors.[78] Patents have also been touted as a means to push back against sanctions by occupying the space of innovation and foreclosing US dominance in the field.[79] Additionally, Chinese courts have nullified patents in cases where foreign assignees hold rights for strategic technologies, such as those applying to silicon chips, pharmaceuticals, or rare earth minerals.[80] Another area where states wield power is in the ability to rein in tech companies, as is evident in the party-state's actions towards firms such as Ant Group and Didi.[81] However, as we shall see

77   'Remarks by Chinese President Xi Jinping at 20th Meeting of SCO Council of Heads of State', *China Daily*, 11 November 2020.

78   Eunji Choung and Min Gyo Koo, 'China's Dream for Chip Supremacy: Seeing through the Lens of Panel Display-Related IC Patents', *Business and Politics*, 24 March 2023.

79   Junwei Luo and Shushen Li, 'Strengthen Building of Basic Reach Capacity for Semiconductor Research to Light Up "Beacon" Towards Realizing the Self-Reliance and Self-Improvement of Semiconductors', *Bulletin of Chinese Academy of Sciences* (Chinese Version) 38, no. 2 (2023), 187–92.

80   Stu Woo and Daniel Michaels, 'China's Newest Weapon to Nab Western Technology – Its Courts', *Wall Street Journal*, 20 February 2023.

81   Andrew Collier, *China's Technology War: Why Beijing Took Down Its Tech Giants*, Singapore: Palgrave Macmillan, 2022.

in the next section, platformization points to a convergence in the forms of power exercised by states and technology firms, as platforms take on roles performed by states and states adopt platformed modes of governance. Much attention has been garnered by the Chinese state's capacity to access data held by tech companies, whether foreign firms operating in China or Chinese firms, although approval processes are complicated and the issue of access to data held by Chinese firms operating beyond the country's borders is complicated. The practice of private technology companies granting the state 'golden shares', small asset holdings that nonetheless offer influence over business directions, is another concern for Western parties made anxious by Chinese data power. However, the company–state nexus in China is variable and needs to be analysed on a case-by-case basis. Moreover, state control over digital infrastructures such as data centres and undersea cables is often patchy, not least because these technologies can span different institutional settings and have transnational ownership patterns that encompass multiple private actors. We need to ask whether digital infrastructures provide opportune technical systems through which powerful states can advance strategies otherwise shaped on the chessboard of international relations, or whether the sociotechnical arrangement of these infrastructures shifts the stakes and modalities of engagement, foregrounding the role of logistification and the operational dynamic of capital in the making of geopolitical and geoeconomic relations.

Data centres are a case in point. These installations are vast hangars full of computers. They collocate servers, switches, and wires that facilitate the storage, transmission, and processing of data in high volumes and at fast speeds. The economic advantages that accrue to parties that place or hire servers in these installations derive not only from opportunities for peering and networking within data centres but also from inputs from client machines that may be situated at vast distance. This means that data centres can operate at cross-border and potentially planetary scales. Yet these facilities have precise locations, often clustering in sites where there is access to energy, skills, land concessions, tax exemptions, or undersea cables. As such, the positioning of data centres within state territories binds them to juridical requirements, such as the Chinese laws mentioned earlier. But depending on operational factors, contractual conditions, and commercial interests, the provenance and ownership of data may be territorially distinct at sovereign and geopolitical levels from its location of storage.[82] Data centres exist within complex assemblages of space, power, and infrastructure that, far from passively reinforcing state sovereignty, generate client footprints, or territories, which follow patterns of networked distribution and cut across the exclusivity and contiguity of state territories.[83] At the same time, they produce operative spaces that fulfil the key logistical task of converting data into capital. These facilities intensify and multiply the extractive capacities of digital technologies, allowing the extraction not merely of raw materials or alienated labour but of patterns of social cooperation which generate data that can be stored, aggregated, analysed, sold, and, importantly, used to train artificial intelligence applications. As Ritajyoti Bandyopadhyay explains, with respect to earlier forms of commodity production and circulation, data centres enjoy a longer lifespan as fixed capital because they support a greater number of turnovers in a reduced time period.[84] No matter that these installations may be built to exist as 'ruins of the future'.[85] They have the capacity to centralize extractive operations in a single site and attract data transactions across wide geographical vistas. Whether they store and process inputs from platform users who contribute data in exchange for the provision of services, keystrokes generated by near or distant workforces, or data collected by remote-sensing or web-scraping technologies, they are indispensable facilities for the production of data power. In this sense, data centres function not merely as technical facilities but also as political institutions that exert influence over the intricacies and convolutions of today's centrifugal multipolarity.

---

82   Brett Neilson and Ned Rossiter, 'Automating Labour and the Spatial Politics of Data Centre Technologies', in Mascha Will-Zocholl and Caroline Roth-Ebner (eds), *Topologies of Digital Work: How Digitalisation and Virtualisation Shape Working Spaces and Places*, Cham: Palgrave Macmillan, 2021, 77–101.

83   Brett Neilson and Tanya Notley, 'Data Centres as Logistical Facilities: Singapore and the Emergence of Production Topologies', *Work Organization, Labour and Globalization* 13, no. 1 (2019), 15–29.

84   Ritajyoti Bandyopadhyay, 'Infrastructuring Data Economy: Data Centres in Historical Context', in Manish K. Jha and Ritam Sengupta (eds), *Data Centres as Infrastructure: Frontiers of Digital Governance in Contemporary India*, Hyderabad: Orient Black Swan, 2022, 60.

85   ARE Taylor, 'Concrete Clouds: Data, Bunkers, Preparedness', *New Media and Society* 25, no. 2 (2023), 405–30.

Doubtless, data centres are only a single class of facility in a complex array of digital infrastructures, and the significance of their location is not exhausted by the observation that they exist in the territory of one state or another. As an analysis of the data centres clustered at Hong Kong's Tseung Kwan O Industrial Estate reveals, the regional placement of these installations within Chinese territory is important not only because different sites offer varying degrees of connectivity to the mainland and the rest of the world but also due to factors such as legislative differences and proximity to financial markets.[86] Insofar as data storage is crucial to the development of artificial intelligence, this local variation is relevant because it contrasts the dominant narrative about machine learning technologies in China being trained towards surveillance and social control.[87] Without question, this narrative is warranted, particularly as regards treatment of minority populations and the issues of ethics, privacy, and cybersecurity surrounding practices such as facial recognition or social credit scoring. But it is not the only story, as a group of researchers investigating automated decision-making in China conclude.[88] The development of automated technologies in China is not exclusively driven by the central government through policy initiatives but also intersects market dynamics, which unfold unevenly across and within subnational regions. Zoning strategies and the introduction of tech bays, which cluster relevant industries in designated areas, are important in this regard. Start-ups and local governments play a role in addressing specific challenges in regional areas. These arrangements have led not only to a heterogeneity of digital-governance models being developed and deployed by provincial and city administrations, including Zhejiang's Holistic Governance model, Hunan's One Thing Once Done system, and Shanghai's One Network for One Office service-delivery platform. China's fragmented system of technological innovation has also resulted in a myriad of

---

86   Brett Neilson, 'Capital Operations: Data and Waste', *e-flux Architecture*, April 2020; Luke Munn, 'Red Territory: Forging Infrastructural Power', *Territory, Politics, Governance* 11, no. 1 (2023), 80–99.

87   On the surveillance narrative, see, for instance, Josh Chin and Liza Lin, *Surveillance State: Inside China's Quest to Launch a New Era of Social Control*, New York: St Martin's Press, 2022.

88   'Decentering Automated Decision Making: Automated Decision Making in China', ARC Centre of Excellence for Automated Decision-Making and Society, 2023.

unique local automation initiatives, such as Guangdong province's digital agriculture programme, which uses drones, platforms, cashless vending machines, and home-cooking machines to trace food supply chains from fields to tables.

The extension of Chinese data and automation technologies beyond the country's borders, under schemes such as the Digital Silk Road Initiative, is likewise a heterogeneous affair. The expansion of Chinese-owned infrastructures for finance, e-commerce, cloud services, data transfer, and smart city projects is definitely part of wider regional and global dynamics by which, as Till Mostowlansky and Max Hirsh write, 'geopolitical ambition, social change, and technological innovation converge and cross-fertilize one another through infrastructure'.[89] Consider the case of the Digital Free Trade Zone (DFTZ) set up by Alibaba on the fringes of Malaysia's Kuala Lumpur airport. A collection of e-commerce warehouses and air cargo facilities, this logistical installation is a part of Alibaba's electronic World Trade Platform initiative, which promotes itself as facilitating 'inclusive globalization' based on collaboration and partnership with SMEs and BRI-participating countries.[90] As Hong Shen explains, such advocacy of inclusive globalization is an important element of China's Digital Silk Road policy vision, alongside cutting industrial overcapacity, enabling corporate China's global expansion, supporting the internationalization of the renminbi, and constructing a China-centred transnational network infrastructure.[91] Yet Alibaba's move into Malaysia also seeks to ward off competition in South-East Asia from US e-commerce giant Amazon, which has set up its Prime platform in Singapore and brokered an agreement with the Vietnam E-Commerce Association.[92] By contrast with Amazon's vertical business model, which involves ownership of assets along its supply chains (from

89   Till Mostowlansky and Max Hirsh, 'Introduction', in Max Hirsh and Till Mostowlansky (eds), *Infrastructure and the Remaking of Asia*, Honolulu: University of Hawai'i Press, 2022, 1.

90   Maximiliano Facundo Vila Seoane, 'Alibaba's Discourse for the Digital Silk Road: The Electronic World Trade Platform and "Inclusive Globalization"', *Chinese Journal of Communication* 13, no. 1 (2020), 68–83.

91   Hong Shen, 'Building a Digital Silk Road? Situating the Internet in China's Belt and Road Initiative', *International Journal of Communication* 12 (2018), 2683–701.

92   Brett Neilson, 'Working the Digital Silk Road: Alibaba's Digital Free Trade Zone in Malaysia', in Mark Graham and Fabian Ferrari (eds), *Digital Work in the Planetary Market*, Cambridge, MA: MIT Press, 2022, 117–36.

inventory to warehouses, logistical networks, data centres, computing applications, and cloud computing services), the DFTZ is a state–private partnership initiated by the Malaysian government and involving collaboration between diverse commercial entities: Malaysian Airports Holdings Berhad, a government linked corporation; Pos Malaysia; Cainiao, Alibaba's logistics arm; and Lazada, Alibaba's South-East Asian retail platform.[93] Significantly, then, in terms of institutional and ownership arrangements, the Amazon model of global expansion is much more top-down than that pursued by Alibaba, a fact that pushes back against the characterization of US business and organizational cultures as less hierarchical and more open than their Chinese counterparts.[94]

In recent times, the Amazon warehouse has become a privileged site for researchers and activists concerned with the implications of automation for labour. We will avoid rehashing the well-trodden arguments about Amazon capitalism, discussions about the impact of Amazon's automation technologies on workforces and labour regimes, and the various writings and struggles surrounding labour actions at Amazon warehouses in countries such as the US and Germany.[95] Suffice it to say that the spread of Amazon's business activities across e-commerce to data centres and web services means that the firm provides an appropriate object for debates and struggles that engage the tendency of automation to reduce workers to what Marx calls 'conscious linkages' of the machine, recognizing that this reduction applies ever more to cognitive labour tasks and not

93   Edmund Terence Gomez, Siew Yean Tham, Ran Li, and Kee-Cheok Cheong, *China in Malaysia: State-Business Relations and the New Order of Investment Flows*, Singapore: Palgrave Macmillan, 2020.

94   Xinyi Wu and Gary Gereffi, 'Amazon and Alibaba: Internet Governance, Business Models, and Internationalization Strategies', in Rob van Tulder, Alain Verbeke, and Lucia Piscitello (eds), *International Business in the Information and Digital Age*, Progress in International Business Research, vol. 13, Bingley, UK: Emerald, 2018, 327–56.

95   Jake Alimahomed-Wilson and Ellen Reese (eds), *The Cost of Free Shipping: Amazon in the Global Economy*, London: Pluto Books, 2020; Armin Beverungen, 'Remote Control: Algorithmic Management of Circulation at Amazon', in Marcus Burkhardt, Mary Shnayien, and Katja Grashofer (eds), *Explorations in Digital Cultures*, Luneburg: Meson Press, 2021; Alessandro Delfanti and Bronwyn Frey, 'Humanly Extended Automation or the Future of Work Seen through Amazon Patents', *Science, Technology, and Human Values* 46, no. 3 (2021), 655–82; Sabrina Apicella, 'Rough Terrains: Wages as Mobilizing Factor in German and Italian Amazon Distribution Centers', *Sozial. Geschichte Online* 27 (2020), S, 81–96; Ruth Milkman, 'The Amazon Union's Historic Breakthrough', *Dissent* 69, no. 3 (2022), 96–101.

simply manual work.[96] In Chapter 5, we turn to assess the role of logistics and tech worker struggles, including the anti-996 movement in China, in opening vistas of internationalism and solidarity in today's multipolar world. Here, we emphasize how technologies of data extraction and automation work to constitute the poles and operative spaces of this world in ways that reach beyond principles of state territoriality. To make this claim is not to deny that such technologies can feed into state or sovereign agendas, as becomes clear for instance in the civil–military nexus of computational development surrounding autonomous weapons, information warfare, space war, and other frontiers of imperial conflict. Contemporary wars make evident 'the complex relationship between the privatization of security and technologically driven automation.'[97] On the one hand, there is a tendency to employ private military and security companies such as Blackwater and the Wagner Group in fighting wars. On the other hand, the increased automation of security and defence technologies means not only that war is becoming less human-centred but also that private contractors are frequently required to operate systems that militaries do not have the expertise to run. Additionally, technologies developed in value chains removed from the military-industrial pipeline can come to play crucial roles in war efforts. Such is the case for SpaceX's Starlink system, which provides off-grid high-bandwidth internet connections via small, low-flying satellites. In their fight against Russia, Ukrainian troops have come to rely on Starlink to pin down and coordinate fire on potential targets. Nonetheless, the channelling of automated technologies towards sovereign imperatives does not remove their propensity to create spaces of capital and power that operate beyond the territorial scale of the national or continental state. In the end, such digital expansion reduces to neither state prerogatives nor capital operations. Central to the modes of power at hand are rather practices of data extraction, analysis, and intervention that transmute relations among geopolitical initiatives, commercial activities, infrastructural installations, and labour-control strategies. These changing and entwined logics become particularly evident in the operations of digital platforms, to which we now turn.

---

96   Karl Marx, *Grundrisse: Foundations of the Critique of Political Economy*, trans. Martin Nicolaus, Harmondsworth: Penguin, 1973, 693.

97   Antonio Calcara, 'Contractors or Robots: Future Warfare between Privatization and Automation', *Small Wars and Insurgencies* 33, nos 1–2 (2022), 250–71.

Platforming capitalism and labour

Digital spaces build privileged sites to test the mutations of territoriality, as well as the frictions and tensions surrounding its relations with a different operative logic and rationality. At the end of the previous chapter, we mentioned the notion of the Stack, introduced by Benjamin H. Bratton to signal 'a transformation in the technical infrastructure of global systems, whereby planetary-scale computation has so thoroughly and fundamentally transformed the logics of political geography in its own image that it has produced new geographies and new territories that can enforce themselves'.[98] There is no need here to discuss the six-layer articulation of Bratton's Stack (Earth, Cloud, City, Address, Interface, User). For our puposes, it is more relevant to note his emphasis on 'planetary-scale computation', which leads him to imagine a unitary Stack structure, characterized by the overlapping of national governments (China no less than the US), transnational bodies, 'and corporations such as Google, Facebook, Apple, Amazon, etc.', to produce 'differentiated patterns of mutual accommodation marked by moments of conflict'.[99] Such an image of a planetary-scale governance of digital spaces, despite the sophisticated and thought-provoking model elaborated by Bratton, appeared as literally utopian even before the escalating geopolitical tensions of recent years. These tensions led the US to stop in 2020 for national security reasons the ambitious project of the Pacific Light Cable Network, a 12,971-kilometre undersea cable involving Facebook and Google, originally planned to connect California and Hong Kong.[100] Even the notion of 'hemispheric Stacks', which registers such tensions, can be misleading since the image of the hemisphere may still 'suggest an intrinsic bipolar split of planetary computation', nurturing the resurgence of a Cold War rhetoric with respect to digital spaces.[101]

---

98   Benjamin H. Bratton, *The Stack: On Software and Sovereignty*, Cambridge, MA: MIT Press, 2015, 375.

99   Tiziana Terranova, 'Red Stack Attack!', in Robin Mackay and Armen Avanessian (eds), *Accelerate: The Accelerationist Reader*, Falmouth, UK: Urbanomic, 2014, 389.

100   Gabriele de Seta, 'Gateways, Sieves, and Domes: On the Infrastructural Topology of the Chinese Stack', *International Journal of Communication* 15 (2021), 2669–71.

101   Ibid., 2684.

Employing a topological approach and a different spatial imaginary, Gabriele de Seta writes that 'the plurality of stacks as projects and projections can instead be understood in terms of domes jostling and occasionally intersecting at different layers'.[102] While the image of the dome describes the way in which sovereign states imagine themselves as controlling digital spaces, de Seta emphasizes that, in the case of China as well as of other countries, such spaces cannot be neatly superimposed with national borders. States, he writes, 'incorporate features of the stack as much as the stack incorporates features of a state'.[103] Analysing the gateways and sieves that articulate the Chinese Stack, de Seta accounts both for the increasing presence of the state in its working and for the stretching of its spatial scope, as for instance in the extension of the use of QR codes for digital payment systems beyond the Chinese jurisdictional domain and more generally in processes of standard-setting.[104] This moment of stretching is key to the working of the Chinese Stack, as we mentioned earlier speaking of the digital Silk Road and the agreement with Kazakhstan, and it builds an important aspect of the spatial constitution of poles in the contemporary world. An uncanny mix of technological homogenization and heterogeneous forms of governance prevails in digital spaces, raising once again the problem of interoperability and of the establishment of gateways among them. Operations of capital crisscross the working of Stacks, while processes of digitalization are steering momentous mutations of capitalism. Issues of surveillance and control are always at stake in digital spaces, as demonstrated for instance by the Aadhaar project established in India in 2009, which employs biometric technologies to facilitate welfare and financial delivery. The vast system of digital infrastructures built on top of it is known as the India Stack, and is managed by governmental bodies that combine financial technology and techniques of population control within a platform-based partnership with private and public actors.[105] In this section we use the platform model, which emerged in the wake of the financial crisis of 2007–8 and became particularly visible during the pandemic, as a lens to analyse how operative spaces intersect the mutations of capitalism.

---

102 Ibid., 2684.

103 Ibid., 2685.

104 Ibid., 2679.

105 Kavita Dattani, '"Governtrepreneurism" for Good Governance: The Case of Aadhaar and the India Stack', *Area* 52 (2020), 411–19.

Besides its political meanings, referring to a programme or plan of action, in the twentieth century the word platform has been used in the economic domain mainly with respect to extraction, and in particular oil extraction (oil platform, offshore platform, and the like). This is an effective reminder of the extractive dimension of the operations of platforms that we discuss in Chapter 1 and to which we will return later. For now, we need to flesh out the peculiarity of digital platforms and of the abstract rationality underlying their operations. Platforms, Bratton writes, 'are generative mechanisms – engines that set the terms of participation according to fixed protocols (technical, discursive, formal protocols). They gain size and strength by mediating unplanned and even unplannable interactions.'[106] Intermediation lies, therefore, at the heart of the working of digital platforms, while the generation of participative settings and the control of their governing protocols describe some of their most crucial operations. Framed in such a way, platforms exhibit a distinct politics that, to follow Bratton, instantiates a 'third institutional form, along with states and market'.[107] Besides their role in labour management techniques, the algorithms shaping platform operations also have important governmental implications.[108] This is, for us, a critical point considering the relevance of the platform model in shaping digital spaces across the globe today. The rationality of intermediation that builds the abstract connection among deeply heterogeneous platforms has a genealogy that needs to be stressed. While it is clear that platforms operating in the fields of transport and delivery are engaged in the execution of logistical tasks, the very rationality of intermediation has in general a logistical origin and imprint. Even from a technical point of view, issues of interoperability and intermodalism (the organization of transportation across more than one mode) can be mentioned as logistical antecedents of the rationality of intermediation implemented by digital platforms.[109] Moreover, logistics has been, over recent decades, a crucial site of experimentation with systems of labour

---

106   Bratton, *The Stack*, 44.

107   Ibid., 44.

108   See Swati Srivastava, 'Algorithmic Governance and the International Politics of Big Tech', *Perspectives on Politics* 21, no. 3 (September 2021); and Claudia Aradau and Tobias Blanke, *Algorithmic Reason: The New Governance of Self and Other*, Oxford: Oxford University Press, 2022.

109   Cowen, *The Deadly Life of Logistics*, 44.

management. The use of key performance indicators to monitor and shape the labour of individuals and workforces, for instance, has anticipated the algorithmic management that is usually associated with the operations of digital platforms.[110]

It is with these aspects in mind that we speak of a platform model, which finds a panoply of radically diverse instantiations in the world. There is in fact no shortage of experiments with 'platform cooperativism', while, more generally, labels such as *gig* and *sharing economy* signal an emphasis on participation and sharing practices; the idea of sharing is indeed a key element of the rhetoric employed by platforms and it may well correspond to the motivations and even to the ethics of many users.[111] Nevertheless, such emphasis has been rapidly obscured by the steady development of corporate platforms, which are clearly driven by the logic of valorization and accumulation of capital. A specific 'platform capitalism' has taken shape in recent years.[112] As Nick Srnicek writes, corporate platforms are constantly seeking out 'new avenues for profit, new markets, new commodities, and new means of exploitation'.[113] To build an effective image of how platforms facilitate processes of capital valorization and accumulation, one has only to add *value* to 'size and strength' in the quote from Bratton we discussed above, where he writes that platforms 'gain size and strength by mediating unplanned and even unplannable interactions'.[114] Indeed, platform capitalism is driven in all its forms, from food-delivery apps to huge infrastructural platforms such as Google or Amazon, by a bulimic will to capture the widest possible spectrum of interactions. Data extractivism is the main tool used in such endeavour, in order to transform interactions into sources of value. Platforms rework the so-called *network effect*, a basic economic notion according to which the value of a product or service depends on the numbers of buyers or users. In the case of platforms, this generates a powerful expansive and even monopolizing push, which

110   Moritz Altenried, *The Digital Factory: The Labor of Automation*, Chicago: University of Chicago Press, 2022.

111   Trebor Scholz, *Platform Cooperativism: Challenging the Sharing Economy*, New York: Rosa Luxemburg Stiftung, 2016.

112   Niccolò Cuppini, Mattia Frapporti, Sandro Mezzadra, and Maurilio Pirone, 'Il capitalismo nel tempo delle piattaforme. Infrastrutture digitali, nuovi spazi e soggettività algoritmiche', *Rivista Italiana di Filosofia Politica* 2 (2022), 103–24.

113   Nick Srnicek, *Platform Capitalism*, Cambridge: Polity, 2017, 3.

114   Bratton, *The Stack*, 44.

leads some scholars to connect platform capitalism to the principle of *antimarket* that, for the French historian Fernand Braudel, runs through the whole history of modern capitalism.[115]

In the West, platform capitalism emerged in the wake of the financial crisis of 2007–8, when the generalized low-interest-rate environment built by central banks reduced the rate of return on a wide range of financial assets and prompted investors, so-called venture capitalists, to 'turn to increasingly risky assets'.[116] It is in this environment that platforms emerged as a new business model and a new type of firm, designed on the principle of intermediation between different user groups and on the infrastructural development that allows capturing and governing an expanding set of interactions for the sake of profit. The platform model, however, was far from remaining restricted to the West or from being simply exported by Western actors across countries and regions. In many parts of the world, including China, Russia, and Latin America, local companies played substantial roles in developing their own variants of the model, making their own contribution to a general process of platformization of economies and societies. The pace of this global process is amazing. If one considers the momentous implications of the platform model for the organization of labour, which we will discuss in a moment, it is striking to compare the decades long process of international transfer of such an important technical innovation as the 'scientific management of labour' with the few years that it took for the platformization of labour to spread across regions and continents. This says something about the nature of global space and contemporary capitalism. But, while platforms have a homogeneous core, what we call the platform model, the ways in which the model is implemented are profoundly heterogeneous and require analytical attention.

We already mentioned the huge variety of platforms operating even within a relatively homogeneous space, the differences in size, sector, and working mode that create frictions and hierarchies among them. At the pinnacle of the Western platform world (we resist calling it the Western Stack, considering the differences between the US and the European Union in the regulation of the digital realm) are the Big Five

---

115   Jamie Peck and Rachel Phillips, 'The Platform Conjuncture', *Sociologica* 14, no. 3 (2020), 73–99.

116   Srnicek, *Platform Capitalism*, 30.

– Alphabet-Google, Apple, Facebook (now Meta), Amazon, and Microsoft – that are often defined as 'infrastructural platforms', since they 'form the heart of the ecosystem upon which many other platforms and apps can be built'.[117] While the peculiar position of these platforms is apparent in their position as gatekeepers of a wide variety of infrastructural services, ranging from search engines to data centres, the reference to infrastructures grasps an important although differentially implemented aspect of *all* digital platforms. Digital space today is increasingly traversed by infrastructural avenues designed and controlled by platforms. As in the case of the highway famously discussed by Gilles Deleuze, such infrastructural avenues enable and intensify connectivity while at the same time multiplying 'the means of control'.[118] This allows us to qualify the meaning of intermediation in the operations of digital platforms. Far from being simply related to existing interactions, intermediation appears here to be structurally linked to the creation of new infrastructural avenues aimed at enhancing connectivity and creating new networks, although always following prescribed control protocols. Connectivity, which also means social cooperation, emerges as a privileged terrain for the valorization of capital today, although this process is far from being smooth.[119] The spread of the platform model across diverse societal domains, including health, education, care, and labour brokerage, transforms the management of connectivity into a crucial field of struggle. Profit-seeking corporate platforms in many parts of the world confront processes of mobilization and experiments of self-management that aim at reworking such platforms to reinvent public policies.[120]

As the Into the Black Box collective writes, platforms are indeed battlefields, 'in which trends of development unfold and with respect to which possible forms of alternative that do not bow to capitalism can

---

117 José van Dijck, Thomas Poel, and Martijn de Waal, *The Platform Society: Public Values in a Connective World*, Oxford: Oxford University Press, 2018, 13.

118 Gilles Deleuze, 'What Is the Creative Act?', in David Lapoujade (ed.), *Two Regimes of Madness: Texts and Interviews 1975–1995*, Cambridge, MA: Semiotext(e), 2006, 322.

119 See Vando Borghi, 'Capitalismo delle infrastrutture e connettività. Proposte per una sociologia critica del "mondo a domicilio"', *Rassegna Italiana di Sociologia* 62, no. 3 (2021), 671–99.

120 See, for instance, Ursula Huws, *Reinventing the Welfare State: Digital Platforms and Public Policies*, London: Pluto, 2020.

take shape'.[121] Platform workers have organized and struggled in many parts of the world, testing the limits of established unionism and inventing new forms of mobilization that work the boundary between circulation and reproduction.[122] While these struggles are vitally important, it is necessary to stress that the operations of platforms do not effect only the lives and labour of the people working for them. If one considers the infrastructural aspects of those operations, it becomes clear that they aim to shape society in its entirety, reorganizing it according to their rationality and logic. This is why it makes sense to speak of a *platform society*, remaining aware of the fact that such platformization is on the one hand a process that confronts a variety of resistances and frictions, and on the other hand it constitutes a project of specific capitalist actors.[123] Digital platforms produce their own operative spaces, which respond to the peculiarity of specific contexts while at the same time being coordinated and synchronized at the level of the cloud upon which the existence of those spaces is predicated. Urban spaces in particular are recoded, reorganized, and in a way 'doubled' by digital platforms, with implications that stretch far beyond the paradigmatic existence of single 'smart cities', with the result of transforming the experience of cities.[124] 'Platform urbanism' is a label that attempts to grasp the impact of digital platforms on these spaces, describing the multifarious ways in which the 'collective intelligence generated by millions of daily interactions with global digital platforms' spurs and transforms the design, experience, and governance of cities.[125] The spaces of platform urbanism are primarily spaces of circulation, striated by technological and social vectors that regulate the access to commodities and services. But they are also spaces in which social

---

121   Carlotta Benvegnù et al. (Into the Black Box), 'Platform Battlefield: Digital Infrastructures in Capitalism 4.0', *South Atlantic Quarterly* 120, no. 4 (2021), 689–702, 699.

122   See, for instance, Jamie Woodcock, 'The Limits of Algorithmic Management: On Platforms, Data, and Workers' Struggle', *South Atlantic Quarterly* 120, no. 4 (2021), 703–13.

123   Van Dijck, Poell, and De Waal, *The Platform Society*.

124   See Into the Black Box, *Futuro presente. I piani di Amazon*, Rome: Manifesto-libri, 2023, ch. 6.

125   Sarah Barns, *Platform Urbanism: Negotiating Platform Ecosystems in Connected Cities*, Singapore: Palgrave Macmillan, 2020. See also Peter Moertenboeck and Helge Moos-hammer (eds), *Platform Urbanism and Its Discontents*, Rotterdam: NAi Publishers, 2021.

reproduction is increasingly entangled with processes of circulation and platform labour, as feminist scholars such as Carlotta Benvegnù and Nelli Kambouri demonstrate in looking both at the increasing platformization of the feminized sectors of cleaning, domestic, and care work, for example, and at the composition of platform labour.[126]

The ways in which the platform model (and the working of specific platforms) have affected labour must be understood within the wider analytical framework of the societal dimensions of that model that we have outlined. Research in different parts of the world has highlighted similar effects of the spread of the platform model, including the further erosion of traditional employment models and established labour rights, the prevalence of piece wages, the blurring of the boundary between formal and informal economy, processes of feminization and racialization, high turnover rates, and participation of migrant labour.[127] Digital platforms clearly have different relations to labour, as it should be clear comparing a food-delivery app with Airbnb, but also in comparing two big infrastructural platforms such as Facebook (Meta) and Amazon. Nevertheless, as we anticipated, they are all supported by the working of algorithms, which play differentiated but equally relevant roles in the management of labour.[128] In Chapter 2 we already touched on debates surrounding the relation of continuity or discontinuity between the algorithmic management of labour and Taylorism. What matters more to us now is to stress that the algorithmic management of labour is a feature that characterizes platform labour but is increasingly reshaping work relations beyond any specific sector. It is from this point of view that it makes sense to use, in general terms, the concept of platformization – to grasp the spillover effects of the platform model, its constitutive tendency to reshape economies, societies, and systems of governance beyond any sectoral divide.[129] A second reason why the algorithmic

---

126   Carlotta Benvegnù and Nelli Kambouri, '"Platformization" beyond the Point of Production: Reproductive Labor and Gender Roles in the Ride-Hailing and Food-Delivery Sectors', *South Atlantic Quarterly* 120, no. 4 (2021), 733–47.

127   Sandro Mezzadra, 'Oltre il riconoscimento: Piatteforme digitali e metamorfosi del lavoro', *Filosofia politica* 35, no. 3 (2021), 487–502.

128   See Altenried, *The Digital Factory*.

129   Antonio A. Casilli and Julián Posada Gutiérrez, 'The Platformization of Labor and Society', in Mark Graham and William Dutton (eds), *Society and the Internet: How Networks of Information and Communication Are Changing Our Lives*, 2nd edn, Oxford: Oxford University Press, 2019, 293–306.

management of labour is important here is that it allows us to hark back to the question of data extractivism, upon which it is predicated. Indeed, looking at processes of valorization of platform capital, data extractivism and related forms of dispossession stand out as a key source of value besides the exploitation of labour. What we need to add is that labour does not refer here to a fixed stock of workers employed by platforms, but rather to a floating multitude of potential workers whose availability shapes the management calculation of platforms and intensifies the exploitation of the 'collective worker', of cooperation.[130]

While the impact of platforms on labour displays some similarities across world regions and continents, the institutional settings, technical operations, and societal positionings vary significantly. The call to 'de-Westernize' platform studies reflects such variegation of political, social, and even technological landscapes.[131] From China to India, Korea to Russia, Mexico to Brazil, we have witnessed a spread of the platform model and a rapid growth of home-based online platforms that challenge the very possibility to take Western instances as a norm. In China, in particular, platforms including Alibaba, Baidu, and WeChat – even before the recent tightening of state control – had to negotiate their operations with 'a plethora of regulatory bodies, interventionist policies, compliance regimes, loan schemes, tax incentives, and censorship measures that helps steer the development of Chinese media'.[132] As the examples of Alibaba and Tencent demonstrate, the peculiarity of state–market relations in China inflects the variegation of platform capitalism, both within the country and across wider regional landscapes.[133] Nonetheless, the platformization of Chinese labour and economy has proceeded in rapid and powerful ways over recent years. Kevin Lin and Pun Ngai provide, for instance, a detailed analysis of the ways in which 'new platform-based companies have been taking over traditional economic activities, including logistics, and restructuring

---

130   Federico de Stavola, 'Al Sur de la plataforma: trabajo y capital en la app latino-americana Rappi', PhD diss., Universidad Nacional Autónoma de México, 2022; Sandro Mezzadra, 'Potenzialità dell'esercito industriale di riserva', *Cartografie sociali* 15 (2023), 167–80.

131   Mark Davis and Jian Xiao, 'De-Westernizing Platform Studies: History and Logics of Chinese and US Platforms', *International Journal of Communication* 15 (2021), 103–22.

132   Ibid., 107.

133   Zhang and Chen, 'A Regional and Historical Approach to Platform Capitalism'.

labor relations and the labor process'.[134] They focus, against the background of a truck drivers' strike across China in June 2018 (consisting
mainly of internal and rural migrants), on the emergence of mega-apps
such as Yun Man Man, which matches millions of truck drivers (mostly
independent contractors) with shippers, and that is profoundly transforming the transportation industry in the country. Importantly, Lin
and Pun understand the 2018 strike as a key instance of new labour
struggle within and against the process that, in the wake of the Great
Recession of 2007–8, has led China to become 'the empire of logistics'.[135]
Such a process is key both to the Communist Party's new theory of
'double circulation', which aims at boosting domestic consumption, and
to the stretching of the economic space of the Chinese pole to create
new markets for Chinese goods. The notion of 'infrastructural capitalism', proposed by Lin and Pun to describe the present socio-economic
situation in China, underscores 'the production and expansion of intersecting physical and digital infrastructures' that disrupt and transform
existing spatial arrangements and spur rapid processes of platformization and a further proliferation of operative spaces.[136] Processes of
platformization run across these spaces, whether reorganizing traditional sectors (such as the garment industry) through the pressure of
e-commerce, promoting platform-based entrepreneurship in metropolitan centres, or through the expansion of digital platforms and labour
into the Chinese countryside.[137]

134   Kevin Lin and Pun Ngai, 'Mobilizing Truck Drivers in China: New Migrant
Struggle and the Emergence of Infrastructural Capitalism', *South Atlantic Quarterly* 120,
no. 3 (2021), 647–54.
135   Ibid., 650.
136   Ibid., 651.
137   Lulu Fan, 'The Forming of E-platform-driven Flexible Specialisation: How
E-commerce Platforms Have Changed China's Garment Industry Supply Chains and
Labour Relations', *China Perspectives* 1 (2021), 29–37; Lin Zhang, *The Labor of Reinvention: Entrepreneurship in the New Chinese Digital Economy*, New York: Columbia
University Press, 2023.

5

Poles of Struggle

Relations of power

Our analysis of war, centrifugal multipolarity, and operative spaces in the previous two chapters has revolved around issues that are usually tackled from the perspectives of geopolitics or international relations. As we discuss in the introduction, such perspectives focus on states, great power, and even landmasses as historical agents. While we emphasize the tensions between territorialism and capitalism in the contemporary world and the need to go beyond a unilaterally territorial understanding of poles, labels such as Russia, the West, China and the US figure prominently in our efforts to make sense of the present conflicts and turmoil at the global level. And rightly so, we can add, since national forces and international alliances (NATO, among others) continue to play important roles in the workings and articulation of capitalism, which become even more pronounced in an age of pandemic and war. Nevertheless, we have methodically attempted to decentre our investigation of states and great powers, showing that their politics is at once enabled and limited, spurred by and enmeshed in a wider fabric of capital flow and operations that we analysed in some detail in the previous chapter. Our concept of political capitalism leads us to interrogate the way in which politics is understood also in the international realm, since states are far from being able to claim a monopoly on its definition. In so doing, we follow the elaboration of a critical geopolitics in the past decades, or more recently 'hidden geopolitics', which unpacks rigid territorial assumptions of mainstream analyses of international politics and challenges the conventional state-centred conception of power.[1] Our focus on capital, however, allows us to go beyond such approaches and to focus attention on the myriad conflicts surrounding the operations of capital, which appear to us as constitutive moments in the dynamics of world politics. Even more generally, we are convinced that, to grasp such dynamics fully, there is a need to move from an analysis of the power relations between states to an analysis of the power relations between classes not simply within states but crucially *across* states, in the emergent constitution of poles.

In the late 1920s, in an age of early geopolitical enthusiasm, the German historian Eckart Kehr claimed in a series of essays the 'primacy of internal politics' as a guiding thread for historical analysis of imperialism, to show 'to what extent German foreign politics before the Great War has been driven by the social structure of the Reich'.[2] Reversing the formula introduced by Leopold von Ranke, who had famously celebrated the primacy of foreign politics, Kehr highlights the crucial relevance of social dynamics underlying the peculiar development of capitalism in Germany, including class struggle, and shifting alliances between the bourgeoisie and agrarian nobles (*Junker*), to understand processes of land and naval re-armament as well as international relations between powers such as England and Russia. Although his work is focused on a single nation-state, the theoretical underpinning of Kehr's research agenda remains valid today and deserves further elaboration both with respect to the power dynamics of specific states and the processes that spur the formation of poles. In doing so, we repeat that we follow Marx in considering capital primarily as a social relation, or as an array of social relations within which 'living labour', famously defined in the *Grundrisse* as the other of capital – as 'non-capital' – plays a constitutive role.[3] Over recent decades, a history of struggles and related

---

1 See Klaus Dodds, Merje Kuus, and Joanne Sharp (eds), *The Ashgate Companion to Critical Geopolitics*, London: Routledge, 2013; John Agnew, *Hidden Geopolitics: Governance in a Globalized World*, London: Rowman and Littlefield, 2023.

2 Eckart Kehr, *Das Primat der Innenpolitik. Gesammelte Aufsätze zur preußisch-deutschen Sozialgeschichte im 19. Und 20. Jahrhundert*, Frankfurt am Main: Ullstein, 1970, 150 (the essay from which we quote was originally published in 1928).

3 Karl Marx, *Grundrisse: Foundations of the Critique of Political Economy*, trans. Martin Nicolaus, Harmondsworth: Penguin, 1973, 272–4.

theoretical elaborations have taught us to expand the understanding of living labour, as well as of class struggle. Our own discussion of circulation and reproduction in Chapter 2 registers such expansion and points to the importance of the very boundary between labour and life as a crucial site of struggle. Once we become aware of the relevance of environmental and natural conditions for the reproduction of capital, movements for climate justice become key actors in any political coalition to confront capitalism. Moreover, there is a need to take stock of the mutations of labour that correspond to the mutations of capital that we have been discussing thus far, of the intensification of social cooperation at the juncture between circulation, reproduction, and production that broadly characterizes the working of contemporary capitalism. While it is important to repeat that such mutations take different shapes across world regions and continents, the further entrenchment of capital operations within wide networks of social cooperation challenges any understanding of so-called standard employment relations and multiplies figures and conditions of labour. 'Floating', 'latent', and 'stagnant' forms of life, to borrow Marx's terminology for 'surplus population' in *Capital*, volume 1, provide today an adequate description of a significant part of the composition of living labour across the divide between global North and South.[4]

When we talk of struggles, with respect to the heterogeneous multitude that composes contemporary living labour and its diverse geographical and political instantiations, we do not have in mind only open moments of dispute, insurgency, and rebellion, such as the ones we analyse in this chapter. Nor do we restrict our analysis to strikes and riots. We understand struggles as the manifold behaviours and practices through which subaltern and exploited populations test the limits of the social relation of capital, inscribe their claims onto existing structures of power, and appropriate spaces to make a living, often in the interstices of capitalism. While open and explicit struggles cannot emerge without the basis laid by these behaviours and practices, there are, of course,

---

4   Karl Marx, *Capital*, vol. 1, trans. Ben Fowkes, New York: Vintage Books, 1977, 794. See also Sandro Mezzadra, 'Potenzialità dell'esercito industriale di riserva', *Cartografie sociali* 15 (2023), 167–80; Sahan Savasli Karatasli, 'Surplus Population, Working-Class Struggles, and Crises of Capitalism: A World-Historical Materialist Reconceptualization', in Adrián Piva and Augustín Santella (eds), *Marxism, Social Movements, and Collective Action*, London: Palgrave Macmillan, 2023, 207–49.

important differences between the two. Nonetheless, no attempt to update Kehr's primacy of internal politics can be successful without taking stock of their interrelation, of the ways in which these diverse forms of struggle and subaltern politics shape the terrain in which foreign politics is forged. Conversely, there is a need to stress that war and regimes of war historically serve as occasions to curb and even annihilate social and labour struggles to reinforce national unity. The Great War, with the proclamation of the Union sacrée in France and the Burgfrieden in Germany, provides a kind of paradigmatic example in this respect. In our present there is no shortage of resonances with this phenomenon, ranging from the reactionary civilizational rhetoric employed by Russia's President Putin to the Westernizing 'identity politics' prevailing in Ukraine during the war.[5] This effect of war demonstrates the constitutive role of social dynamics and struggles for the field of international politics, and vice versa. It also shows the ways in which political backlash creates drastic shrinkage and even erasure of spaces of freedom and equality; war and regimes of war always bring about a violent disciplining of social behaviours.

It may be easy, although not incontestable, to demonstrate the relevance of social struggles in spurring, influencing, and limiting the foreign policy of single nation-states. But what about the formation and dynamics of poles? After all, the common sense goes, there is no class struggle in the international realm. We want to challenge this common sense and make the case for an analysis of the processes of pole formation that emphasizes the roles played by struggles and social dynamics. In doing so, we draw inspiration from theories of imperialism and dependence that stress the need to go beyond the established national nomenclature of spaces, to analyse axes of power and struggle that structurally exceed the political space of the state. These theories, David Slater writes, are 'part of a vital project of *counter*-representation' that we find inspiring, even as we recognize their shortcomings and limits.[6] At least since the Bandung Conference of 1955, notions such as the periphery, the Third World, the Tricontinental, and later the global

---

5   See Ilya Budraitskis, *Dissidents among Dissidents: Ideology, Politics, and the Left in Post-Soviet Russia*, London: Verso, 2022; and Volodymyr Ishchenko, 'Ukrainian Voices', *New Left Review* 138 (2022), 1–10.

6   David Slater, *Geopolitics and the Post-Colonial: Rethinking North-South Relations*, Oxford: Blackwell, 2004, 119.

South have moved to the centre of a geographical imagination that charts emerging spaces of struggle.[7] Anticolonial struggles, while aiming at national independence, were played out in larger spaces, and characterized by a whole set of entanglements foreshadowed by the Pan African tradition and theories of Negritude.[8] Speaking of liberation movements in the African continent, Frantz Fanon wrote in 1958 of 'a kind of illuminating and sacred communication' among the colonized and of the 'necessary interdependence of the liberation movements'.[9] This is not to deny Fanon's focus on national liberation. It is, rather, to signal the wider scope of his politics, which corresponds to widespread tendencies within anticolonial struggles, and which becomes relevant once we acknowledge that the success of anticolonial movements has been severely limited by the 'constraints' of the interstate system.[10]

This is an important point, to which we will return in the concluding section of this chapter, where we also analyse instances of internationalism beyond the imaginary and constraints of the nation and the interstate system. For now, we want to stress that focusing on axes of power and domination that operate beyond the coded spaces of the international world opens an angle on the role of class and social struggles that stretches beyond national borders. What matters here is not only, say, the circulation across national borders of feminist movements or the supposedly global scale of activism for climate justice, on which we will have something more to say in the following pages. Such forms of struggle are important also because they creatively foreshadow and produce new spaces. Beyond that, however, we need to pay attention to more elusive forms of struggle and social dynamics, investigating social behaviours of subaltern and exploited figures that tend to become homogeneous within the space of an emergent pole, or that remain largely heterogeneous – in both cases potentially stoking a source of

---

7   See Anne Garland Mahler, *From the Tricontinental to the Global South: Race, Radicalism, and Transnational Solidarity*, Durham, NC: Duke University Press, 2018.

8   See Gary Wilder, *Freedom Time: Negritude, Decolonization, and the Future of the World*, Durham, NC: Duke University Press, 2015.

9   Frantz Fanon, *Toward the African Revolution: Political Essays*, New York: Grove Press, 1994, 145.

10   Giovanni Arrighi, Terence K. Hopkins, and Immanuel Wallerstein, *Antisystemic Movements*, London: Verso, 1989, 27.

frictions or conflicts. In any case, the formation of a pole generates and is generated by struggles.

While class struggle is rarely analysed in the international realm, the international dimensions of class formation are an unescapable factor in the modern world, considering the relevance of migration for the making and unmaking of the working classes, both at points of departure and at points of arrival. Our previous work on this topic is part of a process of politicization of migration and mobility, which emphasizes that the challenge raised by the movement of migrants to many aspects of international and internal borders should be understood as fully fledged form of struggle.[11] Several scholars and activists participate in this process of politicization, which combines Marxian and Foucauldian insights to come to terms with the role of labour mobility in historical capitalism and to discern the ensuing political stakes.[12] This approach, along with the study of the specific operative spaces within which governmental efforts to steer migration take place, has been influential on the theoretical work and political interventions in migration and border struggles in many parts of the world.[13] From the angle of class formation, migration raises the question of the spatiality of the reproduction of labour power, which becomes even more important considering the relevance of global care chains and female migrant labour for social reproduction across diverse geographical scales.[14] 'For an economy to

11   Sandro Mezzadra and Brett Neilson, *Border as Method, or, the Multiplication of Labor*, Durham, NC: Duke University Press, 2013.

12   See Yann Moulier Boutang, *De l'esclavage au salariat. Économie historique du salariat bride*, Paris: Puf, 1998; and Michel Foucault, *The Punitive Society: Lectures at the Collège de France, 1975–76*, New York: Picador, 2015.

13   See, for instance, Ranabir Samaddar, *Marginal Nation – Trans-border Migration from Bangladesh to India*, New Delhi: Sage Publications, 1999; Nicholas De Genova, Glenda Garelli, and Martina Tazzioli, 'Autonomy of Asylum? The Autonomy of Migration Undoing Refugee Crisis Script', *South Atlantic Quarterly* 117, no. 2 (2018), 239–64; and Sandro Mezzadra, Blanca Cordero, and Amarela Varela (eds), *América Latina en Movimiento. Migraciones, Límites a la Movilidad y sus Desbordamientos*, Madrid: Traficantes de Sueños, 2019. On the operative spaces of migration governance, see Bernd Kasparek, *Europa als Grenze. Eine Ethnographie der Grenzschutz-Agentur Frontex*, Bielefeld: Transcript, 2021.

14   See Arlie Hochschild, 'Global Care Chains and Emotional Surplus Value', in Will Hutton and Anthony Giddens (eds), *On the Edge: Living with Global Capitalism*, London: Jonathan Cape, 2000, 130–46; and Enrica Rigo, *La straniera. Migrazioni, asilo, sfruttamento in una prospettiva di genere*, Rome: Carocci, 2022.

function', Michael Burawoy writes in a now classic essay, 'a labor force has to be maintained and renewed.'[15] In capitalism, the difference between the processes of maintenance and renewal is usually concealed because the same social institutions and the same labour perform the two functions. The organization of migrant labour, Burawoy explains, makes this difference apparent when the national stock of labour force needs to be integrated from the outside, as is often the case in capitalism. In that moment the two processes of maintenance and renewal 'take place in geographically separate locations', because renewal – a crucial aspect of reproduction – is outsourced to the homelands of migrants and an 'international' dimension becomes a constitutive part of class formation.[16]

This internalization of an international dimension within the nation can take many different forms, well beyond those analysed by Burawoy, who was writing at the moment of incipient crisis of Fordism in the US. The geography and temporality of contemporary recruitment schemes of migrant labour are scattered, fractured, and organized according to a 'just-in-time and to-the-point' rationality that reshuffles the geography of class formation.[17] Nonetheless, the question remains crucial. Investigating the movements and composition of labour migration in the Gulf, Adam Hanieh stresses that class formation in that region, which is so relevant for multipolarity today, 'is necessarily spatialized', since it includes not only a multitude of migrant workers but also 'the enormous numbers of *potential* workers who constitute a labour pool for the Gulf' around its multiple peripheries.[18] This is a challenging description of how migration continues to shape class formation across countries and regions. While there is a need to ask whether the geographies of migration will be further reorganized in the emergent multipolar world, it is also important to emphasize that movements of migration are never

15   Michael Burawoy, 'The Functions and Reproduction of Migrant Labor: Comparative Materials from Southern Africa and the United States', *American Journal of Sociology* 81, no. 5 (1976), 1051.

16   Ibid., 1052.

17   See Xiang Biao, 'Labor Transplant: "Point-to-Point" Transnational Labor Migration in East Asia', *South Atlantic Quarterly* 111, no. 4 (2012), 721–39.

18   Adam Hanieh, 'Overcoming Methodological Nationalism: Spatial Perspectives on Migration to the Gulf Arab States', in Abdulhadi Khalaf, Omar AlShehabi, and Adam Hanieh, (eds), *Transit States: Labour, Migration and Citizenship in the Gulf*, London: Pluto Press, 2015, 66–7.

fully contained by governmental practices of steering and acceleration, slowing down, diverting, and even stopping, which often has lethal consequences. This combination of biopolitics and necropolitics may be instantiated by the poles of the 'global compacts for safe, orderly and regular migration' on the one hand, and on the other by myriad forms of detention, kidnapping, and abandonment to death. But while such a combination shapes migration and border regimes across the globe, it must always confront the political dimension of migration, the subjective claims, behaviours, and struggles that permeate its dynamics.[19] Moreover, as studies of transnational migration have signalled since the 1990s, migration is also a creative force in view of its capacity to produce new spaces.[20] Such production of space cuts through processes of pole formation in the contemporary world and opens an angle on the political stakes and social dynamics that at the same time enable and limit those processes. Migration is not simply an important issue in itself, therefore; it also provides an effective lens to investigate emergent multipolarity in the contemporary world.

Issues of coloniality and decoloniality continue to haunt movements of migration. Analysing the new 'planetary' dimensions of migration within the African continent, Achille Mbembe writes that 'decolonization will not be accomplished until every African has the right to freedom of movement throughout the continent'.[21] He stresses the complicity between the 'glaciation of colonial boundaries' in Africa and the border regimes of Europe, which have turned 'the body of the African, of every individual African, and of all Africans' into 'a racial class that is now the border of Europe'. Against the 'bantustanization' of Africa, Mbembe envisages the constitution of a new continental space across borders, sustained by movements of migration and capable of negotiating anew its relations with Europe as well as with China. The reference to China is important here, since Chinese migrants increasingly

---

19   See Claudia Aradau and Martina Tazzioli, 'Biopolitics Multiple: Migration, Extraction, Subtraction', *Millennium: Journal of International Studies* 48, no. 2 (2020), 198–220.

20   See Ayse Caglar, 'Transnational Migration', in Anna Triandafyllidou (ed.), *Routledge Handbook of Immigration and Refugee Studies*, 2nd edn, London: Routledge, 2022, 34–43.

21   Achille Mbembe, 'Les Africains doivent se purger du désir d'Europe', *Le Monde*, 10 February 2019.

settle in Africa, while 'African trade colonies' pop up in Asian metropolises. We find Mbembe's intervention illuminating because it provides an instance of radical imagination that takes seriously the challenges of multipolarity. In continuity with previous traditions of Pan Africanism, it foreshadows the emergence of an African space that becomes a pole spurred and sustained by social dynamics among which migration and mobility figure prominently. Moreover, it points to the need to establish transversal relations with other poles (in this case, Europe and China) in terms that go beyond any traditional understanding of international relations. And, to repeat, it emphasizes the constitutive role of migration in the present multipolar world.

As Mbembe's reference to African bodies as the real border of Europe suggests, the management of migration today takes forms that curtail its creative force and aim simply to produce an exploitable, often racialized and feminized labour force, while restricting spaces of legal protection for refugees. In many world regions, from the Mediterranean to the borderlands between the US and Mexico, from the Bay of Bengal to the southern reaches of Mexico, border regimes are hardening to the point that they intensify what we have called above their necropolitical dimensions, meaning that they produce thousands of deaths each year. Moreover, in the wake of the COVID-19 outbreak, we have witnessed a proliferation of conditions requiring migrants to wait, to be held, and often to be detained.[22] This does not mean that their roles in social reproduction, and, for that matter, in many productive realms, have been lessened. Social relations surrounding migration have become tighter, exacerbating disciplining rhetoric and processes in ways that have in many places become more acute with the war and the related spread of regimes of war. This is a circumstance that raises important questions regarding Russia, where both internal migration and migration from neighbouring countries, including Ukraine, have been in recent decades a key aspect of the composition of labour in production and reproduction.[23] A reorganization of the geographies of migration is clearly a stake in the Ukraine war, and the importance of consolidating

---

22   Sandro Mezzadra and Brett Neilson, 'The Capitalist Virus', *Politics* 44, no. 2 (2024), 188–202.

23   See Aleksandra A. Renoire, 'The Road to the East: Ukrainian Workers in Russia after 2014', Medium, 11 October 2019, alexarenoire.medium.com.

the Russian Federation, often stressed by Putin, must also be considered with respect to the dynamics of internal labour mobility.

In any case, the nationalist rhetoric surrounding war, militarization, and war regimes has a violent impact on movements of migration. This impact is often connected to efforts to reinforce patriarchal regimes through demographic policies that stress the role of women as birth-givers, bearing the burden of the reproduction of the nation.[24] While a 'pronatalist' rhetoric was widespread in Russia long before the invasion of Ukraine, elsewhere in the world conservative discourses proclaiming a so-called Great Replacement incite women to give birth in response to the supposed demographic crisis and civilizational challenge caused by migration.[25] Taken together, these processes and dynamics regarding migration, gender, and nation not only reinforce the borders of specific states but also foster the territorialization of poles, which is to say that they bolster the relevance of the logic of territoriality in their constitution. This becomes clear when we look at the massive exodus from Ukraine in the wake of Russia's invasion of the country, as well as at the attitudes of European states. A few months before the war broke out, in October 2021, the Polish government reacted in a violent and brutal way to the arrival of a few thousand migrants from Africa and the greater Middle East who had crossed the Polish–Belarusian border, an event probably orchestrated by Alexander Lukashenko's regime.[26] Fences, walls, and manhunting were the tools deployed, consistent with an anti-immigration discourse that is particularly strong in Poland. The scene was completely different when hundreds of thousands of Ukrainians, largely women, crossed the Polish border in late February of the following year. They were welcomed as fellow Europeans – and even because 'they look like us' – joining hands against Russia. That race was at stake in these dynamics is exposed by the fact that African students fleeing from Ukraine were denied access to Polish territory.[27] In the

24   Nira Yuval-Davis, *Gender and Nation*, London: Sage, 1997.

25   Michele Rivkin-Fish, 'Pronatalism, Gender Politics, and the Renewal of Family Support in Russia: Toward a Feminist Anthropology of "Maternity Capital"', *Slavic Review* 69, no. 3 (2010), 701–24.

26   See Zahide Erdoğan and Zuhal Karakoç Dora, 'Belarus-Poland Migration Crisis and Supra-National Political Concerns of the Extended Actors', *Güvenlik Bilimleri Dergisi* 11, no. (2022), 417–40; and the impressive film *Green Border* by Agnieszka Holland (2023).

27   See for instance Moustafa Bayoumi, 'They Are "Civilized" and "Look Like Us": The Racist Coverage of Ukraine', *Guardian*, 2 March 2022.

following months, this attitude was reproduced in many European countries by measures that privileged Ukrainians over other refugees, foreshadowing new civilizational and ultimately racial hierarchies in European migration.[28] And while in Ukraine men are not allowed to leave the country due to the patriotic obligation to fight, women continue to escape, joining Ukrainian communities in European countries that have served for many years as crucial reserves of domestic and care labour.

Class writ large

Race and gender are always at stake in the working of border and migration regimes as well as in struggles of migration. More generally, in recent years and in different parts of the world, powerful movements have addressed the constitutive character of racism and patriarchy for the historical development and current formation of capitalism. In Chapter 2, we argued that the question of how social oppression crosses the accumulation of capital is increasingly understood in an intersectional frame. We also explained how approaching labour power as an embodied capacity allows us to go beyond a merely economistic understanding of capitalism, which also means rethinking rather than abandoning the notion of exploitation.[29] From this perspective, intersectionality appears as a crucial tool for analysing the shifting composition of living labour in the contemporary world. This same concept also enables a rethinking of the notion of class from the point of view of what Michael Hardt and Antonio Negri call a 'political theory of multiplicity'.[30] Gone are the days in which class could be conceived in terms of homogeneous categories due to the leading position of a section of the proletariat, be it the working class described by Marx in *Capital*,

---

28   See for instance David De Coninck, 'The Refugee Paradox during Wartime in Europe: How Ukrainian and Afghan Refugees Are (Not) Alike', *International Migration Review* 57, no. 2 (2022), 578–86.

29   Sandro Mezzadra and Brett Neilson, 'Entre extraction et exploitation: des mutations en cours dans l'organisation de la coopération sociale', *Actuel Marx* 63, no. 1 (2018), 97–113.

30   Michael Hardt and Antonio Negri, 'Empire, Twenty Years On', *New Left Review* 120 (2019), 85.

volume 1, in his visionary analysis of 'large-scale industry' or the 'mass worker' theorized by Italian *operaismo* in the 1960s. There is no shortage of analogous processes of homogenization of labour today, and they may well nurture important waves of struggle.[31] But such processes do not foreshadow a general tendency. The composition of living labour is highly heterogeneous and must be investigated in ways sensitive to the peculiarities of the context under scrutiny. To take two important examples: in Chinese as much as in US metropolises, class today is traversed by an array of differences synchronized in various forms by the imperative of the valorization of capital and related manifestations of power and command. The unity of class as a subversive subject and a transformative power is a riddle under such conditions – a riddle that requires a collective investment of theoretical work, analytical investigation, and political invention.

In the next section, we will investigate instances of labour struggle, in particular at the intersection of circulation and reproduction; but in this section, we discuss movements and political dynamics seemingly unrelated to the question of class, or as we prefer to say relevant to the issue of class writ large. Nonetheless, the first two instances of struggle that we address – the Movement for Black Lives in the US in 2020 and the feminist mobilizations that swept Argentina beginning in 2015, and rapidly expanded to the Latin American region under the heading Ni Una Menos (Not One Less) – tackled the question of labour by reframing it from the angle of the radical politicization of a specific difference. In separate but related ways, both movements instantiated the building of powerful intersectional coalitions as relatively new political forms. In the US, there was no shortage of antecedents for such coalitions, in black politics as well as in the history of feminist and queer movements prioritizing what Audre Lorde calls 'the house of difference' over 'any one particular difference'.[32] Moreover, the emergence of Black Lives Matter in 2013, after the acquittal of the murderer of African American teenager Trayvon Martin the previous year, had already transformed the ground of black politics in the US. The protests and riots in the city of

---

31 See Immanuel Ness, *Southern Insurgency: The Coming of the Global Working Class*, London: Pluto Press, 2016.

32 Audre Lorde, *Zami: A New Spelling of My Name*, New York: Crossing Press, 1982, 226.

Ferguson, Missouri, in 2014, following the shooting by a white policeman of Michael Brown, acted as the 'catalyst' for a new movement,
animated by a new generation of young activists against state-sanctioned
violence, and with a 'face' largely 'queer and female'.[33] Ferguson was also
important as a moment to revisit and reinvent histories and traditions of
black internationalism. It reminds us, Angela Davis wrote in the wake of
the riots, 'that we have to globalize our thinking' about issues of racism,
strategies of policing, and the colonial occupation of territories, as in
Palestine, for example.[34] The renewed interest in the notion of 'racial
capitalism' was also an outcome of this political conjuncture.[35]

While the mobilizations and struggles of previous years provided an
important organizational terrain, a political language, and a rich fabric
of street experience, the murder of George Floyd in Minneapolis on 25
May 2020, once more by a white policeman, acted again as the catalyst
for a significantly new movement, concentrated in time but extremely
wide and diverse in composition. The movement for Black Lives that
shook the US, with important resonances in many parts of the world
(from Brazil to France, from the UK the choppy waters of the Mediterranean, where migrant rescue organizations began to use the language
of the US movement), was one of the most visible social and political
struggles amid the COVID-19 pandemic.[36] This movement must also
be understood as a reaction to the disproportionate burden of the pandemic on black communities (as well as on Latinx people and native
Americans). What is striking in the dynamics of the movement is that
the leading role of African Americans, as at other times in US history,
opened spaces within which a multitude of other subjects (starting with
the minorities most affected by the pandemic) could articulate their
claims and contribute to the formation of a diverse and therefore powerful coalition on the streets. The legacy of slavery and the issue of
structural racism as well as police violence were never forgotten in the

---

33   Keeanga-Yamatta Taylor, *From #Blacklivesmatter to Black Liberation*, Chicago:
Haymarket Books, 2016, 153 and 165.

34   Angela Davis, *Freedom Is a Constant Struggle: Ferguson, Palestine, and the
Foundations of a Movement*, Chicago: Haymarket Books, 2016, 13.

35   See Gaye Theresa Johnson and Alex Lubin (eds), *Futures of Black Radicalism*,
London: Verso, 2017.

36   Barnor Hesse and Debra Thompson, 'Anti-Blackness – Dispatches from Black
Political Thought', *South Atlantic Quarterly* 121, no. 3 (2022), 447–75.

thousands of demonstrations that followed the assassination of George Floyd, and his name was repeatedly spelled out along with the names of other victims of police brutality. But wider issues of social justice were also addressed, from the struggle against the violence of the border to migrant workers' claims, from feminist claims to questions of housing, health, and education. The 'horizon' of abolition and 'abolition democracy', a notion introduced in the 1930s by W. E. B. Du Bois that continues to inspire black political thought in the US, was expanded to foreshadow a radical programme of social transformation.[37] To this one may add that, at least in the first phase of the protests, there was a conversation (rather than an opposition) between the nocturnal scene of the riot and the daylight context of massive and largely peaceful mass demonstrations. Both forms of action appear in a different light once this is considered, as distinct from any aestheticization of riots or demonization of violence.

This is not the place to dwell on the aftermath of the Movement for Black Lives in 2020, or to analyse the ways in which it interacted with the presidential elections of the same year and with the defeat of Trump. Nor will we discuss the early adoption and subsequent rejection of such slogans as 'Defund the Police' by sections of the Democratic Party and metropolitan governments. Structural racism remains an issue of heated controversy and hard struggle in the US, while police violence continues disproportionately to target and kill black bodies. Remaining aware of this, our aim here is more limited and consists in fleshing out the contours of a proliferation of struggles that led amid the social crisis of COVID-19 to the emergence of a coalition (or of a number of coalitions) capable of taking the widespread indignation over the murder of George Floyd as a basis for the formulation on the streets of an advanced programme of political transformation. Something similar happened in Argentina under different conditions, beginning in 2015 with the new feminist mobilizations that popularized the slogan 'Ni Una Menos' well beyond the borders of that country. We will have more to say in the concluding section of this chapter regarding the ways in which those mobilizations created new spaces of feminist struggle at the regional scale in Latin America. For now, it is important to stress that the

---

37   Charmaine Chua, 'Abolition Is a Constant Struggle', *Theory and Event* 23, no. 4 suppl. (2020), 127–47.

movement was spurred by indignation about the astonishing number of femicides in Argentina, an indignation that exploded with the murder of the fourteen-year-old teenager Chiara Páez in May 2015. Mass marches in most Argentinean cities laid the basis for the development of a movement that in the following years has profoundly transformed, although not in uncontested ways, a traditionally patriarchal and macho society. Half a decade of Ni Una Menos protests, as well as a targeted mass mobilization on reproductive rights, proved pivotal to the historic legalization of abortion in the first fourteen weeks of pregnancy by the Argentinian Congress in December 2020 – a victory that ultraright president Javier Milei, elected in 2023, will find it hard to reverse.[38] Crucially, the Ni Una Menos agenda has continued to foreground sexual violence. But it has also approached the violence of rape and other forms of sexual abuse in ways that have enabled a deepening and widening of the struggle's scope to encompass social and economic issues as well as the legacy of colonialism in the region. Even more importantly, this 'pluralization of violence' has led Ni Una Menos to break the traditional boundaries of middle-class feminism and to include women working in popular and informal economies, those living in poor neighbourhoods and slums, as well as migrant and Indigenous women.[39]

This heterogeneous and motley composition of the feminist subject in Argentina has shaped the history of social struggles in that country in recent years, compelling labour unions among other political actors to come to terms with feminist language and demands. A crucial element of the Ni Una Menos mobilization has been the appropriation and reinvention of a traditional labour movement tool: the strike. Taking inspiration from the women's strike against the criminalization of abortion in Poland in 2016, Argentinian feminists made 8 March a day of feminist strike, with mass participation and international resonances in several places, including the US, Spain, and Italy. Claiming the strike as an 'exercise of withdrawal and massive sabotage' was primarily a way to refuse a condition of victimhood. At the same time, in the words of Verónica Gago, the feminist strike 'shaped an organizational horizon

---

38   Camilla Reuterswärd and Cora Fernandez Anderson, 'Why Milei Won't Succeed in Repealing Argentina's Abortion Policy', *The Loop*, 5 December 2023, theloop. ecpr.eu.

39   See Verónica Gago, *Feminist International: How to Change Everything*, London: Verso, 2020, chapter 2.

that allowed for hosting multiple realities that resignified, challenged, and updated the dynamic of what constitutes a strike itself'.[40] The feminist strike politicizes intersectionality, demonstrating the limits of the traditional labour strike by shedding light on profound mutations of labour as well as on figures and activities that have long remained invisible to unions. In this way, feminism provides an angle on emerging intersections of labour and life, which cut through the boundaries between production and reproduction, and the formal and informal economy, and instantiate in an effective way what Marina Montanelli calls 'the unforeseen subject of the feminist strike'.[41] In an age in which the feminization of work extends even beyond the crucial domain of social reproduction, the feminist strike in and beyond Argentina is for us a crucial experience and at the same time an invaluable contribution to the rethinking of class politics in the present.

Feminist and women's struggles are manifold and widespread across the globe, crossing national spaces and necessarily intersecting processes of pole formation. The mass mobilizations in Iran in the wake of the assassination of Mahsa Amini in September 2022 stand out as particularly relevant, considering both the dramatic nature of the confrontations (that led to hundreds of dead and wounded demonstrators) and the country's peculiar position in the Greater Middle East. In Chapter 3, we mentioned the processes of neoliberalization and precarization of labour that have characterized the peculiar capitalist formation in Iran since the 1990s. Such processes have profoundly transformed Iranian society, from the metropolitan spaces of Tehran to the country's manifold peripheries. The determination of the young people who participated in demonstrations that went on for months, the tactics employed to confront the regime's security forces, and the creative language and performances within the movement bear witness to processes of subjectivation deeply rooted within the new conjuncture. These factors enabled a qualitative leap with respect to previous instances of mobilization such as the 2009 Green Wave. Women, more often than not young girls, were at the forefront of struggle, performing such

---

40   Verónica Gago, '#WeStrike: Notes Toward a Political Theory of the Feminist Strike', *South Atlantic Quarterly* 117, no. 3 (2018), 663.

41   See Marina Montanelli, 'The Unforeseen Subject of the Feminist Strike', *South Atlantic Quarterly* 117, no. 3 (2018), 699–709.

defiant acts as the removal or even the burning of headscarves in public or the cutting of hair. As Eskandar Sadeghi-Boroujerdi explains, there is a long history of women's activism for human and civil rights in Iran. But such visible roles and defiant attitudes were new and 'left much of the world mesmerized, at least for a time'.[42] Sparked by the murder of a Kurdish Iranian woman and characterized by women's leadership, the movement clearly took on feminist characteristics, but its composition cut across several sectors of Iranian society, involving, for instance, contract workers at a major petrochemical complex and refineries. Following Sadeghi-Boroujerdi, we can say that the struggle emerged at the intersection of 'gender oppression and social reproduction', but quickly reverberated across the main political, religious, and economic axes composing the Iranian social formation.

The fact that Mahsa Amini was Kurdish opened, at least potentially, a vital space to critique the prevalent ethnocentric understanding of the Iranian nation, which has a long history of giving way to specific forms of Persian nationalism. The slogan of the movement was, not by accident, a Kurdish one: 'Woman, Life, Freedom' – more specifically, it is a slogan associated with the Women's Protection Units (YPJ) in north-eastern Syria (Rojava) and with the political project developed over recent years by Abdullah Öcalan, which is not only against any form of nationalism but is radically critical of the very form of the nation-state. Chanted in Kurdish, *Jin, jiyan, azadi*, or translated into Persian, *Zan, zendegi, azadi*, this slogan continues to echo as we write. And it is a valuable political resource, since the issue of nationalism is particularly relevant in the multipolar globe we inhabit. In different parts of the world, processes of pole formation are crossed and shaped by an understanding of the nation that often takes on absolutist tones and privileges civilizational homogeneity. To put it in the classical terms of debates on nation and nationalism, the *ethnic*, however reinvented and manipulated, takes precedence over the *civic* dimension. This tendency applies not only to imperial or continental states such as Russia and Turkey, but also to small- and medium-sized nations such as Ukraine and Poland, which resort to the language of nationalism and to related identity politics to

---

42 Eskandar Sadeghi-Boroujerdi, 'Iran's Uprising for "Women, Life, Freedom": Over-Determination, Crisis, and the Lineages of Revolt', *Politics*, published online 23 March 2023, 2.

claim their place in the international world (and in these cases, in the European and Western pole).[43] In this conjuncture, minority and Indigenous struggles acquire new meanings, going beyond a mere politics of recognition and at least potentially opening spaces for the emergence of a political articulation of the multiplicity that today characterizes the fabric of labour and life. This possibility exists despite the fact that such multiplicity is often disciplined in violent ways by nationalist rhetoric, measures, and governmental devices.

India is a good case in point. The protests against the Citizenship Amendment Act from November 2019 to March 2020 reveal, on the one hand, the spontaneity and power of a movement that swept the subcontinent. On the other hand, the developments of those weeks are telling as regards the nature of the Hindu nation-state under construction in India: Ranabir Samaddar has written aptly of a quick and dramatic entwinement of 'revolution and counterrevolution in India'.[44] We may first note that the movement emerged in a situation of acute political and fiscal-economic crisis, in the wake of the general election of April–May 2019 (which led to Narendra Modi's second term as prime minister) and ended with the start of the epidemiologic crisis of COVID-19. Beginning in the 1980s, the constitutional emphasis in India on *jus soli* with respect to citizenship has been increasingly criticized by nationalists who advocate a shift towards *jus sanguinis*, leading in 2003 to the recognition of the status of Overseas Citizens of India. As Partha Chatterjee explains, this change 'created a large pool of affluent diasporic converts to the cause of Hindu nationalism'.[45] At the same time, the selective management of migrants and refugees coming from the region (for instance, Tamil refugees from Sri Lanka or Rohingya escaping ethnic cleansing in Myanmar) has been put under pressure by the rise of Hindu nationalism.[46] The Citizenship Amendment Act that was pushed through parliament in early December 2021 opened an expedited

---

43   See again Ishchenko, 'Ukrainian Voices'.

44   Ranabir Samaddar, 'Revolution and Counterrevolution in India', *South Atlantic Quarterly* 120, no. 1 (2021), 190–3.

45   Partha Chatterjee, 'The State of Exception Goes Viral', *South Atlantic Quarterly* 120, no. 1 (2021), 196.

46   Sabyasachi Basu Ray Chaudhury, 'Dispossession, Un-Freedom, Precarity: Negotiating Citizenship Laws in Postcolonial South Asia', *South Atlantic Quarterly* 120, no. 1 (2021), 212.

process for the naturalization of non-Muslims coming to India from Pakistan, Afghanistan, and Bangladesh while excluding Muslims entrants from this same process. Associated with the establishment of a new National Register of Citizens, the act was widely perceived as a threat by Muslims all over India. This was largely due to the perceived risk of a mass illegalization of people living the country for decades, based on experiences of the registration process in Assam. The mobilization of Muslims prompted the rapid development of a mass movement across the country, with the participation of disparate groups of citizens, minorities, human rights activists working with migrant communities, and student organizations, as well as left, populist, and regional parties.

The movement against the Citizenship Amendment Act was, of course, diverse and even contradictory in its composition. Nonetheless, it instantiated, in powerful and unique ways, the upsurge of an India irreducible to Modi's Hindutva, open to regional dynamics, and struggling for a reinvention of democracy and welfare beyond any nationalism. It was met by the government and the ruling BJP (Indian People's Party) with violence and brutality: first with mass shooting and mass arrest by the police, then with the so-called Delhi riots in February, whose official death toll was fifty-three, thirty-six of them Muslims. When the nationwide lockdown was ordered as a pre-emptive measure against COVID-19, the movement was over and 'counterrevolution', to put it with Samaddar, had prevailed. Nonetheless, the movement against the Citizenship Amendment Act in India remains important for anybody interested in issues of minority politics and struggle against nationalism amid processes of pole formation. The critique of nationalism is, for us, a political and theoretical razor for the analysis of the conflicts and tensions that shape the emerging multipolar world. While the US is not exempt from such critique in an age of Trumpism and resurgent white supremacy, China also deserves critical attention in this respect. Conflicts and repression of the Uygur minority in the Xinjiang are well known, but, even more generally, we have been confronted over recent years, and in a pronounced way since the rise of Xi Jinping, with an entrenchment of Chinese nationalism – with an emphasis on the majoritarian Han group that may even take racist tones. We do not need to go into the details of such nationalism, analysing, for instance, how the rhetoric of the 'century of humiliation' is used in today's China. We note only that the vibrant debates on minority politics within China's

Communist Party, which led to the establishment of the Regional Ethnic Autonomy System in the wake of the revolution, seem to have been completely forgotten.[47] And the unity of the nation hangs over any form of social mobilization in China, including proliferating struggles at the intersection of circulation and reproduction.

Reproducing struggles

A hoodie with the words French Tech stamped on the chest – this was the clothing reportedly worn by French President Emmanuel Macron as he declared the 'strategic autonomy' of Europe to journalists during a flight to Guangzhou after a state visit to Beijing in April 2023. Macron's meeting with Xi Jinping, held with European Commission President Ursula von der Leyen, had yielded no concessions on the Ukraine war. However, he had managed to sell more aircraft, cosmetics, financial products, and pork to China. Then, mid-flight, he took the opportunity to declare that European countries should avoid becoming 'vassals' by following the US on Taiwan and accepting the 'extraterritoriality' of the dollar, tendencies that he worried would prevent Europe emerging as a 'third pole'.[48] Unsurprisingly, the US reaction was harsh, especially because Macron's comments came on the brink of Chinese military drills around Taiwan, triggered by Taiwanese President Tsai Ing-wen's meeting with Republican US House Speaker Kevin McCarthy. Many commentators, including in China, sought to explain the situation by placing Macron's remarks in continuity with an *étatisme* that extends back to De Gaulle. But, in light of our reflections on Eckart Kehr's notion of the 'primacy of internal politics' in the first section of this chapter, we think other factors need to be considered. We are not simply suggesting that Macron was playing to a domestic French audience, because the internal politics of the European Union is also surely at stake here, particularly considering its reconfiguration since the beginning of the Ukraine war, which has granted more power to staunch US

---

47   See Wang Hui, *La questione tibetana tra est e ovest*, Rome: Manifestolibri, 2011, 74–90.

48   Nicolas Barré, 'Emmanuel Macron: "L'autonomie stratégique doit être le combat de l'Europe"', *Les Echos*, 9 April 2023.

allies such as Poland and weakened the France–Germany power axis. Nonetheless, it is hard to ignore that Macron's geopolitical exhortation came at a period when France had been experiencing its deepest social upheaval in decades, in the form of widespread protests against the government's pension reform plans. We will have more to say about these struggles in due course. For now, we want to note that they were not just an indignant reaction to government reforms requiring people to work for two more years before pensionable age – a change primarily affecting those workers with fewest qualifications, including women who provide services in education, heath, cleaning, and care. Nor were the protests merely a response to the government's use of a peculiar constitutional measure to push the legislation through without parliamentary debate, although this surely increased the level of anger and drew youth and student movements into the struggle. The issue of pensions goes to the core of social reproduction in contemporary capitalism because it raises questions of labour, time, health, population, gender, and care rooted in the social and biological propensity of the body to age.[49] The question is how struggles that address this reproductive dimension of capitalism intersect the realm of geopolitics.

To grapple with the nexus of reproduction and geopolitics, we need to return to the question of circulation and its relation to productive processes in contemporary capitalism. In Chapter 2, we argued that the blurring of production and circulation is an important aspect of the current formation of capitalist accumulation and valorization. Reproduction, we explained, organizes and articulates production to circulation, making it a particularly potent domain of social and political conflict in today's world. This critical importance of reproduction in the present is due not only to the reduced capacity of states to guarantee the turnover and replenishment of capital at the national level, under financialized conditions in which accumulation tends to pass through transnational circuits. It also derives from the increasingly politicized ways in which processes of reproduction intersect with the production of subjectivity, perpetuating the antagonism between labour and capital while also crossing and complicating it with multiple additional markers of difference, among which race, gender, sexuality, age, and ability are

---

49   Brett Neilson, 'Globalization and the Biopolitics of Ageing', *CR: The New Centennial Review* 3, no. 2 (2003), 161–86.

only the most commonly mentioned. These two aspects of social reproduction are often analysed separately, but to understand how current
labour struggles mutate beyond forms that were prevalent under
national industrial capital and how these changes relate, in turn, to state
transformations, geopolitics, and pole formation, we must grapple with
both of these factors, theoretically as well as empirically.

Returning to the pension struggles, we can note two aspects of the
mobilization that shadowed Macron's mid-flight proclamations based
on a cycle of struggles that includes the protest against the new labour
law in 2006 and the rise of the *gilets jaunes* in 2018–19. First is the
composition of the movement. Important in this regard was the presence of women at the forefront of the struggle, a factor related not only
to the economically precarious position in which many women in
France find themselves but also to specific elements of the reform, most
notably the fact that under the new pension law maternity leave does
not count as part of one's working years.[50] This strong female participation was surely a crucial element in galvanizing a massive social struggle
linked more to questions of social reproduction than traditional capitalist production. David Gaborieau notes the prevalence of logistics
workers and what we earlier called circulation struggles in the movement, observing that the number of workers in strategic sectors such as
logistics and energy now equal those employed in France's manufacturing industries.[51] He emphasizes the tactic of blocking flows deployed by
these workers, noting that these methods bring an element of continuity
with the *gilets jaunes*. By contrast, Romaric Godin and Juan Chingo
suggest that too heavy a reliance on workers in strategic sectors is a
mistake.[52] Workers in key sectors such as the aerospace industry did
not join the protests, and France's economy is by now populated largely
by service workers. For Godin and Chingo, these facts need to be
accounted for in organizing a robust and effective movement. A further
question concerns the possibility for circulation struggles to feed reactionary political agendas, as they did in the Canadian truckers' blockade

---

50   Morteza Samanpour, 'The State and Global Capital: "Retirement Reforms" in
France', *e-flux*, 5 April 2023.
51   Filippo Ortona, 'In tutti gli strati del movimento sociale si è alzato il livello di
conflittualità. Intervista a David Gaborieau', *Il Manifesto*, 7 April 2023.
52   'France on the Eve of a Mass Strike? Interview with Juan Chingo and Romaric
Godin', Verso blog, 28 March 2023, versobooks.com.

of 2022.[53] This issue, and the related matter of the involvement in the movement of migrants and unemployed youth from the *banlieues*, is never far away in France, where the extreme right National Rally (Rassemblement National) has exploited the anger directed against Macron and may even benefit from it electorally. But aside from the issue of electoral prospects, the French pension protests spanned a wide heterogeneity of living labour, marking the emergence of a mass workers' movement that intervened on the terrain of reproduction rather than production. The potential for the movement to shift from the defensive protection of rights onto more offensive grounds remained open, although the escalation of repression and brutal state violence – a kind of internal war regime, as several observers noted – worked to forestall such a development. In any case, the claim of the priority of life over labour that prompted the movement has continued to echo in France and beyond.

The second matter to raise with regard to these struggles is the analysis offered by their organizers of the radicalization of bourgeois class in France and how it relates to wider economic and geopolitical factors, including the Ukraine war. That protestors organized a large mobilization on the day of Macron's meeting with Xi, and even set fire to the upmarket brasserie La Rotonde in Montparnasse, one of the French president's favourite restaurants, is significant. It marks a strong consciousness that the struggle shapes and is in turn shaped by international politics and global dynamics. Pertinent factors here include France's position in the European Union; rising military spending and the militarization of society in response to the Ukraine war; the deep indebtedness of France and related processes of financialization in the wake of the 2007–8 crisis; state transformations in the global North driven by more general changes in the reproduction of capital; and the shifting workings of capitalism in the global South, which impel the emergence and changing global position of countries such as China. Seen in this context, the French pension struggles become something other than a rearguard action by labour forces in the global North seeking to maintain a privileged position in the world system. As Morteza Samanpour points out, the increasing radicalization and

53   See Joshua Clover, 'The Political Economy of Tactics', Verso blog, 16 March 2022, versobooks.com.

violence of the Macron regime needs to be seen in continuity with forms of so-called authoritarianism in the global South, not because liberal democratic traditions can be discounted but because the reconfiguration and refunctionalization of the state is an important aspect of current capitalism.[54] In this light, it is relevant that pension struggles have also been part of the social landscape in countries such as Vietnam, India, Brazil, Chile, Russia, Nicaragua, and China. Elaine Sio-ieng Hui and Chris King-chi Chan, for instance, investigate the rise of pension strikes in China's Pearl River Delta, detailing how female migrant workers have organized to claim pension rights, and in so doing, have shifted the terrain of struggle away from wages and working conditions into the sphere of reproduction.[55]

It would be easy to expand this account of pension struggles, noting, for instance, the massive street protests, riots, general strikes, and police violence that accompanied the 2019 pension reform passed by Brazil's Jair Bolsonaro government. But reproduction struggles extend way beyond pensions, encompassing issues of education, health, and environment, among others. In the Bolsonaro years, Brazil was a veritable laboratory for such struggles, with student protests against education cuts playing a prominent role and the movement to save the Amazon from deforestation assuming a special importance. The latter is a particularly complex matter, related to land-grabbing extractive economies, Indigenous claims, agribusiness supply chains, price signals, funding rollbacks for programmes of satellite monitoring, on-the-ground personnel, and the demarcation of conservation areas.[56] Considered in the expanded sense intended by Marx in *Capital*, volume 2, however, reproduction encompasses not only the provision of the labour forces and environmental conditions necessary for capital turnover but also the sphere of accumulation. At a theoretical level, this expansion of the concept of reproduction helps to explain the link between reproduction and circulation struggles. The latter have, as we outlined in earlier chapters, become prominent at a time in which relations among

54 Samanpour, 'The State and Global Capital'.

55 Elaine Sio-ieng Hui and Chris King-chi Chan, 'From Production to Reproduction: Pension Strikes and Changing Characteristics of Workers' Collective Action in China', *Journal of Industrial Relations* 64, no. 1 (2022), 3–25.

56 Heriberto Araujo, *Masters of the Lost Land: The Untold Story of the Amazon and the Violent Fight for the World's Last Frontier*, New York: Mariner Books, 2023.

production, circulation, and reproduction are shifting due to factors such as the platformization of the economy and the designation of essential work in the pandemic. The struggles of riders, or platform delivery workers, are emblematic of these changes. Assuming different forms across the heterogeneous legislative and social environments in which platform economies have burgeoned, these struggles reach way beyond campaigns for reclassification, which seek to move the contractual relationship between platform operators and platform workers into the structure of waged employment. At stake in these struggles is not only the question of how exploitation can be established under relations of independent contracting in which the worker appears more as an entrepreneur than an employee, but also the regulation or political control of labour under conditions of algorithmic management and data extraction. These issues have made platform struggles a particularly potent and contested area of organizing and debate, with the pandemic moment acting as an important factor of visibility. Exploring resistance among ride-hailing drivers in Lagos, for instance, Daniel Arubayi documents practices such as the use of geofencing applications to fool the platform, running the platform application on devices with insufficient processing power to manipulate trip data, using battery settings to interfere with GPS signals, and working in collusion with other drivers to raise prices by simulating surges.[57] Julie Yujie Chen reports the use of similar algorithm-manipulating tactics in China, involving the use of multiple devices and platform subscriptions.[58] By contrast, Jamie Woodcock worries that too great an emphasis on algorithms and data, both as strategies of capital and tools of worker resistance, detracts from a focus on workers' experiences and changing class composition, preventing the 'development of new forms of collective, organized power'.[59]

Clearly, platform labour struggles will continue to test the practical and conceptual boundaries between circulation and reproduction. Yet they

---

57   Daniel Arubayi, 'Documenting the Everyday Hidden Resistance of Ride-Hailing Platform Drivers to Algorithmic Management in Lagos, Nigeria', *South Atlantic Quarterly* 120, no. 4 (2021), 823–38.

58   Julie Yujie Chen, 'Thrown Under the Bus and Outrunning It: The Logic of Didi and Taxi Drivers Labour and Activism in the On-Demand Economy', *New Media and Society* 20, no. 6 (2017), 2691–711.

59   Jamie Woodcock, 'The Limits of Algorithmic Management: On Platforms, Data, and Workers' Struggle', *South Atlantic Quarterly* 120, no. 4 (2021), 711.

also have a geopolitical aspect due to the spread and use of platforms with different national affiliations across regional, geographical, and national settings. The task of mapping the diffusion of platforms across the variegated spaces of global capitalism, comparing for instance the use of Chinese ride-hailing platform Didi to Uber, is not one we undertake here. Suffice it to say that, while the spread of Chinese platforms often evokes the country's Digital Silk Road Initiative, seeking to coordinate flows of goods and services through specific zones and countries, the presence of significant platform players from countries such as India, Singapore, and Sweden belies the narrative of a zero-sum competition between Chinese and US platforms. Even in the area of e-commerce – as we discussed in Chapter 4, the competition between Alibaba and Amazon is acute in South-East Asia – the national affiliations of these companies do not mean they can be understood straightforwardly as proxies for other forms of geopolitical rivalry. These companies pursue different models of international expansion, with Amazon vertically organizing its ownership of all elements of its supply chain and Alibaba partnering strategically with local companies. With regard to labour struggles, these organizational factors have a special relevance, particularly because Amazon's warehouses have emerged as sites of intense class conflict over recent years, with automation technologies, the use of agency workers, union busting, and new strategies of organizing all at stake. In the US and Germany, the struggles at Amazon facilities have been particularly intense, leading to experiments in transnational labour organizing and campaigning such as the Make Amazon Pay initiative.[60] In the case of Alibaba, it is more difficult to trace labour conditions and struggles down to particular sites and initiatives, although the company was certainly at the centre of the 996 tech workers movement that swept China in 2019. Named for the long hours expected of workers in China's technology industries (9 a.m. to 9 p.m., six days a week), the flames were fanned when Jack Ma, Alibaba's founder and erstwhile chairman, declared: 'To be able to work 996 is a huge bliss. If you want to join Alibaba, you need to be prepared to work 12 hours a day, otherwise why even bother joining?'[61] At its height, 996

60   Sarrah Kassem, *Work and Alienation in the Platform Economy: Amazon and the Power of Organization*, Bristol: Bristol University Press, 2023, ch. 7.

61   Quoted in Lulu Chen, 'Jack Ma Draws Controversy by Lauding Overtime Work Culture', *Bloomberg*, 12 April 2019.

attracted denouncements of tech company labour practices from Chinese
state media and solidarity statements from US tech worker collectives.
However, its decentralized and networked organization, which began on
the software development platform Github and was largely restricted to
online activity, never involved stoppages and was unable to force workplace changes.[62] In ensuing years, 996 has evolved into more passive forms
of resistance that encourage slowing down and rejecting work pressures.
Known as *tang ping* (lying flat) and *bai lan* (let it rot), these silent practices
of refusal, which are prevalent among young people and shared through
social media memes, have been amplified by the economic and psycho-
logical effects of COVID lockdowns.

Geopolitical conditions and discourses certainly feed into the domain
of labour struggle in the tech industries. In the US, tech companies have
regularly raised fears about China to repel threats of government regulation, arguing that they need free reign in innovation to continue to
outstrip their competitors on the other side of the Pacific.[63] Such was
the logic, for instance, behind Mark Zuckerberg's claim that if 'another
nation's platform sets the rules, our nation's discourse could be defined
by a completely different set of values'.[64] Likewise in China, corporate
leaders have invoked the rhetoric of the tech war to justify exploitation
of their employees, and in particular the requirement for long working
hours. Regimes of war, as we know, curb and discipline labour and
social struggles. Insofar as movements such as 996 and its subsequent
meme iterations predominantly involve media-literate youth, they need
to be understood in relation to their relevant temporalities, causes,
demands, class compositions, and interests. The same applies to the
anti-lockdown protests that hit Chinese cities in November 2022 in
reaction to a building fire in Ürümqi, Xinjiang that killed ten people.
Widely characterized as the A4 rebellion after the blank sheets of paper
held by some protestors, these apparently spontaneous actions, which
seemed to embody a political rejection of the Xi Jinping regime, were

62 Kevin Lin, 'Tech Worker Organizing in China: A New Model for Workers
Battling a Repressive State', *New Labor Forum* 29, no. 2 (2020), 52–9.

63 J. S. Tan and Moira Weigel, 'Organizing in (and against) a New Cold War: The
Case of 996.ICU', in Mark Graham and Fabian Ferrari (eds), *Digital Work in the Planetary Market*, Cambridge, MA: MIT Press, 2022, 209–28.

64 Quoted in Will Feuer, 'Watch Mark Zuckerberg Deliver a Speech on Free
Expression at Georgetown University', CNBC, 17 October 2019.

also largely composed of urbanites and students. However, as a young Chinese activist writing from outside the country points out: 'When the white paper is cited as the emblem of the whole movement (both within China and overseas) discussions about the movement in its entirety become solely oriented around the political protests of urbanites and students, or to the solidarity campaigns held in overseas Chinese communities, but this narrative ignores entirely the struggles happening among migrant workers and within urban villages.'[65] Eli Friedman explains how these worker protests targeted the closed-loop approach to lockdown by which workers were confined to factory and dormitory spaces without the possibility to leave.[66] Among these events were a May 2022 riot at Apple supplier Quanta Computer in Shanghai, where workers fought with guards and breached a checkpoint outside the factory, and more prominently the massive escape of workers from Foxconn's locked-down Zhengzhou plant, where just days before the so-called A4 protests broke out hundreds of migrant workers scared for their health scaled walls and squeezed through gaps in the fence to run for their hometowns. As Friedman argues, these events need to be placed in with the context of many other struggles in the sphere of reproduction carried out by proletarians in China's urban villages and industrial districts since the 2000s.

Understood in this way, the November 2022 lockdown struggles in China that importantly softened the government's approach, express deeper problems related to the circulation of capital and the dynamics of social reproduction, which were only amplified by the pandemic. A similar point can be made about another of the most important protest movements that unfolded during the COVID years, the Indian farmer protests of 2020–1. Ostensibly a reaction to three laws passed by the central government seeking to liberalize India's agricultural markets and encourage contract farming, these actions, which eventually took the form of a months-long blockade of four highways leading to Delhi, had deeper roots in 'dynamics of agrarian change and reconfigurations of

65   Zuoyue, 'Why Were the White Paper Protests Comprised of Three Movements? Understanding the Revolutionary Features and Limitations of the Anti-Lockdown Protest Wave', *Chuang* (blog), 23 December 2022, chuangcn.org.
66   Eli Friedman, 'Escape from the Closed Loop', *Boston Review*, 28 November 2022, bostonreview.net.

class and caste.[67] One of the puzzles surrounding the protests is why they broke out when they did, as by all accounts Indian agriculture has been in crisis for decades. The answer seems to lie in the fact that many farmers can no longer live off the land alone and have been forced to supplement their incomes with wage labour. Compounded by the effects of the pandemic, this situation has led to 'a multi-pronged squeeze on the social reproduction of increasingly diversified households whose livelihoods cross the rural-urban divide.'[68] Although the laws that sparked the protests focused on transforming markets for agricultural produce, which is to say on issues of circulation and exchange, wider issues of reproduction were at stake. These matters extended to environmental and ecological concerns about the sustainability of the land under conditions of chemical and fossil fuel–intensive agriculture – matters left largely unaddressed in the farmers' claims. Nonetheless, the movement comprised a wide coalition of farmers' organizations, labour unions, Dalit groups, the Punjabi diaspora, and progressive civil society organizations, which, combined with robust female participation far exceeding that in previous farmers' movements, posed a severe political challenge to the Modi administration. In the end, the government relented by repealing the laws under question, a significant victory for the farmers but one that left the underlying issues of social reproduction that drove the protests unchanged.

Doubtless, there are many other reproduction and circulation struggles that have unfolded in different parts of the world in recent years. For instance, the successful result in the Berlin housing referendum of 2021, which came on the back of years of tenants' and anti-gentrification struggles, endorsed a plan to expropriate properties owned by large corporate landlords.[69] Although it is important to note that the left municipal government did not implement the plan, the movements that accomplished the positive referendum outcome succeeded in making issues of social reproduction and financialization mainstream concerns in the city. In the US too, reproduction and circulation struggles have

---

67   Amita Baviksar and Michael Levien, '"Farmers" Protest in India: Introduction to the JPS Forum', *Journal of Peasant Studies* 48, no. 7 (2011), 1342.

68   Ibid., 1345.

69   On the background of the referendum, see Manuela Bojadžijev, 'Housing, Financialization, and Migration in the Current Global Crisis: An Ethnographically Informed View from Berlin', *South Atlantic Quarterly* 114, no. 1 (2015), 29–45.

been a prominent part of the social landscape. Nurses' and teachers' strikes have unfolded across the past decade, while successful unionization struggles in businesses such as Amazon and Starbucks have more recently been heralded as new models of labour organization.[70] On the outskirts of Los Angeles, the incredible growth of warehousing has given rise to logistics and reproduction struggles in the area known as Inland Empire, a kind of shadow space that gives material form to the US's role as consumer of last resort for commodities produced in and imported from China. The district has become a hotbed for labour organizing and unionization campaigns among predominantly migrant temporary and contract workers, as well as community struggles directed against the area's transformation into a 'diesel death zone'.[71] As in other parts of the world, the pandemic has intensified and highlighted these struggles. Paul Apostolidis, a committed researcher of migrant worker centres in the Inland Empire and beyond, hopes that 'sensitisation to occupational health and safety threats due to the pandemic could provide a point of departure for more far-reaching critique and opposition' to biopolitical and racialized modes of control in hazardous work settings such as the meatpacking and warehousing industries.[72] But, whatever the changes to labour struggles brought by the pandemic, the outbreak of war and the intensification of regimes of war have introduced new challenges. We must repeat that war typically brings the suppression of labour struggles and an attempt to escape from domestic contradictions in the name of imperial confrontation. It is to the stakes of such confrontations for struggles for freedom and equality that we now turn, keeping in mind not only the imperial dimensions of current geopolitics that we discussed in Chapter 3 but also the ongoing legacies of colonialism that continue to ring in the extractive and exploitative dynamics of contemporary capitalism.

---

70   See John Logan, 'A Model for Labor Renewal? The Starbucks Campaign', *New Labor Forum* 32, no. 1 (2023), 87–97.

71   See Julian Emmons Ellison, Joel S. Herrera, Jason Struna, and Ellen Reese, 'The Matrix of Exploitation and Temporary Employment: Earnings Inequality Among Inland Southern California's Blue Collar Warehouse Workers', *Journal of Labor and Society* 21, no. 4 (2018), 533–60.

72   Paul Apostolidis, 'Labour Biopolitics and Covid-19: Lessons from Latinx Migrant Workers in the USA', *Greek Studies Now* (blog), 22 March 2021, gc.fairead.net.

'Be Water'

'Stability, Prosperity, Opportunity' – this was the slogan chosen by the Hong Kong government to celebrate the twenty-fifth anniversary of the city's return to the Chinese mainland in 1997. In mid-2022, the slogan featured prominently in posters pasted all over Hong Kong as well as in advertisements placed across the world in sites such as Frankfurt Airport, gentrified areas of Australian cities, and the sides of trams in Brussels and Milan. The campaign aimed to signal that Hong Kong had entered a new era after the social unrest of 2019–20 and the subsequent pandemic. Above all, it wanted to send the message that Hong Kong was open for business. However, members of the Hong Kong diaspora were quick to protest on social media. In Brussels, the two trams fully wrapped with the slogan were removed after twenty-four hours in circulation. Billboard advertisements in Sydney were covered with posters that included catchphrases such as 'Stop Beijing's Propaganda' and 'Stand with Hong Kong'. Ted Hui, a former Hong Kong opposition politician and democracy street protester exiled in Australia, asked: 'If Russia . . . put an advertisement in major cities in Australia promoting that it is a peacemaker, promoting their military actions for the peace of other countries, would that ever be allowed?'[73] Clearly, the ads were read as something more than city branding and had entered the fray of current geopolitics and regimes of war.

Hui's comment ventures an implicit comparison between Russia's invasion of Ukraine and the violent quelling of the protests that swept Hong Kong in 2019–20, generally considered to have ended with Beijing's promulgation of the Hong Kong national security law in June 2020. We will not examine the rhetorical force of Hui's statement by making observations about the tested line between police and military actions; since 1997, Hong Kong has been a Special Administrative Region (SAR) of the People's Republic of China (PRC), and, although police brutality and military tactics were features of the protests, the legal means by which the party-state bypassed the Hong Kong government to impose the security law differ from the military assault that

---

73   Quoted in Sally Brooks, 'Hong Kong Diaspora Say Billboards in Australia Are Beijing Propaganda and Spread Lies', ABC News, 11 August 2022, abc.net.au.

occurred in Ukraine. This remains the case even if the presence of People's Liberation Army troops in Hong Kong was conspicuously expanded during the most intense months of protest, and members of the People's Armed Police, the mainland's core paramilitary and anti-riot force, reportedly accompanied Hong Kong police to the frontlines.[74] The national security law established the crimes of succession, subversion, terrorism, and collusion with foreign organizations. Understandably, the legislation raised grave concerns in Hong Kong about the continued applicability of the 'one country, two systems' principle. Beijing's decision to implement the law displayed flagrant disregard for the movement's success in forcing the withdrawal of the previous year's Anti-Extradition Law Amendment Bill, proposed by the Hong Kong government and allowing the removal of people to the mainland for trial. Subsequent arrests, prosecutions, and imprisonments represented a harsh defeat of the Hong Kong democracy movement. However, as with other powerful movements that have experienced equally harsh defeats over recent years – from the so-called Arab Spring to the struggles around Gezi Park and Taksim Square in Istanbul, from the democratic uprising in Sudan starting in December 2018 to the 2019 mass demonstrations in Lebanon – it deserves careful investigation with respect to its composition, impact, and potential for the future.

In what sense do the Hong Kong protests of 2019–20 intersect processes of geopolitical transformation, even beyond the obvious resonances with the tensions surrounding Taiwan? These intense social struggles, which reached an apogee with the siege at the Polytechnical University of Hong Kong in November 2019, need to be understood in the context of Hong Kong's wider colonial and economic predicament. This is not the place to rehearse the history of China's ceding of Hong Kong Island at the barrel of British guns in the wake of the First Opium War. Suffice it to say that the British interest in enforcing the sale of Indian-grown opium to Chinese consumers was asserted under cover of an economic liberalism that would find its intellectual justification in the writings of Adam Smith and leave an indelible mark upon Hong Kong's political and social life. Designated a free port, Hong Kong's economy would be driven by the drug trade. In 1860, after the Second Opium War,

---

74 Greg Torode, 'Exclusive: China's Internal Security Force on Frontlines of Hong Kong Protests', Reuters, 18 March 2020.

Kowloon, across the harbour, would become part of the colony. It was the era of concession colonialism, in which European powers gained extraterritorial rights in cities and ports dotted up and down China's east coast.[75] The Japanese joined the fray in the 1890s, seizing Taiwan and unleashing a further scramble for concessions, amid which Britain would lease Hong Kong's New Territories for a hundred years in 1898. In many ways, this concession system, which imposed what is now known in the PRC as the 'century of humiliation', provided a precedent for the kinds of zoning and graduated sovereignty that would take grip around the world with the globalization wave of the 1990s.[76] Hong Kong's economy thrived under these conditions, particularly after the British took the territory back from the Japanese in 1945 and the Chinese revolution of 1949 brought a flood of cheap labour.

In the next fifty years, Hong Kong not only punched above its weight in manufacturing but also became an important financial centre, where market freedoms were combined with strong legal privacies. Enamoured of Milton Friedman and other neoliberal economists who favoured economic above political freedoms, the colony housed a subject population, which, aside from uprisings such as the anticolonial riots of 1967, was doubly abandoned and doubly occupied by contesting political, juridical, cultural, and linguistic forces.[77] Although the British introduced elections in the years immediately preceding the handover, these did not involve universal suffrage and gave disproportional voting rights to business sectors. Hong Kongers had no say in the 1997 transfer of sovereignty, the terms of which were settled directly between China and Britain. These historical circumstances set the stage for the growing restiveness of large segments of the Hong Kong population in the post-handover period, when the premise of 'two systems' often seemed to slip under the imminent arrival of 2047 and the encroachment of mainland political control. Movements such as that which protested the closure of the Star Ferry terminal in 2006, the anti–High Speed Rail movement of 2009, Occupy Central in 2011, and the Umbrella movement of

---

75   See Barry Naughton, *The Chinese: Transitions and Growth*, Cambridge, MA: MIT Press, 2007.

76   Quinn Slobodian, *Crack-Up Capitalism: Market Radicals and the Dream of a World Without Democracy*, New York: Metropolitan Books, 2023.

77   See Jamie Peck, 'Milton's Paradise: Situating Hong Kong in Neoliberal Lore', *Journal of Law and Political Economy* 1, no. 2 (2021), 189–211.

2014 gave impetus to the events of 2019–20. This latter movement, the largest of them all, would rally under five demands: withdrawal of the extradition bill; retraction of the 'riot' label for protests; amnesty for all those arrested during the protests; an independent commission of inquiry to look into the political crisis and police operations; and universal suffrage – meaning direct elections – for the Hong Kong chief executive and all legislature members.

Understanding the struggles of 2019–20 means not only situating them with respect to the forms of capitalism and political rule that developed in Hong Kong over the late twentieth and early twenty-first centuries but also in relation to momentous changes in the PRC over the same period. Not least the creation of Shenzhen as the privileged zone of China's export-oriented economy, just across the border from the New Territories, brought new pressures to what is now known as the Greater Bay Area, and, to a large extent, overshadowed Hong Kong's role as an economic powerhouse. If the 'two systems' referred to in the Hong Kong Basic Law introduced in 1997 designate Hong Kong's capitalism on the one hand and PRC socialism on the other, it is now necessary to grapple with the variegated forms of political capitalism that have arisen on the mainland and how they have affected and spilt over into Hong Kong itself. Although it is true that Hong Kong has served as a gateway between the PRC and the world economy, that role is now less pronounced in a period in which cities like Shanghai and Shenzhen host important financial markets, which, as we explored in Chapter 4, have increasingly opened to foreign investment. Appended to a geopolitically resurgent China, Hong Kong's economic growth has faltered, and increasing inequalities have curtailed the opportunities of the working classes and young people in its aging society. Many so-called Hong Kong localists blame this situation on the PRC, attributing for instance the city's exorbitant real estate prices to the arrival of investors from the mainland, and underestimating the role of austerity politics in diminishing its once strong public housing system. In reality, Hong Kong's widening economic inequalities have a longer genealogy, rooted in the oligarchy of a few influential business families, who do indeed harbour pro-China sympathies, but whose power was consolidated in the period of British rule.[78] The situation has created a

---

78   See Jun Zhang, 'Is Mainland China the Source of All of Hong Kong's Problems?', *HAU: Journal of Ethnographic Theory* 10, no. 2 (2020), 313–18.

political tinderbox, which in 2019 exploded in reaction to Beijing's direct, institutionalized influence on the Hong Kong government and growing efforts to control speech codes and modes of political expression that have become second nature to many Hong Kong people. The struggles that ensued thus crossed the geopolitical field created by China's rapid economic rise, even if the social and economic factors that kindled them are not fully captured by the protestors' five political demands.

For us, images of young protestors facing off riot police armed with water cannons, tear gas, rubber bullets, and sponge grenades elicit immediate sympathy and solidarity, rooted in our own political experience. Nonetheless, we think it is important to emphasize the multiplicity and contradictions of the Hong Kong protests, whose participants in some instances threw bricks and petrol bombs but were more generally characterized by the slogan 'Be Water', lifted from a Bruce Lee film and meant to signify the movement's adaptability, decentralization, and inventive use of technologies.[79] There has been much critical talk about the sentiment against mainland migrants that pervaded the protests and how this aspect of the movement reinforced bordering technologies and epistemologies that 'sustain the colonial-imperial cartography of the capitalist world'.[80] We cannot deny the accuracy of this analysis, which to some extent takes inspiration from our previous writings. Nor can we disavow its grounding in important research that demonstrates the collaborative bent of Hong Kong people in the context of British colonialism, and the 'northbound colonialism' exercised by Hong Kong-based capitalists, managers, and professionals in the mainland during the 1990s.[81] Nonetheless, we are hesitant to reduce the movement to the moment in November 2019 when, in recognition of the two Hong Kong–related bills signed into law by the US president, protestors brandished US flags and posters of Donald Trump. Doubtless many protestors saw political opportunity in courting the US government and

79   Yong Ming Kow, Bonnie Nardi, and Wai Kuen Cheng, 'Be Water: Technologies in the Leaderless Anti-Elab Movement in Hong Kong', *Proceedings of the 2020 CHI Conference on Human Factors in Computing Systems*, 2020, 1–12.

80   Jon Solomon, 'Hong Kong, or How Social Struggles Can Reinforce the Cartography of Capitalist Enclosure', *Critical Legal Thinking* (blog), 14 January 2020, criticallegalthinking.com.

81   See Law Wing Sang, *Collaborative Colonialism: The Making of the Hong Kong Chinese*, Hong Kong: Hong Kong University Press, 2009.

media in a situation that seemed otherwise hopeless, as if the party-state was biding its time, waiting to move at a moment in which the world was not looking, as indeed turned out to be the case when the pandemic scattered attention. But to reduce the geopolitical dimension of the protests to a zero-sum choice between the US and the PRC is to misperceive the terrain of global power in which Hong Kong finds itself. Even after the clampdown of 2020, the city-state remains embroiled in financial, logistical, and extractive dynamics that make claims of national interest or democracy versus autocracy difficult to disentangle from capitalist relations in which decoupling is far from an economic reality.

To recognize this predicament is not to claim that all strains of the 2019–20 movement accepted such bipolar geopolitical terms. Nihilistic currents cannot be ignored, even if the claim of the Chuang collective that 'the least overtly political grouping – the one that seems to want nothing more than for the city to burn – is, in fact, the only one with an accurate intuition of the real political terrain' verges on the aestheticizing the riots.[82] An adequate account of the movement's composition cannot fail to mention a minoritarian but strongly anticapitalist element that split between the advocacy of consumer activism and the organization of political strikes.[83] It would be a mistake to attribute a coherent factional identity to these fragments, given the predilection for decentralized organization through social media channels such as Telegram. Nonetheless, there was a push among leftist currents to coordinate an alternative institutional base through the formation of grassroots trade unions, some eighteen of which came into existence between June and December 2019. The plan was to 'reassert the importance of class-based organization and to reconnect political demands with socioeconomic rights'.[84] In general, these leftist strains tended to contrast the localist emphasis on Hong Kong identity and independence by voicing solidarity for labour struggles on the mainland and offering a clear-eyed view of the close government-business ties in Hong Kong as well as the links

82   Chuang Collective, 'The Divided God: A Letter to Hong Kong', *Chuang* (blog), January 2020, chuangcn.org.
83   Debby Sze Wan Chan and Ngai Pun, 'Economic Power of the Politically Powerless in the 2019 Hong Kong Pro-democracy Movement', *Critical Asian Studies* 52, no. 1 (2020), 33–43.
84   Pun Ngai, 'Reflecting on Hong Kong Protests after 2019–20, *HAU: Journal of Ethnographic Theory* 10, no. 2 (2020), 337.

between the PRC party-state and Hong Kong-based conglomerates. This is not to say that the left backed away from the movement's five claims or the wider outrage at the PRC's impingement upon Hong Kong's civil liberties and legal autonomy. Rather, these elements sought to contest not only the Chinese party-state but also the forms of political and variegated capitalism that link Hong Kong's institutional and economic predicament to wider processes of exploitation and extraction in the PRC and beyond. Necessarily, this perspective involved an effort to see beyond the dead end of 2047 and to articulate the movement to other islands of struggle in the world, portending a vision of geopolitics based not in great power rivalry but in patterns of solidarity and translation that contest and work through territorial limits and bordering practices.

Needless to say, the democracy movement had its opponents within Hong Kong, including not only pro-Beijing government and business elites but also working-class people who run small businesses or have family connections with the mainland. This is not to say that all working-class people refused to side with the mêlée, especially youth harassed by the police or troubled by the claim that mainland migrants eat up public housing and social welfare resources. Interestingly, given the prevalence of localist discourses among the protestors, one group that disagreed with the movement is the so-called Indigenous Hong Kongers, whose presence, especially in the New Territories, supposedly predates British colonial rule.[85] Granted special privileges or *ding* rights allowing them to build residences on land passed down through the male line, these villagers have been sheltered from Hong Kong's high real estate prices and have amassed wealth through the sale or leasing of such land.[86] In the years leading up to the protests, these *ding* rights were subject to legal challenges, which succeeded for a period in rolling them back, before they were restored by means of a 2019 appeal. Unsurprisingly, the Indigenous villagers sided with Beijing, opposing modifications

---

85   Emily Feng, 'Hong Kong "Indigenous" Villages Mirror Tensions of an Increasingly Divided City', NPR, 17 October 2019, npr.org.

86   See Say H. Goo and Heather Lee, 'Lawful Traditional Rights and Sustainability: An Unbalanced Interest in the Customary Ding Right in Hong Kong?', *Hong Kong Law Journal* 50, no. 3 (2020), 961–82; and Malcolm Merry, *The Unruly New Territories: Small Houses, Ancestral Estates, Illegal Structures, and Other Customary Land Practices of Rural Hong Kong*, Hong Kong: Hong Kong University Press, 2020.

to voting rights that might result in changing the laws, unpopular among Hong Kong residents coping with the world's highest housing costs. One group of village strongmen even took matters into their own hands, violently attacking protesters with sticks and metal bars at the Yuen Long metro station in July 2019. One of the darkest incidents of protests, the Yuen Long attack was ironic given that the granting of *ding* rights by the British colonial government in 1972 was linked to measures that aimed to prevent a repeat of the 1967 riots. Moreover, these rights, which passed into the Hong Kong Basic Law in 1997, affirmed concessions granted by the British in 1899 after the six-day war in which colonial forces quickly put down a rebellion mounted by villagers in the New Territories. Siu Keung Cheung convincingly argues that Hong Kong's 'local Indigenous' population is a colonial construct which not only excluded women but also provided the British with a population-management technology that incorporated local elites into mechanisms of rule.[87] The claim to traditional lifestyles anchored to land and unchanged by colonialism skewed property relations in ways that accorded the idiosyncrasies of colonial administration. Chueng's contention is worth remembering at a time when localist sentiments in Hong Kong have once again given impetus to vanquished rebellion and opened the door to governance strategies that promote social stability and capitalist opportunity.

Shifting the analytical focus of section away from the Hong Kong protests, we can note that such an argument about New Territories villagers need not invalidate the struggles of Indigenous people in other parts of the world, which for centuries have been at the forefront of battles against the extractive dynamics of capitalism and colonialism. Whether in the face of the settler colonialism that resulted in the pillaging of Indigenous land and communities in and beyond the countries now known as Australia, Canada, and the United States, or in the *latifundia* and *encomienda* systems that proliferated in Latin America, such struggles have provided paradigms of resistance and survival that resonate beyond the local contexts in which they are necessarily rooted. Important to these struggles are the reflexive dynamics of colonial dispossession identified by Rob Nichols, who argues that, rather than

---

87 Siu Keung Cheung, *Gender and Community under British Colonialism: Emotion, Politics and Struggle in a Chinese Village*, London: Routledge, 2006.

assuming prior possession in ways that perpetuate proprietary and com-modified social relations, Indigenous claims regarding stolen land rest on retrospective forms of ownership that generate property only in the wake of colonial violence and land grabbing.[88] These processes are important to keep in mind at time in which a fresh round of extractive activities, based in the mining of critical minerals to support the energy transition, creates new geographies of Indigenous dispossession and struggle. In sites as diverse as the lithium triangle spanning Argentina, Bolivia, and Chile; the Middle Arm Sustainable Development Precinct in Larrakia country in Australia's Northern Territory; or Namibia's southern coast where Germany seeks to initiate green hydrogen projects – the prospect of energy imperialism has reignited Indigenous struggles along the extractive frontier.[89] At stake in these mounting struggles is not only land, although that remains a primary point of contention, but also knowledge, law, and data, making them political initiatives that pertain not only to mining but also to extraction in an expanded sense.[90] Yet because the question of renewable energy intersects issues of supply chains, friendshoring, and strategic competition, these struggles also have an irreducibly geopolitical element. In this aspect, Indigenous struggles are inseparable from dynamics of political capitalism, because they are both shaped by these processes and continue to impact upon them.

To make this point is not to reduce the multiplicity of Indigenous struggles to a single source or to attribute them a coherent enemy. These struggles have always been shaped by the peculiar qualities of the colonialism against which they are cast. Among these, settler colonial-ism is prevalent because the expropriation of Indigenous land and labour is central to its workings. But, while settler colonialism experienced a

88   Rob Nichols, *Theft Is Property: Dispossession and Critical Theory*, Durham, NC: Duke University Press, 2020. See also Brenna Bhandar, *Colonial Lives of Property: Law, Land, and Racial Regimes of Ownership*, Durham, NC: Duke University Press, 2018.

89   See respectively Michael Hardt and Sandro Mezzadra, *Bolivia Beyond the Impasse*, Brooklyn, NY: Common Notions, 2023; Kirsty Howie, 'Porous Jurisdictions: Sacrifice Zones and Environmental Law in the Northern Territory of Australia', paper presented at Western Sydney University, 30 March 2023; and Pia Eberhardt, *Germany's Great Hydrogen Race: The Corporate Perpetration of Fossil Fuels, Energy Colonialism, and Climate Disaster*, Corporate Europe Observatory, Brussels, March 2023.

90   See Sandro Mezzadra and Brett Neilson, 'On the Multiple Frontiers of Extrac-tion: Excavating Contemporary Capitalism', *Cultural Studies* 31, nos 2–3 (2017), 185–204.

moment of expansion in the late nineteenth century, when its practices and categories contributed to the making of international law, a story told in part by Lauren Benton and Lisa Ford in *Rage for Order*, it is not the only form of colonialism to have reached beyond its initial contexts.[91] Above, we mentioned how the concession colonialism that emerged in China, and of which Hong Kong provided a prominent example, offers a precedent for the zoning technologies that have proliferated under global capitalism. Similar claims might be made for other forms of colonialism, of which Nancy Shoemaker identifies ten, including planter colonialism, transport colonialism, legal colonialism, and missionary colonialism, to which we might add the data colonialism that has recently been proposed as a means of explaining 'the conversion of daily life into a data stream'.[92] Yet, while Shoemaker situates these varieties of colonialism in the historical past, giving examples with firm spatial limits, we think that the continuation of these forms of colonialism into the present has involved their mixing, spatial dissemination, and in some cases diminution or expansion. Seen in this way, concession colonialism can no longer be restricted to China, and settler colonialism can be seen to influence liberal claims for a rules-based international order with implications that, at once, reach beyond and deepen the logics that legitimate and perpetuate the dispossession and genocide of Indigenous people in white settler colonies.

By analogy to the notion of variegated capitalism, which relates to and subtends this proliferation and hybridization of colonial forms, we might speak of a variegated colonialism that spans the scales and spaces of the contemporary world system. Returning to the question of renewable energy, for instance, there is at stake not only the desiccation and toxification of Indigenous lands on which mining occurs but also the zoning and legal technologies that enable such extraction, the global trade rules that govern the export of critical minerals, and the missionary rhetoric that justifies the rush to commodify these substances as a means of saving the world. Doubtless, the intensity and admixture of

---

91   Lauren Benton and Lisa Ford, *Rage for Order: The British Empire and the Origins of International Law, 1800–1850*, Cambridge, MA: Harvard University Press, 2016.

92   Nancy Shoemaker, 'A Typology of Colonialism', *Perspectives on History*, 1 October 2015, historians.org; Nick Couldry and Ulises Mejias, 'Data Colonialism: Rethinking Big Data's Relation to the Contemporary Subject', *Television and New Media* 20, no. 4 (2019), 336.

colonialisms subject to such variegation differs drastically across sites, depending on operations of capital as well as on other factors such as regulation, corporate governance, infrastructure, supply chains, and degrees of militarization. But we think the perspective of variegated colonialism offers an important analytical angle on the kinds of imperialism involved in contemporary pole formation, which, as we have already argued, do not neatly coincide with territorial demarcations, and cannot accurately be labelled according to the continental powers with which they are commonly identified: the US pole, the Chinese pole, the Russian pole, the Indian pole, and so on. Struggles within and against such pole formation, as in the case of Hong Kong, are likely to be riven with contradictions and limits, but, as we shall see in the next section, they offer powerful means of contesting, and even breaking, the nexus of capital and geopolitics that marks the current world conjuncture.

Continental intimacies

How is it possible for struggles to have an impact on geopolitical scenarios? And how do the latter become an internal moment in the former? The questions we raised in the previous sections have key political implications in a world where the existing centrifugal multipolarity is increasingly crisscrossed by the spread of war regimes. Where are the spaces for a new politics of liberation (which must also be a politics of peace) in such a scenario? Critical regionalism and continentalism, the legacies of Pan Africanism, anticolonialism, and Tricontinentalism may provide at least fragments of a political imagination to be reactivated in contemporary disputes and conflicts. But we do not need to turn to the archive to discern dynamics of struggle that cross the formation of poles contesting the rule of capital and foreshadowing new horizons of social and political cooperation beyond it. Recent political experiences in Latin America provide a noteworthy testing ground. If one thinks of the 1980s and 1990s, when military dictatorships in many countries gave way to a process of transition to democracy, the region seemed caught in the Washington Consensus, which meant continued dependency on the US and further experimentation with the neoliberal policies inaugurated with terror and blood by the Pinochet regime after the 1973 coup. The situation changed quite dramatically towards the end of the twentieth century, when a concatenation of uprisings at the regional scale (from Ecuador to Bolivia and Argentina) was followed by a proliferation of new movements and struggles in most Latin American countries. Since 1994, the Zapatista rebellion in Mexico has played a fundamental role within this process, providing movements with a new language that circulated across and beyond the region and underscoring the leading role of Indigenous movements in the new cycle of struggles.[93]

The composition of the Latin American movements in the early 2000s was different in many of the countries involved. Nonetheless, taken together, those movements display a set of characteristics that continue to be relevant today. Struggles of the unemployed and urban poor politicized the transformations of labour that had marked the end of *desarrollismo* ('developmentalism'), the specific Latin American instantiation of a model of state-led industrialization and nation building. Processes of self-organization and mobilization of workers in the informal and popular economy further signalled the crisis of that model. Urban struggles reinvented neighbourhoods, often cooperating (for instance in Argentina) with workers who had occupied and recuperated (as they put it) a panoply of enterprises abandoned by owners. The protracted struggle for justice in the face of the crimes and mass murder perpetrated by past dictatorships took on new accents within this dense fabric of mobilizations, giving new meanings to the language of human rights. At the same time, Indigenous movements and insurgency re-opened a much longer chapter in Latin American history, politicizing the persistent legacy of colonization and targeting centuries-old forms of exclusion and racist domination. In Bolivia and Ecuador, where Indigenous struggles were particularly powerful, they led to new constitutions characterized by an innovative approach to issues such as interculturalism, pluri-nationalism, and the environment.[94]

Crucially, the uprisings and movements of the 1990s and early 2000s were able to re-open a regional political space in Latin America that had been envisaged several times since the age of independences but was

---

93   See Verónica Gago and Sandro Mezzadra, 'In the Wake of the Plebeian Revolt: Social Movements, "Progressive" Governments, and the Politics of Autonomy in Latin America', *Anthropological Theory* 17, no. 4 (2017), 474–96.

94   See, for instance, Marco Aparicio Wilhelmi, 'Nuevo constitucionalismo, derechos y medio ambiente en las constituciones de Ecuador y Bolivia', *Revista General de Derecho Público Comparado* 9 (2011), 1–24.

then restricted and even demolished with the building and consolidation of nation-states that also built the framework for the contested processes of democratization that shaped the twentieth century. In several countries, including Bolivia, Argentina, and Ecuador, the insurgent moment that started in the late 1990s prepared the ground for the establishment of new 'progressive' governments that formed what is often called a 'pink tide'.[95] The relation between such movements and these governments was far from direct, linear, or unproblematic, and the former were often caught between conflict and co-optation.[96] Nonetheless it is important to note that, at least in the first phase of their history, the progressive governments scaled their action to the regional space opened by these uprisings and movements, launching ambitious projects of regional integration in the fields of trade, infrastructures, and even monetary politics. Chávez and Lula, often considered at the opposite edges of the progressive governments' spectrum, played key roles in prompting those projects, which were made possible by the commodity boom that preceded the financial crisis of 2007–8 and the related processes of entrenchment of extractive activities that have occasioned heated debates, radical critiques from the left, and political and social clashes in several Latin American countries.[97] We have written extensively elsewhere about these developments and conflicts.[98] The important point here is that, once the financial crisis hit Latin America towards the end of the first decade of the century, the issue of regional integration was downplayed and even disappeared from the agenda of progressive governments. A new nationalization of politics and rhetoric emerged, instantiated by Cristina Kirchner's project of 'pesification' of the economy (the denomination of all exchanges in the national currency) in 2012 and related disputes between Argentina's and Brazil's central banks.

---

95   See Franck Gaudichaud, Jeffery R. Webber, and Massimo Modonesi, *Los gobiernos progresistas latinoamericanos del siglo XXI. Ensayos de interpretación histórica*, México: UNAM Ediciones, 2019; and Steve Ellner, *Latin America's Pink Tide: Breakthroughs and Shortcomings*, New York: Rowman & Littlefield, 2019.

96   See, for instance, Gary Prevost, Carlos Oliva Campos, and Harry E. Vanden (eds), *Social Movements and Leftist Governments in Latin America: Confrontation or Co-optation?*, London: Zed Books, 2012.

97   See, for instance, Thea Riofrancos, 'Extractivismo Unearthed: A Genealogy of a Radical Discourse', *Cultural Studies* 31, nos 2–3 (2017), 1–30.

98   See Sandro Mezzadra and Brett Neilson, *The Politics of Operations: Excavating Contemporary Capitalism*, Durham, NC: Duke University Press, 2019.

Nonetheless, vectors of regional integration have continued to cross and shape the Latin American space. Formal organizations abound, including Mercosur (a trade bloc whose full members are Argentina, Brazil, Paraguay, and Uruguay), UNASUR (the Union of South American Nations, set up in 2008 on Hugo Chávez's initiative), and CELAC (a regional association of Latin American and Caribbean countries). Perhaps less known, but equally important, is the Initiative for the Integration of the Regional Infrastructure of South America (IIRSA), which was launched in 2000. Functioning as a logistical platform, IIRSA's structure was originally designed as a blend of multilateral cooperation among governments and public–private partnerships, with the aim to attract foreign capital to the region.[99] Described as a 'logistical and capitalist utopia', IIRSA's plan is articulated around ten 'axes of integration and development' that encompass the whole region and aim at cross-disseminating what we called in the previous chapter operative spaces.[100] While this infrastructural initiative has encountered a multitude of resistances since its inception, due to its association with extractivism but also to the ecological consequences of its projects and to their impact on Indigenous populations, in recent years it has also been compelled to negotiate the increasing presence of Chinese capital.[101] Since the establishment in 2014 of a China–CELAC forum and the inclusion of many Latin American countries in the Belt and Road Initiative, China's activism has intensified and focused on big infrastructural projects, such as the Bi-Oceanic Railway Corridor from Brazil to Peru. While this raises important challenges, not only for IIRSA but also for national governments, the region becomes one of the sites of confrontation between China and the US, whose historical and imperial influence in Latin America continues through organizations such as the OAS (Organization of American States) and free trade agreements with countries such as Chile, Colombia, and Peru.

However relevant, these are not the only vectors of integration or the only conflicts at stake in the Latin American space. We discussed above the new wave of feminist mobilization that has swept the region in

---

99 Alessandro Peregalli, *IIRSA entre integración y racionalidad logística*, New York: Peter Lang, 2022, 97.

100 Ibid., 182.

101 Ibid., ch. 6.

recent years, challenging the rule of patriarchy and establishing new forms of communication and struggle well beyond national boundaries. What is just as striking is the continuity in the waves of uprising that traverse Latin America, moving from country to country. The big revolt in Chile of October 2019, which remains a threshold in that country's political history despite the defeat of the new project for constitution in the referendum of September 2022 and the subsequent turn to the right, was soon followed by popular revolts in Ecuador, with huge Indigenous participation, while in May 2021 a mass social movement against fiscal reform in Colombia gave way to a general mobilization against the prevailing social and political system that created the conditions for wider change and for the electoral victory of President Gustavo Petro.[102] To this we should add that, in December 2022, the impeachment and removal of President Castillo in Peru led to a widespread movement of insurgency led by peasants and Indigenous people and violently repressed by security forces. Even the election of anarcho-capitalist Javier Milei to the presidency of Argentina in October 2023, which shows the uneven and stochastic quality of political developments in Latin America, has been met by a strong round of resistance, protests, and strikes. Movements and struggles continue to repoliticize the Latin American space, raising old and new issues, among which feminism and antiracism figure prominently. At the same time, while political commentators and pundits maintained that the pendulum of Latin American politics had swung to the right by the middle of the last decade, progressive governments are again popping up across the region. Today's conditions are quite different from those of the first decade of the century (as the presence of a figure like Milei and more generally the rise of an aggressive right in many Latin American countries clearly demonstrate). Nonetheless, in a multipolar world, there may also be new chances for a process of integration driven by a kind of antagonistic cooperation between governments and movements.[103] As the former Brazilian foreign minister under President Lula (2003–10), Celso Amorim, contends, 'multipolarity is at the

---

102   See Andrea Fagioli, *Ottobre cileno*, Rome: Manifestolibri, 2023; and the special section of *South Atlantic Quarterly* 122, no. 4 (2023), dedicated to the revolt and to the constituent process.

103   See Hardt and Mezzadra, *Bolivia beyond the Impasse*.

same time a tendency and an objective', which requires political will and struggle.[104]

Latin America is neither the solution nor a model for a politics of liberation in a multipolar world. It is just an instance that illuminates a horizon of possibilities, whose actualization remains an uncertain wager. There is no need to insist on the peculiar history and conditions of that region of the world, which is moreover profoundly heterogeneous within its own space. Operations of capital, as we stressed in the context of IIRSA, play key roles in the reorganization and governance of the architecture of power in the region, providing an effective instantiation of what we call political capitalism. The question is: how to confront those operations; how to foster processes of appropriation and distribution of wealth that can support a more general transformation of social relations in a feminist, antiracist, and ecological direction? These are key issues for the forging of a new politics of liberation, and we believe that the history of the past two decades in Latin America demonstrates that the scale of the nation and the state cannot provide fully fledged answers. This is not to say that the nation does not matter any more. While it can be an important scale of struggle and political invention, it is necessary to remember that it can nurture forms of nationalism that may facilitate operations of capital even when they rhetorically oppose them. This is particularly the case in what we have called imperial states, and in Latin America this regards above all the position of Brazil, which was accused of playing a hegemonic role in the region in the first decade of this century.[105] Negotiating such balances and imbalances is an important task if we are to imagine a positive politics capable of occupying and qualifying the tendency to multipolarity, inscribing within this tendency a programme of social and political transformation that may turn it into an 'objective', to echo Amorim. Confronting, at the same time, operations of capital and powers such as China and the US as *internal* to the Latin American region, requires the invention not only

---

104   Sergio Lirio, 'América del Sur en la Nueva Geopolítica Global. Entrevista a Celso Amorim', *Nueva Sociedad* 301 (2022), 82–92. See also Celso Amorim, 'Política Internacional e o Brasil no Mundo: Da Unipolaridade Consentida à Multipolaridade Possível', *Revista Centro Brasileiro de Relações Internacionais* 1, no. 1 (2022), 19–32. On 5 January 2023, Lula appointed Amorim chief advisor of the presidency.

105   See Raúl Zibechi, *The New Brazil: Regional Imperialism and the New Democracy*, Oakland, CA: AK Press, 2014.

of a new programme of political and social transformation but also the establishment of new spaces of action, both for struggles and for governments.

We do not deny that states and governments, under specific conditions, can contribute to the forging and deployment of the politics of liberation that we have in mind. But this is possible only when their action is embedded in and sustained by a variegated fabric of struggles and powers that retain their autonomy, and when they aim to inscribe their action within wider political configurations beyond national boundaries. Movements themselves have the capacity to instantiate a geography of struggles that exceeds the nation. The issue of migration is again relevant here. To shift our geographical focus for a moment, take the City Plaza Hotel in Athens, Greece, a seven-floor building that was occupied by hundreds of activists and migrants in April 2016.[106] Rooted in Athens, traversed by the dreams, desires, and needs of migrants arriving from Afghanistan, Syria, Kurdistan, and Iran, as well as those of transnational activists from across and beyond Europe, the City Plaza Hotel effectively instantiated until the end of the occupation in July 2019 what might be called a countergeography of struggle. Such intermingling scales, languages, and cultures foreshadow the kind of political labour that is key to the formation of a politics of liberation and peace in a multipolar world. In quite different conditions, amid a bloody war with the involvement of the Islamic State, Russia, the US, and Turkey, the Kurdish movement in north-east Syria, in Rojava, has struggled with weapons and civil determination to establish a form of social cooperation and a system of institutional arrangements that in general terms resonates with the City Plaza Hotel. In Rojava too, managing differences (mainly between ethnic groups and religions) has become a revolutionary art, spurred by feminist struggles, and sustained by an ecological awareness. This has been possible due to political developments within a section of the Kurdish movement in which 'the emphasis on the Kurds as a people *without* a state became one on the Kurds as a people *beyond* the state'.[107] Abdullah Öcalan, the leader of the Kurdistan Workers' Party

---

106   See Olga Lafazani, 'Homeplace Plaza: Challenging the Border between Host and Hosted', *South Atlantic Quarterly* 117, no. 3 (2018), 896–904.

107   Joost Jongerden and Ahmet Hamdi Akkaya, *Die Entwicklung der kurdischen Freiheitsbewegung. Gesammelte Texte zur Einführung in Geschichte und Gegenwart*, Frankfurt am Main: Westend Verlag, 2022, 18.

(PKK) who has been imprisoned in Turkey since 1999 (and who has already been mentioned), played important roles in those developments.

The City Plaza Hotel and self-government in Rojava are just two instances of localized struggles and practices that can nurture the radical political imagination in a multipolar world. It should be clear that we are not conflating them – that we remain aware of the incommensurability of the challenges one has to face squatting a building in the centre of a European city and taking weapons to establish and defend forms of life and cooperation under military attack. The point is to demonstrate that, in imagining the reinvention of a politics of liberation with the capacity to challenge processes of pole formation, we do not need to remain trapped in grand scenarios of regional or continental integration. Localized struggles and practices have become even more important: what matters is their articulation within wider coordinates and projects, their translocal circulation and resonances. It remains true that, to confront operations of capital whose scope is far from local or even national, we need political inventions that reach not only beyond the nation, but also across and beyond regions and continents. Writing in 2010 about decolonization and 'deempirialization' in Asia, Kuan-Hsing Chen contends that 'Asian regional integration is strategically central'. He adds, however, that 'this integration cannot be understood simply in regional terms; it has to be placed in the context of global politics since September 11. It is a regionalism, but also an internationalism and a globalism.'[108] Although the conjuncture has significantly shifted since 2010, this remains true in an age of pandemic and war. And it makes the task of rethinking internationalism particularly urgent.

We do not know whether the term *internationalism* is still valid today. The twentieth-century history of internationalism is characterized by memorable episodes of solidarity across countries and continents that may be evoked by geographical labels such as Spain, Ethiopia, and Vietnam (we could, of course, mention many other episodes). Nonetheless, it is also true that communist internationalism has served too often as an instrument to cover up for the national interests of the USSR – with catastrophic implications in the age of Stalin (the label *Spain* is of course redolent here). Even beyond that, it is important to stress that

---

108   Kuan-Hsing Chen, *Asia as Method: Toward Deimperialization*, Durham, NC: Duke University Press, 2010, 15.

throughout the history of socialist, anarchist, and communist internationalism it has been taken for granted that the unit of organization is
provided by the nation. It should be clear from our argument that we
need to go beyond such a focus, working towards a variable geometry of
spaces for political action and an intertwining of those spaces through
organizational and institutional processes of networking. It is important
to stress that such spaces are not given in advance, as would be the case
in a simplistic understanding of multipolarity. We do not contend that
existing poles, with stable boundaries, provide the coordinates within
which a new politics of liberation and peace should be established. On
the contrary, such a politics must invent and create its spaces and may
thus contribute to shifting the geography of multipolarity. Moreover,
the presence of the US and China in Latin America, as well as Kuan-
Hsing Chen's understanding of regional processes of integration in Asia,
suggest the need to politicize what we call, citing Lisa Lowe's remarkable
book, regional and continental intimacies.[109]

As we have already argued, there is no shortage of historical instances
of political projects and practices that foreshadow an internationalism
beyond the nation. New research on the Third International and the
global South, starting with the Baku Congress of the Peoples of the
East in 1920, present the Comintern as 'the fulcrum of a multi-centered
global history of twentieth century anti-colonial insurgencies and revolts
with long-standing implications for present-day political organizing'.[110]
There is much to learn, indeed, from such historical excavations. Struggles across continents resonate through the history of anti-imperialist
movements. Think for instance of the slogan 'Fiat is our Vietnam',
popular in Italy in the early 1970s, or of the words employed by M.
Hoang Minh Giam, North Vietnamese minister of culture, to greet the
BPP delegation led by Bobby Seal at the 1968 Montreal Hemispheric
Conference to End the War in Vietnam: 'You are Black Panthers, we are
Yellow Panthers.'[111] The list could easily go on. Such historical exercises

---

109   See Lisa Lowe, *Intimacies of Four Continents*, Durham, NC: Duke University
Press, 2015.

110   Paolo Capuzzo and Anne Garland Mahler (eds), *The Comintern and the Global
South: Global Designs/Local Encounters*, London: Routledge, 2023, 7 (the quote is taken
from the introduction).

111   Joshua Bloom and Waldo E. Martin Jr, *Black against Empire: The History and
Politics of the Black Panther Party*, Oakland, CA: University of California Press, 2016, 267.

are important to forge a political imagination capable to reinvent or reframe internationalism. There is also a need to map contemporary movements and struggles from this angle. To give an example, what Verónica Gago calls the new 'feminist international' is built upon a dense web of bodies in struggle, territorial and subjective specificities, situated practices of anticolonial and antiracist politics that defy the limits of nation-state geometry without ever becoming abstract.[112] Over recent years, the movements that build the backdrop of Gago's theoretical elaboration have been able to assert in new ways the Latin American scale of their action, producing powerful resonances both in the US and in South European countries such as Italy and Spain.

Again, this is just an example, and at the same time it is a conjunctural opportunity for a new internationalist politics to come, whatever its name will be. Eventually, its spatial coordinates are given by the 'terrestrial factory' we inhabit, while its temporality is structurally altered by climate change and related ecological crises.[113] In this book, we have attempted to illuminate some of the conditions for such a politics, while signposting the troubles and pitfalls it has to face. Our analysis of emergent multipolarity has underscored the nested and complicated geography of the contemporary world, where processes of pole formation cut through international maps centred upon the nation-state and proliferating operative spaces of capital. The pandemic and the Ukraine war have further complicated such geography, while the spread of war regimes across countries and regions reminds us that the issue of peace is at the heart of any politics of liberation – a proposition only more clear following the events in Gaza and their ricochet effects across and beyond the Middle East. Our concept of political capitalism emphasizes the governmental and political dimensions of capital's operations and raises new questions regarding how they can be effectively confronted. Crucially, our analysis of circulation and reproduction opens an angle on the transformations of the composition of living labour that must be investigated carefully in different places but goes beyond the model of a standard labour relation embodied by a privileged subject. What we call the multiplication of labour is relevant here, while factors such as gender

---

112 Gago, *Feminist International*, ch. 6.

113 See Davide Gallo Lessere, 'Nine Theses on Internationalism Today', forthcoming in *Historical Materialism*.

and class are significant concerns for any coalition. This is not a time for easy optimism, but, to play on the words of Lauren Berlant, the cruelty of the world does not allow us the luxury of pessimism.[114]

Although we have emphasized the terrestrial and global dimensions of political capitalism and multipolarity, our perspective has always been alert to the planetary crises of environmental and health catastrophes. Indeed we insist, as does Dipesh Chakrabarty, that bringing analytical attention to the nexus of the global and the planetary is a necessary condition for any future politics.[115] Doubtless, such visions can go wrong, as we would argue they did in the geopolitical romance of China saving the earth from a collision with Jupiter, as conceived in Frant Gwo's 2019 film version of Liu Cixin's short story 'The Wandering Earth', celebrated by Chinese cybernationalists long before it was picked up by the US streaming platform Netflix. The dreams of Elon Musk and Jeff Bezos, to make Mars a site for the unlimited expansion of the frontiers of capital, are an equally dystopian prospect. Human beings are earthlings, and we do not take seriously the fantasy of survival beyond the atmosphere and biome on which we rely. Nonetheless, we are convinced that escape can be a political act, particularly in the form of movements that desert capitalist relations of exploitation and extraction. In 1970, in the wake of the clashes and dreams of the 1960s, Paul Kantner and Jefferson Starship released a visionary album entitled *Blows against the Empire*. One of its signature songs is called 'Hijack'. The lyrics describe a plan to revolt against the mighty by hijacking a starship from orbit and journeying into space to find a new home. Carrying 7,000 'gypsies' past the sun, the songwriters imagined an afterlife among the stars for the counterculture of the 1960s – a dream on which we look back, after more than five decades, with tenderness. But as it echoes from the past, the call to 'hijack the starship' might find resonance today, to reinvent internationalism and inspire a politics of liberation across the globe.

---

114   See Laurent Berlant, *Cruel Optimism*, Durham, NC: Duke University Press, 2011.

115   Dipesh Chakrabarty, *The Climate of History in a Planetary Age*, Chicago: Chicago University Press, 2021.

Acknowledgements

For conversations and companionship invaluable in writing this book, we thank Manuela Bojadžijev, Joyce Chi-Hui Liu, Elisabetta Magnani, Enrica Rigo, Ned Rossiter, Ranabir Samaddar, Susan Zieger, and the members of EuroNomade and the Into the Black Box Collective. For institutional and financial support, we acknowledge the Institute for Culture and Society at Western Sydney University, the Australian Research Council Discovery Program, the Department of the Arts at the University of Bologna, and the European Union's Horizon 2020 Research and Innovation Program. For reading and commenting on the text, we thank Michael Hardt and Toni Negri, the latter of whom sadly did not live to see its publication: we mourn him and celebrate his communist life, the life of a teacher, a comrade, and friend. *Grazie, maestro*. On a more personal note, we would like to mention Rossella and Giovanna, whose loss only reinforces their presence, and Mila, whose journey into adulthood traversed the interval in which the writing took shape.

Index